The Fabu
Matter of Fact

The Poetics of Neil M. Gunn

Richard Price

EDINBURGH UNIVERSITY PRESS

© Richard Price 1991

Edinburgh University Press
22 George Square, Edinburgh

Set in Linotron Garamond by
Koinonia Limited, Bury, and
printed in Great Britain by
the Alden Press, Oxford

British Library Cataloguing-
   in-Publication Data
Price, Richard
   The fabulous matter of fact: The poetics of Neil M.
   Gunn.
   I. Title
   823

ISBN 0 7486 0259 3

The publisher acknowledges subsidy
from the Scottish Arts Council towards
the publication of this volume.

Contents

Preface

Despite the arrival in 1981 of F. R. Hart and J. B. Pick's authoritative biography, *A Highland Life* (John Murray), in recent years there have been only two book-length studies entirely devoted to the work of Neil Gunn. The first, Margery McCulloch's *The Novels of Neil M. Gunn* (Scottish Academic Press, 1987) dismisses almost all of Gunn's novels after 1944 as artistically unsatisfactory. John Burns' *A Celebration of the Light* (Canongate, 1988) acts as a substantial corrective to this view, but deals only with the later novels, employing a knowledge of Zen Buddhism that runs the risk, despite the elucidation it achieves, of making Gunn appear more influenced by Zen than he actually was. Almost before anyone else, Kurt Wittig in *The Scottish Tradition in Literature* (Oliver & Boyd, 1958) recognised the stature of Gunn's work. He not only placed Gunn within a continuity of Scottish literature, he saw his novels as the quintessence of Scottish Renaissance achievement. Hart's *The Scottish Novel* (John Murray, 1978) gives special prominence to Gunn, too. Also by Hart, the essay, 'Neil Gunn's Drama of Light', in *The History of Scottish Literature* Volume 4 (Aberdeen University Press, 1987) is an excellent point of departure for those new to Gunn, as is Douglas Gifford's *Neil M. Gunn and Grassic Gibbon* (Oliver & Boyd, 1983). *Neil M. Gunn: the Man and the Writer*, edited by Gifford and Alexander Scott (Blackwood, 1973), was the first book of criticism, biography, and appreciation entirely devoted to Gunn and it is still a key critical text. Nevertheless, a study with a cohesive overview that also incorporates more detailed analysis has so far been lacking.

Today, a hundred years after Gunn's birth, it seems timely to offer such a book. Almost all of his novels are now in print again, and many of his essays and letters have been collected. His non-fiction has seen some handsome reprinting, an extensive bibliography has appeared, and Alistair McCleery has written a fine history of the publishing house whose principal author Gunn was: *The Porpoise Press, 1922–39* (Merchiston, 1988). Yet Gunn's popularity far outstrips the critical attention he has received. This is all the more surprising given the importance he has within the Scottish Renaissance, an area increasingly drawing interest among scholars and the public alike. It is no accident, for example, that Grieve's letters to Gunn are among the most quoted in studies of Mac-Diarmid. Gunn was recognised by Grieve as an equal if opposite force in the Renaissance in particular and in literature in general, and their letters to each other are often their most revealing.

One reason for this neglect may be that Gunn has the appearance of being a rather 'unliterary' author. In a sense Gunn's writing is so much 'of itself' that it is felt that research can hardly do anything but cloud his rather deft 'natural' prose. This attitude pays a respectful homage to Gunn's skill, and he himself poured scorn on those he felt were part of a merely cerebral literati. But Gunn's intricacies, I feel, still warrant discussion. This book attempts to reconsider Gunn, therefore, as the consummate novelist he was, and in doing so interprets him not only as a writer, in the earlier years, more firmly within the Scottish Renaissance than has generally been realised, but also as one of our most challenging and sophisticated novelists. The approach I have taken is one that relates close textual criticism to Gunn's wider concerns. Though the greatest of the novels are discussed here, room is given to all his extended fiction.

The best books from the first half of his writing career, *Morning Tide* with its beautiful portrayal of boyhood, *Highland River* with its experimentation in form, and *The Silver Darlings* with its concentrated layering of meaning, have been placed in the context of Gunn's specifically personal historical perspective, a perspective at its most bitter in his novel of the Highland Clearances, *Butcher's Broom*. The later great books are wide in thematic scope: *The Serpent*, the Young Art books and, last of all, *Bloodhunt* and *The Other Landscape*, deal in a sophisticated way with the large human issues with which all the finest literature is concerned. For any serious enthusiast or student of Gunn the above-named novels are essential reading. Together they exemplify the astonishing range of Gunn's work, his technical skill, and his ability to make the novel a philosophical medium without also making it a poor read.

Clearly inferior works, even the serialised *The Poaching at Brianan*, as well as poorly-realised books such as *Second Sight* and *The Drinking Well* are included here because they are important for our understanding of Gunn's work as a whole. A pivotal book such as *Wild Geese Overhead*, for example, is of more significance in this way than in itself: Gunn's worst books are often his most revealing. Finally, though *The Atom of Delight* (1956) is in many ways a 'fictional' autobiography, it is not extended fiction in any accepted sense. Though I duly recognise its achievement, not least in crossing the filaments of genres, there has not been sufficient space to consider it here. It obviously offers a *post factum* reflection on Gunn's works, but it was felt that essays more strictly contemporaneous with his fiction, and less conscious of their place in a wider structure, would be more trusty guides to Gunn's themes. Nevertheless, the reader is referred to *The Atom of Delight* as a rich if slightly more oblique handbook to his poetics. *The Fabulous Matter of Fact* is offered in the hope that it, too, may be companionable for those with an interest in Gunn, in Scotland and its novels, and in literature in general.

Acknowledgements

Many more people than I can thank here have helped in the writing of this book. I owe especial thanks to Andrew Noble of the Department of English Studies, the University of Strathclyde, and to the late Martin Spencer of Edinburgh University Press. Robert Crawford, Leona Esther Medlin, and Edwin Morgan read various parts of the manuscript, and offered thought-provoking comments. J. B. Pick has been particularly generous with his time, and his advice and criticisms have proven invaluable.

For computer know-how I am indebted to Hunter Steele and to Rob Price. I owe much to Donny O'Rourke for encouragement and support. Martin Scarrott helped with very specific queries. Thank you, too, to the staff of the Mitchell Library, Glasgow, the British Library, the National Library of Scotland, and the Andersonian Library (University of Strathclyde).

I am delighted to acknowledge Dairmid Gunn's kind permission to quote from Gunn's work, and Neal Ascherson's permission to quote from *Games with Shadows*. I am grateful to my employers in the British Library for helping to fund my higher degree, and for allowing me to work temporarily part-time. *Gairfish*'s co-editor, W N Herbert, has been sympathetic towards my conflicting attentions.

Most of all, I would like to thank Dereck Price, Jackie Canning, and all my family.

This book is dedicated to the memory of my mother.

1

Crawling from out the Hinterland

The Grey Coast

I

O, Sun!

I have seen a black adder
Pour out his cold-blooded length
From the unfrozen earth,
And in a lascivious arabesque
Lie gleaming-coiled,
Sun-drunk, by matted roots
Of the wild rose tree,

Crawling from out the hinterland
Of earthy gloom,
Past the cold stones
Of dreams and old desires,
Comes my soul to the roses
Like a black adder.[1]

When Christopher Grieve gave Neil Gunn's 'O, Sun!' the first page in *The Scottish Chapbook* of July 1923 he was acting in the self-appointed capacity of Impresario to the Scottish Nation.[2] A useful volunteer for the Scottish Literary Corps, Gunn was encouraged to become more versatile and to develop his prose. Though Grieve was enthusiastic about the Caithness man's verse, and indeed included Gunn's work in his own public readings, from the beginning of their long association he was eager to see Gunn write more fiction.[3] On the evidence of one short story, which he published in another of his journals,[4] Grieve recognised a writer of considerable potential: 'I don't know if you've written much prose yet, but you certainly should! I look forward with confidence to exceptionally fine stuff from you.'[5]

By the end of 1924 Gunn had published about a dozen short stories, and not only via his new friend in Montrose. *Dublin Magazine* and *The Glasgow Herald* (which had refused earlier work) had by then both published him.[6] In January of the next year Grieve gave further support to Gunn's plan for a compilation, and he praised the stories' international validity.[7]

The collection, however, was put aside. There had been a rejection from Chatto and Windus, but also Gunn had begun work on a larger canvas – 'sketches' had become inadequate for the psychological depth and scale he wanted. In June 1926 *The Grey Coast* emerged from Jonathan Cape.

The smaller pieces that precede *The Grey Coast* reveal the unhappy landscape from which the novel sought to be liberated. 'O, Sun!', for example, reads like a distillation of Gunn's ambition and art. The desire for newness and energy, even at overdose level, the longing to move beyond a past jaded and desolate, the necessity of finding sensual release from mental numbness – all the aspirations of the poem reappear with vigour in *The Grey Coast.*

'O, Sun!' is a statement of intent. In the early 1920s Gunn found the earth still frozen in his rediscovered Caithness. Harbours were silting and houses still emptying of their youth 'for good'. In the Gaelic culture with which he identified, and in the politics and art of Scotland at large, there, too, was stagnation. *The Grey Coast* attempts to break from such enervation, but his short stories of this period show how hard Gunn felt the task. Of particular interest are 'Half-light' and 'Hidden doors'.[8] In the former, a headmaster, Iain, returns to the bleak harbour village he had earlier forcefully rejected ('I'm going to get warm with colour and sun and snakes!'). His death in a swimming accident follows, and much of the story is taken up with the narrator's investigation of the cause, particularly via what amounts to a literary criticism of Iain's poetry.

The verses Gunn 'quotes' show an opposition between a grey landscape with its grey past and a longing for a sensual, golden, state of being. The narrator interprets Iain's opposing fantasy of exuberant colour, sound, and sex as the yearning and extreme reaction to life on the northern coast:

> Nothing 'twilight' about it. On the contrary, a savagery – sometimes more concealed than may appear. For these

things have been denied by the unpoetic grey years that lie about him like inescapable grey boulders. And he misses nothing, as though every forbidden, sensuous thing had to be savoured. Colour cannot be left alone [...].[10]

The result of this experimental mix of short story, poem, and analysis, is not unlike Grieve interpreting MacDiarmid.

The word 'twilight' is not used lightly. One of Iain's intentions, in the narrator's words, was to provide 'a more realistic counter-blast to the Fiona Macleod twilights, and from the land of Gaeldom.'[11] The Celtic Twilight, deriving its name from Yeats's nineteenth-century miscellany of Irish tales, had its Scottish counterpart in the works of 'Fiona Macleod' (real name, William Sharp), Neil Munro, and others, and shared an at times morbid interest in the reiteration of Celtic myth, particularly tragedy. Iain had had Fiona Macleod in his collection, and the narrator finds a plan for a satirical attack on the Twilight there, too. Where traditional tragedies did not exist, the Twilighters invented them. Most stories had either a crude sentimentality alien to authentic Celtic legend or supplied a conclusion that indulged in death. This was seen as in keeping with the real feeling of the Gaelic-speaking people. Macleod asserted, for instance, that in the Gaelic world there was 'the unconscious knowledge of the lamentation of a race, the unknowing surety of woe.'[12]

Having said this, some of the Twilight writing was better than third-rate. Macleod's 'The Sin-eater' for instance, is a particularly good example of a more realistic and engaging story.[13] Gunn was right to be cautious in condemning the Twilight out of hand – in fact his artistic problem was how to develop from the Twilight a more satisfactory literary politics. At the end of 'Half-light' the narrator realises that Iain was finding a saving quality in the grey coast, and in the motivation of the Twilight writers. In the same way, Gunn wanted to make the 'movement' with which he partially identified more artistically, and politically, muscular. His reaction to the Twilight was quite distinct from the anti-Kailyard fiction of *The House with the Green Shutters* or *Gillespie*. *The Grey Coast* certainly takes cognisance of anti-Kailyard ideas with its grim realism, but Kailyard concerns are not heightened to anything like the intensity reserved for the Twilight. McCulloch has tentatively recognised the importance of this. Writing of 'Half-light', she remarks: 'I am not sure [...] that Gunn's references to

Fiona Macleod should be taken as jokes.'[14] In fact, Gunn makes the Celtic Twilight the central literary concern of most of his earlier fiction.

Several of the early short stories have the bleak outlook of Gunn's perceived predecessors, but without the sentimentality or the 'Gaelic' hokum. In 'Symbolical',[15] snow consumes a crofter's neighbour, and the incident becomes 'the symbol or vision of all their lives'. In 'Hidden Doors', an Englishman, Turner, tries to find a metaphysical music that will express the Highland experience but he dies at the foot of a hill, Cnoc-an-druidh, whose Gaelic name, meaning 'The Druid Hill', suggests a link to a pagan past. This shows the distance in artistic sensibility Gunn had to travel before rendering the fairy knoll a vital component of his regenerative vision in *The Silver Darlings*.

Where Gunn's tragedy differs from the Twilight is in the precision of the sorrow. The real problems he depicts are not done so with the 'sentimental meaningless ineptitude' that Turner had discerned in Macleod and others.[16] J. B. Salmond made a similar point when reviewing *Morning Tide* : 'Gunn shows consummate art in his power to describe in its place and to keep in its place the ferocity of emotion.'[17]

The Grey Coast presents a fierce anti-Twilight voice, but also announces itself as more than just a reaction. It is the first novel of the Scottish Renaissance, a novel with a self-confidence, a drama, and a psychological grittiness which, had it been the only work Gunn produced, would have earned it a much more central place in the Scottish twentieth century canon than it currently maintains.

II

The centre of *The Grey Coast* is Maggie, a young woman living with her uncle, Jeems. He has saved her from the Poorhouse following the death of her mother (her father having died a long time ago). Jeems has led the rich landowner, Daun Tait (known as 'Tullach' after the name of his land), to believe that Maggie will be his to marry and in so doing he has drawn many favours from him. He is now dependent on Tullach because he has become too old to wholly manage his croft. Maggie loathes Tullach and has a more attractive suitor in the young fisherman, Ivor, but he is tortured by his own poverty, and eventually decides to leave the village altogether. At the last minute he comes back, uniting with Maggie as Jeems dies in his own rabbit-snare (his will securing a small fortune for his niece). Tullach is thwarted, and is left with the intense memory of Maggie and Ivor's passionate embrace.

Though the location is never made specific, *The Grey Coast* is a Caithness novel. When Ivor abandons his village he returns via Skye and 'the east coast and the north road' (303). This is a symbolic commitment to the homeland Gunn called 'a grey strip of crofting coast, flanked seaward by great cliffs, cliffs "flawed" as in a half-sardonic humour of their Creator to permit of the fishing creek ...' (14).

That this is really Caithness he confirmed in 1935 when he wrote a similar description, but with more naming detail.[18] Gunn also used examples of Caithness dialect to define the location in the novel (one expatriate enthused over 'the very great pleasure to have the old Caithness phrases repeated once more'.[19] A 'blockie' (118), for example, is a small cod, and 'clocking' (85), is sitting idly for a long time (as well as the sound of a broody hen). Both are words spoken in Caithness at the end of the nineteenth century, and therefore within Gunn's childhood experience.[20]

Of all his work, *The Grey Coast* is Gunn's largest concession to the use of Scots. He uses other Scots words in more general currency in the north-east, too. Grieve's letter to Gunn, dated 1 November 1923 (i.e. about two years before Gunn began work on *The Grey Coast*), shows that Gunn was interested in a 'handy dictionary' of Scots, so it seems that what Scots Gunn could not remember or recover on visits to his mother in Caithness, he may have plundered from one of Grieve's suggested texts.[21]

Dunbeath in Caithness was Gunn's place of birth, and in 1922, newly-wed, he moved back from work in England to Lybster, just north of there. The stay was brief, however, and within eighteen months Inverness was his new home, and would be so for the next eleven years.[22] Gunn did not write *The Grey Coast* in Caithness. A perhaps natural tendency to mythologise worked in Gunn's favour. The avoidance of place-name evidence, but the depiction of a landscape and speech formed from remembered experience allowed him to have his cake and eat it, too. Here a novel rich with a feeling of locality, but without an easily identified locale. Though to the more resourceful reader it was certainly somewhere in Caithness, it was also to some extent anywhere. These are exactly the conditions that allow certain Scottish novels allegorical strength; what Gifford has called 'a serious historical-metaphysical synthesis which can do justice to the writer's conception of Scotland.'[23] Gunn indicates his national concern first of all by using MacDiarmid's poem 'Glog-hole' as the novel's epigraph. That this was the poem's first place of appearance and that Grieve had given Gunn the poem (a fact confirmed by their correspondence [24]) show the author's wish to appear committed to Grieve's Scottish literary movement. This was at a very early stage – so early, indeed, that Grieve's pseudonym appeared in the non-standard form 'M'Diarmid'. Grieve-as-MacDiarmid was still very much a literary fledgling. At the time of *The Grey Coast*'s release neither *Penny Wheep* nor *A Drunk Man Looks at the Thistle* had been published (though Gunn knew that they were going to arrive).

Another pointer to a particularly Scottish intent is to be found in Gunn's mention of the decay of the fishing. This occurs in the schoolteacher's conversation with Peter Sinclair, a retired fisherman, about the dilapidated fish cooperage.

> What industry, carried on at what speed, with gaiety like blown spindthrift on the crest of it! Vanished – as a race vanishes! Why? The schoolmaster stirred. 'I hear the Fishery Board won't do anything,' he said. 'Just that!' said Peter. And then after a moment, 'Nor the proprietor nor the County Council nor any council o't!' 'I suppose it's had it's day and it's dying.' said the schoolmaster. 'I suppose just that,' said Peter ... (174–5)

Not only does this attack the lack of investment from Council and owner (the community against itself), it makes a jibe at the British Government, too – the power behind the Fishery Board. Once again Gunn's later work makes the point more clearly.

> The export of cured herrings to the Baltic was lost when Russia began her social experiment. Not that Russia no longer required herrings, but that the British Government kept changing its mind about dealing with her. The herring is immensely more important to Scotland than to England. But Scotland could not deal separately in this matter.

Norway, however, could and did. The Norwegian Government guaranteed Russian payments to the Norwegian fishermen to the extent of many millions of pounds. The Norwegian Government never lost a penny and the Norwegian fishermen got the market. It is interesting to reflect how the attitude of some politician seven hundred miles away may affect a seaboard and its people.[25]

Though Gunn was very much more involved in Nationalist politics in the 1930s, when this piece was written, than in the decade before, it seems unlikely that a man whose job it had been to visit areas of Caithness on Government business would remain unaware of how the southern masters were regarded. His own fishing background makes such insensitivity even less probable, and his involvement with Grieve makes a failure to recognise a national sensibility impossible.

That said, considerable blame is laid in the novel with the people of the grey coast themselves. If the Celtic Twilight romanticised a fatal flaw in the idealised Celtic peoples, Gunn accepted the flaw as decidedly unromantic. Jeems is both whore-master and voyeur while Tullach is mean, rich, and lascivious. Even Ivor and Maggie verge on a dangerous passivity. The real Gloom, Gunn argued, is economic and social, but also psychological. The reader is smothered in this crushing and complex twilight throughout *The Grey Coast*. The landscape reiterates the theme: the colourlessness of Maggie's surroundings seem eternal. 'Grey' is repeated over and over and for Maggie the greyness is spatial and temporal. Landscape and her future coalesce in numbness. 'Life was mean, mean and bare, with no colour to it, no warmth but the eternal greyness, that was a poverty, an exhaustion as of animal hunger' (113). In fact, the name of the location, Balriach, subtly reiterates this: 'riach' (from the Gaelic 'riabhach') is a Scots word for grey-white or drab. Greyness, it seems, is rooted in the very identity of the village. Gunn's grim pun near the beginning of the novel carries that suggestion, too: '[…] the rule was the small croft with its low grey dikes built of the boulders which the land in labour never failed to give forth' (13). Here it is as if the very earth is the beginning of the cultural still-birth; as if human effort, 'labour', is also the 'labour' of the earth's giving birth – to rock. Gunn makes it clear that the physical environment has its psychological correlative, with Maggie suffering in a kind of defensive limbo, 'as though the mind had got plunged in a grey vacancy, where reality was a matter of muffled echo' (11). Thus, while Jeems, Ivor, and Tullach are characters of varying degrees of action, albeit in a usually self-destructive manner (as befitting in the 'land of knotted rheumatism and dead things' (39)), Maggie is manifestly passive.

The bargaining piece in Jeems' deal with Tullach, she is servile to her uncle out of a loyalty and a distant gratitude, and this makes her behaviour towards Tullach evasive rather than confrontational. As we shall see, her attitude of acceptance has its equivalent in the attitudes of Celtic Twilight writers. That she eventually rises above it, rejects Tullach to his face, is Gunn's illustration of futility overcome, and it is significant that in the scene in which she does so (when at the milking) Gunn employs colour and light to accompany the feat.

> Through the blood mist in his eyes and the darkling atmosphere of the byre, her face blazed whitely at him like a lit-up corpse face. Her body had been a pillar of ice. His husky grunt of triumph, of further intention, wavered and broke. His glower wavered. He stooped and slashed the milk from his trousers-leg. 'That bluidy milk has wet me through!'
> (269)

White seems to break through Tait's psychological darkening. It is Maggie's 'whiteness' that sears him into defeat, and it is white milk (Gunn juxtaposing intensity with humour) that permeates to Tait's leg. His sexual gluttony, in effect, is spilling back on him, this being the last of the sexual associations Tullach makes at the thought of Maggie milking (16, 141, 147). But equally important is the fact that Gunn is showing Maggie's assertion of her rights as a thing of light. The continual grey of Gunn's descriptions in the novel (most of the novel takes place in the gloaming, and inside where the light is unclear) is here breached.[26]

Gunn's literary concerns tie in well with his use of light and colour. The seemingly self-contained drama is productively interpreted as an allegory of the youthful defeat of sexual repression, miserliness, economic hardship, and the arrogance of power, but *The Grey Coast* also binds these themes to the artistic defeat of the old Celtic Twilight. There are more explicit indicators, however, that this is what is happening. The first overt reference to the Twilight arrives via the character of the local schoolteacher,

Moffat. At first insensitive, Moffat is a prototype for Gunn's later benevolent but often misguided observer characters. The village intellectual – likable, though, for his willingness to be part of the community – he is disturbed by the possibility that common humanity may have become disconnected from art. Of course, this is a theme for Gunn, too. When Moffat quizzes Ivor on whether recent Celtic poetry has meaning for the reality of Ivor's life it seems clear that Gunn is asking a similar question. Does literature make any difference?

This theme is central to the Scottish Renaissance, and Gunn's early airing of it anticipates, for example, MacDiarmid's doubts. 'The trouble is that words / Are a' but useless noo / To span the gulf atween / The human and "highbrow" view'.[27]

Unfortunately, Moffat's manner of speculation seems in itself to reinforce the 'gulf'. He sees Ivor, for instance, as a 'sample, looming at him in a primal self-sufficiency, even positively with the air about him of brooding emotion!' (41). This flourish of pseudo-analytic racial stereotyping underlies the atmosphere Moffat creates, distancing himself from Ivor, who is visibly uneasy. For Moffat, Ivor is 'the Gael', a character from a Victorian 'Celtic' tragedy incarnate. Intoxicated with the writing of Fiona Macleod, Moffat dwells on one particular phrase from the preface to 'The Sin-eater': 'It is destiny, then, that is the Protagonist in the Celtic Drama' (43).[28] This, we are told, 'haunted him meaninglessly like an echo', implying that Moffat himself is uneasy with Gunn's acknowledged antecedent. An echo, after all, is simply more indistinctness, the grey that dominates with seemingly eternal squalor the eastern sea-board, yet behind the nihilism and defeat recalls a time of more vitality.

For Macleod, beauty and tragedy interlocked formed the appropriate subject for fiction of the Celtic fringe: 'The beauty of the World, the pathos of Life, the gloom, the fatalism, the spiritual glamour – it is out of these, the inheritance of the Gael, that I have wrought these tales'.[29] Such a theory of art has clear dangers. Macleod's enthusiasm for the abstract idea of 'destiny', of 'fatalism', was precisely the creed of resignation above which Gunn sought to rise, especially as Macleod's identification with Gaelic culture was so close to Gunn's sympathies. Art based on death-wish is hardly a healthy basis for a wider politico-literary rejuvenation. On top of this Macleod argued, like Muir in *Scott and*

Scotland,[30] that Scottish separatism was fundamentally over-ideal-
istic, and was in any case irrelevant to the development of a
Scottish artistic identity.

> I am ever but the more convinced that the dream of an
> outward independence is a perilous illusion – not because it
> is impractical, for that alone is a fascination to all of us, but
> because it does not, cannot alas, reveal those dominant ele-
> ments which alone can control dreams without actualities.
> Another and greater independence is within our reach, is
> ours to preserve and ennoble.[31]

The phrase 'cannot alas' typifies the tone of resignation that
pervades Macleod's writing. He consistently maintains that Scot-
land as a Celtic country has an inherent cultural weakness that will
always incapacitate it in any attempt at self-determination. The
'greater independence' of which he talks is roughly what Muir
would call 'an automonous literature', but Gunn refuses to make a
distinction between nationhood and cultural wealth. Instead, he
insists that art and political vitality are closely linked. He looks
abroad for a model that 'proves' art and nationalism can ascend
together, finding culmination in radical change.

That model is Ireland. It is no coincidence that the poetry
which finally acquires meaning in *The Grey Coast* is by Yeats.
While Macleod often cites Yeats in his non-fiction prose as the
best example of current-day Gaelic genius, distinctively Celtic
despite the language employed (only 'the instrument is English'),[32]
Gunn's position as regards Yeats seems more nationally aligned.
In his essay 'The Hidden Heart', the Abbey Theatre is seen as a
vital example of the joint rise of nation and art. The survival of
Irish culture beyond the pale is seen as hopeful for Scotland, too:

> The dissatisfied Scot may be feeling back for a potency
> greater, more imperatively needed by humanity at large,
> than he knows of. His stirring to a sense of receding na-
> tionality may also be an instinctive reaction against a world-
> wide gathering of mechanistic forces, his Celtic unconscious
> rebelling against the tyranny of the iron wheel.[33]

If this essay is not quite contemporaneous with *The Grey Coast* –
it was published two years after the novel – its argument was
nevertheless clear to Gunn from at least 1924, when Grieve had
written to him encouraging him to see himself as part of the
Scottish literary movement and, more practically, to contribute to

what he hoped would be 'equal to the Dublin Mag. – the splendid merits of which I concede'.[34] Gunn had also a very close friendship with the Irishman Maurice Walsh which began long before his association with Grieve. All through the 1920s and 1930s Gunn made visits to Ireland, and despite the tendency in current critical commentary to separate Gunn from the other writers of the movement, Cairns Craig's observation about the Renaissance is highly appropriate to Gunn: 'The great wave of Scottish literary reassertion in the 1920s which we now call the Scottish Literary Renaissance took both name and some of its impetus from the more politically focused Irish movement of the previous decade.'[35]

Gunn's use of Yeats in *The Grey Coast* puts forward this broad connection between art and politics, though, as always with Gunn, politics had to start very locally, ideally at the personal level of experience. Moffat is therefore on more solid ground with 'The Lake Isle of Innisfree' than with Macleod (45). Ivor is initially unable to understand Yeats's poem but this has more to do with Moffat's manner than anything else – a comment in itself. With the experience of physically detaching himself from his community Ivor comes to realise, however, that the poem's latent aspiration has potency.

> The schoolmaster, then, had his queer longings – and the
> poets who wrote the lines were men, with longings, too!
> And so all that stuff about the cabin and the bean-rows was
> a sort of longing thrown out towards that land there. (182)

In this there is a parable for Gunn's own art. The reader who may be as unfamiliar with Gunn's northern villages as Ivor is with Yeats's cabin and bean-rows need not dismiss the essence of the fiction. Moreover, the fact that Yeats's poem, especially in contrast to Macleod's voice of mourning, is aspirational – 'I *will* go' – makes it all the more accommodating. We recall Maggie's view of the pessimistic Mrs Hendry whose 'murning', her 'insincere art', 'breathed of the feelings with such expert facility that everything of grief but its heart trembled before one' (98).

Greater sincerity, greater verve, is to be found in the West, as Ivor discovers. Gunn portrays the Western Isles retaining the dances and songs dead in the east, and his particular interest in the Outer Hebrides (re-expressed in *The Silver Darlings*) may derive from a perceived anthropological link between them and Caithness. Thus Carmichael, whom Gunn had read, found the richest area of folk tradition on the Atlantic fringe, but he identified its connections with the east:

> The greater portion of the collection has been made in the Western Isles, variously called 'Eileana Bride', Hebrid Isles, Outer Hebrides, Outer Isles, 'Eilean Fada', 'Innis Fada', Long Island, and anciently 'Iniscead', 'Innis Cat', Isle of the Cat, Isle of the Catey. Probably the Catey were the people who gave the name 'Cataibh', Cat Country, to Sutherland, and 'Caitnis', Cat Ness, to Caithness.[36]

Ivor is deeply affected by the fiddle-playing and songs he hears 'abroad' (301), and soon after comes to a better understanding of himself. He resolves to return home. That this occurs 'on a rounded knoll' shows another early use of the Druid Hill motif. Relevant to the Twilight problem is Gunn's use, again, of the 'seeing' metaphor – of things becoming distinct despite the mist. Notice the indulgence of Twilight diction, too.

> It was a strange mood of cold exultation that followed, with its eyes seeing himself, life, everything, in a stark clarity, seeing beauty with a vision that was remorseless. The moon and the dim night and the loneliness about him, swimming in about him in swirls, like swirls from the secret, invisible passing of Beauty's self … And remorseless vision could see only the beckoning loveliness. His manhood came upon him then, and he shivered before it, and felt his breath cold on his lips. He saw himself, and he saw Maggie, and he saw his desires. The moment of realisation was absolute. (302)

It is with this new resolve that Ivor finally unites with Maggie. That they come together with 'the passion that had at last burst intolerable suspense and swept body to body' (320) is surely more physical than McCulloch's coy suggestion that they 'declare their love for each other' (this, in fact, they never do).[37] The sexual liberation is Gunn's symbol for the possibility of a much wider freedom; in its eroticism and metaphors of light it is anti-Twilight.

Though Tullach makes an attempt on Maggie's virginity, and Jeems delights in voyeuristic tales of sexual titillation, a sexual embrace occurs only at the end of the novel, separate from the dark claustrophobia of the gloomy byre where all the other erotic scenes take place. The very last words of the novel are 'searing clarity'. This is the freedom of light that Maggie and Ivor have won from the worst possibilities of darkness. It is what Gunn called elsewhere 'a counterblast to the Fiona Macleod twilights and from the land of Gaeldom!'[38] *The Grey Coast* relies on sexual frustration to instil the final embrace with greater force. Gunn constructs a series of erotic scenes that simmer on the edge of intercourse until the consummation of the last page. Parallel to these are Jeems's stories which increasingly inflame Tullach. Maggie's response to her own sexuality is dealt with at some length. Gunn makes the byre the place where Maggie's virginity is most threatened, and it is Tullach who does the threatening.

It is a subtle irony that Tait's land-inherited name is from a Gaelic-derived Scots word found in some places in Caithness. 'Tulloch' is a Scots word for a mound or hillock, specifically a fairy hill. It is also a disdainful Caithness colloquialism for a 'heap of money'. Gunn uses both fundamental senses: Tullach has become only a man of substance, and in so doing he has lost the connection with the culture that gave him his name's other meaning. Introduced to us following Jeems's hint at Maggie's proposed marriage to him, Tullach from the start is portrayed as Maggie's furtive (and then not-so-furtive) ogler as she stands in the light. Tullach takes 'a swift, sly, appraising look at the finely made, lithe body as it bent to the blaze' (10). But he also has a sense of importance that prevents him, initially, from undignified action. His desire and his social position conflict, so that despite this obsessive attention to Maggie – 'For all his talk and short gusty laughs, Tullach had listened to every sound from her first movement' (15) – he pauses before following here to the byre.

> And he hesitated because of some subtle forbidding sense of the dignity due him. He was no farm hand, no penniless, jaunty young fisher fool. What he was doing he was doing solidly, with the dignity of a man of substance, and the end was inevitable. (15)

Ironically, it is a 'penniless young fisher fool', unknown to Tullach, who is his chief rival. Importantly, Tullach's belief in the 'inevitable' – a sexual manifestation of Celtic Twilight fatalism – is equally misplaced. It is Tullach's arrogant assumption of omnipotence, paradoxically, that serves to frustrate him: his hesitations allow Ivor and Maggie to come closer together.

Instead of an assumption of an inevitable sexual possession, Ivor is shown to have profound self-doubts, feeling himself 'Of no more substance or weight in the eyes of men than a boy at the school.' (33). In contrast to Tullach, it is Ivor's low estimation of himself that causes him to hesitate in his approaches to Maggie. Maggie, on the other hand, seems to understand herself and her 'suitors', and, following another of Tullach's unsuccessful attempts on her virginity, she looks out to the sea with the growing knowledge of the extremity of Tait's lust

> knowing nothing beyond the flooding of dark revelation, an embodied shadowing of unspeakable things, enveloping, smothering gestures. She had not only read Daun Tullach: in a swift moment of awakened instinct she had known what he had felt. Known what he had felt, what had made his voice hoarse; and had escaped from his and it as if from a destroying ... (123)

In what follows Gunn introduces three motifs that are to reappear in most of his other novels: the hunt, the snake, and the circle. Gifford is technically incorrect when he says that the snake and the circle are first introduced in *Highland River*[39] – these exist indeed in earlier poetry, though *Highland River* expands their significance. Maggie realises that she is Tullach's sexual prey – 'that she was his game and he was after her – in that way' (127); earlier he had been likened to the traditionally vicious stoat (122). However, her deepening awareness of her own allure, and of Tullach's attraction to her, is a 'black snaky knowledge' (124) like the black snake of 'O Sun!', and Gunn makes it clear that in such serpent knowingness lies a strange pleasure: 'Yet is there a subtle fascination in a certain sort of danger more frightful than the danger itself, more compelling. The awakening heart knows it, burying deep the knowledge. And through that fascination there worms a thin nervous thread that throbs as with a curious sense of elation...' (127). In this embryonic duality of response to the serpent we see Gunn's bifocal perception of violence as both life-destroying and life-giving. Thus, for instance, Jeems' pathetic death is also liberation; the 'little mound of grey boulders' (319) that causes his death is in a sense the greyness liberating itself – it guarantees the release of his small fortune for Maggie.

Out by the cliffs the image of the circle is also raised: 'For a long time she lay very still caught away from her adventure of the byre into this circle of refuge, of strange freedoms; a magic circle of daring and fear, and in some inscrutable way of self-knowledge'

(127). It is this idea and symbol of psychological integrity that is to dominate Gunn's poetics in later novels. Here, Maggie's enjoyed alone-ness is akin, perhaps, to Joanna's in Catherine Carswell's first novel, *Open the Door!* (1920). As a girl, Joanna moves up the Perthshire hillside to lie by the 'haunted pool', enjoying 'the early stirrings of womanhood',[40] and on the same hillside, where the novel ends, Joanna finally finds a satisfactory partner.

In *The Grey Coast*, the cliff-edge is important for revealing the sexual parallels between character and landscape: 'Hypnotic in an awesome way, the eternal mating of cliff and sea' (126). Maggie's fascination for the rugged coast is partly to do with the contemplation of sheer size. She has a justified 'terror', after all, of 'being inside any place' (123), and much of the novel takes place in the cramped confines of croft, byre, hut, and box-bed. Measuring them against the sea, Maggie finds 'Her uncle, Tullach, herself – small dots of figure in comparison!' (126). This is also belittlement by comparison of age – the sea's foreverness shows the individual's insignificance – but most of all it is the vast metaphoric copulation of the elements, and Maggie's identification with its energy, that renders the sea, paradoxically, a comforter. In the coast's dynamic metaphor Maggie is made momentarily tiny, her profound anxieties and aspirations are given sufficient parallel: 'To feel as much was to have a sense of taking refuge in this mating of sea and cliff, a sense of being privy to its dark strengths, its perilous eternities' (126). Such enduring sympathy in Gunn's novels between humanity and landscape begins in *The Grey Coast*: 'And presently there came upon her a merging sense of oneness with the elements about her' (127). In particular, Gunn is interested in moments when 'communion' with the environment – sea, river, or hillside – precipitates a realisation of some aspect of character development. Here it is a crystallisation of Maggie's understanding of both the disgust and excitement of sex.

Such ambivalence is not just a simple Tullach–Ivor antithesis. Sex with Tullach is, briefly, a *warm* possibility (238) and Maggie's '*healthy* body' enjoys the thought of Tullach's. A male (Lawrentian) authorial fantasy, perhaps, but while her conquering emotion is rejection of Tullach, it should be understood that there has been opposition from the other camp. The choice is cruel because Tullach is physically attractive, and offers the lure of financial stability. Maggie's final rejection of Tullach is, on the one hand, a rejection of the lust and complacency of the powerful by the victimised. On the other, it is a denial of a safe way of life, however demeaning, and also (for all she knows) of the glorious spontaneity of sex.

That Jeems ignores Maggie's emotions for most of the novel (until her brave-faced No) may seem to illustrate an assumption in Jeems that women are irrelevant as sentient beings, but there is also the issue of security. Gunn's point, I think, is that on the grey coast debasement occurs because survival is the grotesque imperative (57-8). It is security, after all, which Jeems can guarantee Maggie as long as she is seen to be Tullach's intended, as Jeems genuinely sees her. It is true, too, that Jeems appears to incite Tullach to approach Maggie, as if to make the marriage more certain, or (more feasibly) because Jeems enjoys baiting the man who, in all but cunning, is his 'better'. The first dialogue between them shows the contrasts of temperament between Jeems and Tullach. Jeems feigns mental frailty by 'losing' his tobacco, and Tullach, sitting in 'the most comfortable chair' (9), is manipulated into offering his (superior) plug (10). The rich landowner boasts of his triumph against the County Council, and objects that the parish representative had been impartial (12). 'Decidedly a man of substance on the strip of grey coast', Tullach tries to live up to 'some subtle forbidding sense of the dignity due him' (15), but his every moment betrays him when he enjoys Maggie in his reverie (39). Tullach simply can't control himself – his breath, his hands, his face. Contrast this with Ivor's reticence when he is with Maggie: Tullach, on seeing them together, assumes with cynical ease that Ivor has sexual standards below Tullach's dubious ones. And sexuality for Tullach seems inextricable from dominance – 'Realisation would be the more absolute and crushing – then!' (17). It is Jeems who dominates Tullach, however, and he does so by retelling the taunting stories of his younger days. The bawdiness of the three yarns strikes at Tullach's forty-year bachelorhood while their exoticism attacks his insularity. The momentary 'searching puckishness' (17) of Jeems shows that the old man is very much in control.The tale he then tells, of one seaman introducing another to an Oriental whore, parallels exactly the relationship between the storyteller and his uncouth listener. Tullach is the attracted but tense ingenu and Maggie is the proffered piece. Thus, when Tullach says of the yearning sailor 'I jalouse he was anxious to go back' (20) he is expressing what he would have wanted to do. His comment about the sailor's ambiguous intent, 'So you could never be sure what he meant, eh?' (20) is similarly precisely how Tullach feels when trying to gauge to what extent Jeems teases him intentionally; his transparent humours contrast with Jeems' wiliness. The pattern is repeated later (149-50). The fact of Jeems' impotence (sexual and financial) and his past enjoyment of sex, albeit voyeuristically, is what most offends Tullach. As the narrative infected with Tullach's view shows, Jeems' ploy of depicting women as gifts-for-the-taking – literally *present*ing themselves to men – is exactly in tune with Tullach's sexism. Women with beauty are 'made for' man's enjoyment (150); women exist to be devoured by men; Maggie is 'ripe' (211).

Jeems achieves another victory over Tullach in the third and last major dialogue between them, when Tullach begins to glean Jeems' ingenuity. Here he insinuates, 'conversationally', that Ivor's desertion of Balriach is in fact a noble act (263-5). This in itself hurts Tullach because he is included among the 'women left behind' (265), but there is also a charged innuendo in Jeems' phrasing. When he says Ivor is 'better oot the way' this means, on the face of it, that the grey coast has nothing to offer Ivor; its subtext, however, is that a strong rival for Maggie has now been neutralised. His remark that 'it needs a little spunk' (265) to leave, as well as implying that Tullach boringly plays safe, more pointedly suggests sexual inadequacy. Naturally, Tullach is touched to the quick: the 'done cratur' is attacking his virility (266).

Despite Tullach's pride, it is difficult not to sympathise momentarily with his difficult, embarrassed proposal of marriage immediately after his humiliation by Jeems. 'Like one stricken to an intolerable poise,' Tullach is portrayed as nervous and (astonishingly) delicate, even if showing false modesty: ' "Tullach is no' a bad little croft. What?"' (267). His faltering speech gives way to a lunge, however, when he realises Maggie will never consent to marry him (269).

Tullach's punishment in the morality schema of the book is to become evermore an onlooker. The ferocious ending shows the young couple emerging from the psychologically barren hinterland Tullach had helped to sustain, and Tullach is 'sentenced' to ultimate frustration. The 'hinterland' is still his prison, and it is made all the worse because he has seen the lovers go beyond it.

2

Twilight and New Morning

The Poaching at Grianan, The Lost Glen and *Morning Tide*

I

The Poaching at Grianan was probably the second novel Gunn wrote. Serialised over eight months in *The Scots Magazine*, from 1929 to mid-1930, it was actually written before *The Lost Glen*, which finished its serialisation in the same magazine a few months beforehand.[1] It has never been published in book form, and if it ever were at less than 150 pages it would be Gunn's shortest novel. It is at times uneven, unpolished, and clumsily expressed. Yet a study of the extended fiction of this period would be incomplete without it, and certainly it adds to our understanding of the framework of ideas within which Gunn was working.

The novel opens in a grimly depicted Edinburgh, an immediate departure from the wholly rural *The Grey Coast*. Don M'Allister, originally from the Highlands but now working in the city as a journalist, impulsively follows his friend Callum, a middle-aged antique dealer, to the Highlands. There Callum plans to enjoy and hunting and fishing holiday at Grianan, an estate. Finla, an activist of what appears to be the underground left accompanies Don. They all become involved with the problems of a father and daughter come upon hard times: the Laird of Grianan, a MacDonald, has been forced to occupy only the Lodge of his once vast property, while the American Maines, with rights to most of the land, live in the Castle. Eilidh, MacDonald's daughter, is aware that her father's deteriorating mental health is a result of his 'fall' and she sees her marriage to the young Maine, Cyril, as a possible cure. Cyril Maine has a passion for Eilidh (Don comes to love her with more restraint). He arranges a dinner party at the Castle for both MacDonalds, but with the real intention of becoming more intimate with Eilidh. The humiliation of the dinner forces MacDonald to insanity. He shouts out his clan's Gaelic shibboleth and a little later disappears – heading into the remoter outreaches of the estate. Soon after, unable to see that it is the old man who is hiding in a bothie, Cyril shoots him as a poacher. Though Callum manages to see the old man home quickly, MacDonald actually wants to die and the novel finishes with his demise. The last paragraphs, however, show a delicate coming together of Don and Eilidh at the height of their sorrow.

The depiction of a debased Edinburgh, 'the slum that was once the Royal Mile of Scottish Kings',[2] shows earlier and more detailed engagement with the subject of the city than is generally perceived in Gunn's work. As the rather crude reference to an eminent past suggests, the nationalist point of view is more explicit than anything in *The Grey Coast*. Callum's antique shop, crammed with Highland memorabilia, is a deathly 'catacomb', and his shutting the door on it is for the better. Correspondingly, when he thinks of the fine weather expected at Grianan (Stokoe notes Grianan is Gaelic for 'the sunny place'[3]) it is with 'the thrill of an opening door'.[4] Callum and his sister Kirsty are living in a cramped apartment and have very little money. To a rather arrogant Callum the people about him are 'dark stunted growths below the level of his far look', the stench of a 'slum fish-and-chip shop' has a 'revolting warmth' which carries with it a heavy parcel of grievances.[5] Don and Callum share a Gaelic background, and the Edinburgh section of the novel is full of anticipation of a Highland idyll.[6] There is a much greater commitment in this novel to the idea of a whole Gaelic ethos. I will discuss more fully in the next chapter Gunn's qualified acceptance of Grieve's belief in a Celtic-based alternative to the pattern of established European culture, which was at work from an early stage. The opening paragraph in fact celebrates the 'fact' that the Gaelic language is void of 'those meaningless English swears'.[7] It is not a linguistic preference alone. Don sees the Gaelic culture as very much a Scottish one, indeed almost as *the* Scottish culture – 'not from any little-nationalist point of view but profoundly as a spiritual inheritance', – and this 'had brought him into friendly relations with the capital's underworld – more particularly on its Gaelic side'.[8] It is this that suggests to him an ambition that seems close to Gunn's: 'And at rare moments M'Allister dreamed of what he might do with his pen, intensely recreating as an artist the picture of a lost inheritance – as a new goal'.[9] Unfortunately Gunn's ambitions outstrip his skills. The fabricated Celtic-Gaelicism in the novel can be very clumsy, in particular Don's turns of phrase – witness his 'By the great Cuchulain!',[10] his 'echo of a Druidic chant', and 'I have put a circle around you'.[11] True, Don is aware that he is using '"poetic" or toy forms',[12] and he says such things only to himself, but Gunn is much more successful when he describes the diminished reality of the Scottish Highlands. As we soon learn, they are no idyll – if they have been forgotten they have also been neglected, and the deterioration contrasts with the recollections of Callum's sister who remembers her northern home as 'respectable', 'smoothly ordered', and 'a paradise'.[13]

Gunn focuses most intensely on the Gaelic predicament in his treatment of the Laird and his daughter. His description of the Americans who have taken over the Castle is occasionally fierce: 'If he had screwed down the Trust, over the estate deal, to the last unsqueezable pound, and left its nominal owner with a charity pittance, that was all in the matter of business.'[14] Existing only intermittently in the world of sanity, MacDonald's mental crisis shadows his usurpation, so that when Cyril invites him to the Castle for dinner, he takes a turn for the worse. Eilidh realises that her father's stepping foot in the Castle under such circumstances would be 'to have the past, the ghosts of the past, rising up before him'.[15] She sees the possibility of redemption in her own partnership with Cyril, and Gunn expresses this in the fatalistic vocabulary of the Twilight: 'she had experienced the fatal sensation of drifting helplessly towards him, of forces combining to fulfil her destiny, which was once more to be mistress of Grianan Castle'.[16] It is this danger of finally giving in that Eilidh eludes, but unfortunately her father's effectual suicide (he deliberately neglects his gunshot wound) is the old generation's way of defence. At Cyril's dinner part, MacDonald's traditional dress had already assumed 'the best characteristics of a death's head',[17] even if it was a gesture of defiance. The Laird's frustration at Grianan Castle – 'The brain was gathering a slow, a cunning knowledge of being trapped by ghosts' – finally surfaces in his Gaelic outburst.[18]

MacDonald's disappearance and flight to the wildest parts of the estate, the psychologically 'healing places', is his final retreat into what Gunn would have us see as an instinctual core of self-protection. When Cyril accidentally shoots the old man, Gunn distorts the popularly-conceived Highland world, the icon of which must be Landseer's *Monarch of the Glen*. Showing us inside MacDonald's bothie, he reveals a rather more sordid, though no less symbolic, view of what the Gael has become

> The interior was not unlike a Landseer composition seen in a nightmare. The laird with his close-cropped white beard, his commanding glance, his bare hairy chest and blood-soaked bandaged shoulder, was seated on a form against the gable wall, the out-thrust delicate nostrils of the extended stag touching his right foot.[19]

Gunn is also at pains to recognise that the enervation in Gaelic culture has partly been self-inflicted, an ambivalence that will recur in almost all of the novels up until and including *Butcher's Broom*. MacDonald's death-bed speech admits:

> It's a sad thing to see a race dying out. It's a bitter thing – to have assisted. Those of us who in our time had the knowledge, the power – we are responsible. And now the foreigner comes and builds his fire on our hearths. We have betrayed the trust in us. The day of the Gael is passing from these hills, his voice is dying. And now that it is so and all effort unavailing – we would cling – too late. Too late.[20]

Against this pessimism of the old generation, however, Gunn again uses the symbolism of light and colour so effectively deployed in *The Grey Coast*. This is most sensitively handled at the end, when a delicate grey dawn leaves Don and Eilidh alone together. There is none of the physical intensity of the union between Maggie and Ivor, which would have been inappropriate in the circumstances of MacDonald's recent death; even so there is a feeling of cautious optimism. Cyril has literally been ditched, wounded in a car crash precipitated by the sight of Finla. Though calculated to recover, Cyril can no longer wield power over Eilidh because her wish to see her father back in the Castle obviously no longer stands. Don, who has been only a little more than an interested observer for the large part of the novel, becomes a participant by moving to comfort Eilidh, and it seems that the younger generation of Scots have broken free from their fixings. Gunn, however, had not broken free. *The Poaching of Grianan*, despite isolated snatches of finer writing, lurches and flounders between a paranoid view of urban Scotland and a crudely

fictionalised view of Gaelic decay in the countryside. His next
novel not only pays more attention to reality, and in so doing
embraces its own symbolic drama, it is more even in delivery and
more accurate in its satire.

II

Dear Sirs,

  Against my better judgement I am prompted to thank you
for your critical note accompanying the return of my Ms,
The Lost Glen. [...]

  Those of us who are interested in what is sometimes called
the Scottish Renaissance Movement must, I suppose, be
sanguine enough to keep looking for the publisher who is
prepared to take risks! Though why we should expect him
to, heaven knows! for we are aware how comparatively easy
– and acceptable – it would be to supply the staple fare of
kilts, sporrans, and Romance, in island dawns and Celtic
twilights – not omitting a helping of cabbage from the
'kailyard'! But, amusing as it may seem, we are sufficiently
moved by the emergence of new forces in Scottish life to
keep blasting away at the new claim. Possibly, after all, it is
the only merit of *The Lost Glen* that it stands for the first
honest attempt, as far as I know, at introducing the High-
lands as they are today.Though honesty is not literature, I
grant you, even if it's satire, or irony, or anguish.

  Letter to Hodder and Stoughton, 18 May 1929[21]

Though *The Lost Glen* (1932) was published in book form only
after *Morning Tide* (1930/31), it was in fact written some years
before and serialised in embryonic form in 1928.[22] As McCleery
suggests, it was probably written in late 1927 and, like the lost
novels *The Lobster Pot* and *Cavern'd Echoes*,[23] it belongs to that
extraordinarily productive period when Gunn was writing not
only novels but poetry, drama, prose-sketches, and short stories,
and all the time working full-time for the Civil Service.

  It is the bleakest of all Gunn's novels, and seems out of keeping
with the ultimately more hopeful novels of the same period. The
plot centres around Ewan, a divinity student who has been finan-
cially supported by his maternal uncle but who has returned in
disgrace from Edinburgh. His sententious benefactor had caught

him having a rowdy though innocent drink with friends at his student lodgings, and that was the end of his divinity career. Returning to his Highland home for what he intends to be only a short stay before emigrating altogether, he finds his mother embittered and the whole community seems to have turned their backs on him. His father and, as we see later, Ewan's piper-friend, Colin McKinnon, are sympathetic, however. The worst happens when Ewan persuades his father, against the elder's better judgement, to go to sea for a fishing, and though the two are reconciled when Ewan explains what had happened in Edinburgh, the storm that has meanwhile mounted tips their boat over and Ewan's father is drowned. The first section ends with Ewan coming out of the sea alive.

Part Two opens about a decade later. Ewan now works as a ghillie for the rich visitors to the local hotel who require instruction for fishing on the lochs. Clare Marlowe, an Englishwoman, is one such. Apart from the holiday itself she is up north to visit the hotel's resident Englishman, Colonel Hicks, her uncle. He is a bigoted, condescending, and lascivious ex-colonial, and he and Ewan have a mutual antipathy. Clare is intelligent and very much her own person, even if she seems to romanticise Celtic life via the works of Yeats and 'Fiona Macleod'. She is attracted to Ewan, who in turn still harbours a secret self-frustrated love for Mary McKinnon, piper's daughter. In the course of this section we are also introduced to Colin and his sublime pibroch, 'The Lost Glen', a modern composition which apparently puts the tartanry of other airs to shame. In the background is a 'land raid', a crofters' sit-in on sheep-farming land they claim is ancestrally theirs, in which Ewan pessimistically refuses to get involved. Gunn also draws attention to the trade union movement's rejection of the crofters' cause on the grounds that the crofters are actually self-employed. At the end of this section, Ewan realises what an earlier unclear 'second sight' experience had been: the vision of his own death at sea.

The third section, 'Interlude', is given over to a brilliant, satirically realised village concert, in which locals give potted recitals for the benefit of the American laird and patronising guests. Its delivery in a script-like shorthand emphasises its staged artificiality, and shows Gunn willing to break form. Part Three resumes the story proper at the ceilidh held after the concert, where music and sensuality are liberated. Ewan explains to Clare the genesis of

Colin's 'The Lost Glen', but ruins the moment by clumsily kissing her. On another day the Colonel tries to rape Mary, though Mary does not report it. Later, suspecting he has become the subject of gossip, he flies into a temper when he overhears the ghillies speaking in Gaelic to each other. The sexual theme is continued when Ewan's sister, Jean, begins to act out of character. Only much later do we learn that she is pregnant. Her mother, now reconciled with Ewan, points out that she has been avoiding her, and Ewan determines to find out what's wrong. In this he fails.

Meanwhile the land raid has intensified. Ewan is finally drawn into the debate and delivers first a vision of how the Highland folk could profit from taking the Highlands back into their own control, and second, a fierce condemnation of the Liberal agent who is supposed to be defending them. It is just after this that Colin confides in Ewan the details of the Colonel's attack on Mary, and then circumstances lead Ewan to believe that the Colonel is also having an affair with Jean. Ewan is wrong, however, and we are shown Jean's real boyfriend, a student. When he finally learns that Jean is pregnant, Ewan assumes that Hicks is to blame. Despite his earlier resolution not to kill the Colonel for trying to rape Mary, when he happens on the Colonel he tries to strangle him. The old man's heart gives out before Ewan is finished. He disposes of the body with difficulty over the cliff-edge, and then, as if fulfilling his own second sight, he clambers into a boat. Colin can be heard playing 'The Lost Glen' as Ewan heads for his presumed suicide.

Though McCleery surveys some of the revisions of the serialised *The Lost Glen* made for final publication in 1932,[24] he does not mention the biggest change of all: the creation of Part 1 of the 1932 novel. The book's first section details Ewan's return to the village, the Edinburgh 'debauchery', and his father's death (the serial passes these over in a small flashback). The new section expands the serial description of Ewan's delicate relationship with this father, compressing their time together into days rather than the weeks of the serial, and showing more clearly that it is because of the special nature of his friendship with them that Ewan feels his father and Colin are profoundly disappointed in him.

> [...] What Colin would despise him for most was not carrying his undertaking through. There was something mean about his defeat, and weak. A hidden pride would never have allowed it. Something worthless at the core, turning soft and

rotten. Not the fine, secret Gaelic temper. [...]

For Ewan had betrayed something more than himself. And not to many is the awful power of betrayal given. To less and less in this ancient land. Therefore how jealously must the few guard it! The secret of the heather ale! ... hardly even a parable for the secret of the hidden steel. (27-8)

[...] His father was a grown man, like Colin: the final arbiters of that secret spirit which he had betrayed. (34)

The 'parable' Ewan is thinking of is Neil Munro's short story, 'The Secret of the Heather Ale'.[25] In this a defeated Highlander, Calum Dubh, defies a marauding clan by taking himself and the secret of his hidden whisky into death over a high cliff. Ewan is grimly punning, then, when he uses the phrase 'secret spirit'. As we soon learn, Ewan had not lost his 'fine, secret Gaelic temper', had not done anything to be ashamed of, and like Calum Dubh had protected the folk pride. Moreover, as *Whisky and Scotland* (1936) showed, whisky to Gunn was literally and symbolically the very best distillation of the 'Gaelic temper' or 'character'.

Ewan's disgrace, his moment of 'betrayal', occurred when he and some Highland friends had been taunted by their student friend, Lothian (whose name seems to underline the Lowland–Highland conflict at work). Mimicking a Highland accent, Lothian immediately raises the Highlanders' hackles and as the evening wears on one student, significantly called Munro, begins to sing a Gaelic song. At this Lothian declares that 'he detested that "maudlin Celtic-fringe much"' (39). Ewan responds only with a smile, which in turn produces Lothian's shouted obscenity. It is this which brings Ewan's furious uncle into the room.

Despite his uncle's overblown anger and hypocrisy, Ewan responds mutely (a significant change from the serial version, where Gunn had made Ewan much more vocal, telling his uncle 'to take his stinking money to the devil'.[26]) Ewan seems to a greater extent to act the quiet martyr, a textual change which is in keeping with the literary echo working through the whole of the new first section. For Gunn is making a very specific literary point in the Edinburgh scene. Lothian's taunt against the 'maudlin Celtic-fringe muck' is an attack on the Celtic Twilight values he (wrongly) ascribes to Munro's authentic Gaelic song. The other Munro, i.e. Neil Munro, was and still is associated with the Celtic Twilight. At the time of *The Lost Glen*, Neil Munro was *the* Highland author. Though he was a romancer and an adventurist, he also had a fine command of Gaelic–idiomatic English, and a sensual language as distinct from the vagueness of the worst of the Twilight. Wittig said of his best novel, *The New Road*, that 'There is a genuine effort to understand the Gael in terms of his country, of his tradition of story, *ceilidh* and poetry, of his history, of the indelible vestiges of the past where his race trod.'[27] However, 'Munro could have dealt with the fate of the modern Gael, but he never did', and it is with this that Gunn seems to be finding fault. The character Munro seems unable to move on from his heritage; to sing a Gaelic song is 'the last defiant thing he could do' (38). But, as Gunn said in his letter to Hodder and Stoughton, *The Lost Glen* 'stands for the first honest attempt, as far as I know, at introducing the Highlands as they are today'. In addition, the novel's reference to trade unionism and land raids, and to the fund to commemorate the Macrimmons' piping school (108), suggests a very contemporary setting.[28]

Tied up in *The Lost Glen* is this conscious sense of being a cutting-edge artist within a movement of like-minded artists in an enervated Scotland. When Gunn was corresponding with Salmond about serialising the novel, he stressed that his 'modernism' was also founded on a sense of nationality. 'There is such a lot waiting to be written about auld Scotia at the moment, too; rather vital, modern stuff, it seems to me.'[29] In this Gunn had been encouraged by Grieve, who had earlier made a comparison with Munro : 'Neil Munro is after a fashion representative enough [as a contemporary Scottish novelist] and has a solid body of work behind him [...] but I wouldn't give two brass farthings for anyone who duplicated his achievement.'[30] In Grieve's exhortation to Gunn to reach up to things unattempted yet in prose, something of worth in Munro, even so, is acknowledged. This is Gunn's attitude to him, also – one made all the more conscious in *The Lost Glen*, perhaps, by the fact of Munro's death in December 1930, the very time Gunn was revising the serial for Porpoise Press (no explicit reference is made to Munro in the serial).[31]

The character Munro's retreat to things Gaelic is to Gunn an understandable gesture of pride, but it is voiced by a drunk. Vomit and tears follow. Ewan, on the other hand, does not lose his dignity. He stoically accepts the responsibility his uncle wrongly places upon him, paralleling the silence Calum Dubh in 'The

Secret of the Heather Ale' keeps when he sacrifices himself on a point of integrity. Both Calum and Ewan would rather be suicides than submit to a demeaning power. Unfortunately this pride is its own destroyer, as the novel as a whole shows, and as the Edinburgh incident dramatises in microcosm. When backward-looking and suicide become the fabric of commitment, the result can only be tragic – the desolate conclusion of the book is the logic of Twilight poetics worked through.

Ewan finally believes, like the Twilight writers (but *not* like Gunn), in a pervasive futility, so he offers no help to the crofters in their uprising, though he chastises the establishment politicians and has contempt for the Glaswegian trade unionist, Duffy. The political context for this can be found in Ireland in the actions of early Sinn Fein. They actively encouraged land agitation before they realised that it alienated their more wealthy supporters. Henry Patterson has described the pre-Easter Rising Sinn Fein as 'a small if energetic alliance of Irish language and cultural revivalists, economic nationalists and a smattering of representatives of the underground physical force tradition'.[32] The nationalists in Scotland were a ragbag of all these types, except the last, and Gunn would seem to be flirting with the land rights parallel, too. Sinn Fein had a firm grasp of agrarian politics, and they were able to outmanoeuvre their political opponents by manipulating this 'revolutionary nationalism with a conservative social content'.[33] It would be wrong to think that Scotland's social fabric was anything like as rural as Ireland's, and though Ewan describes what could be done with the Highlands if the crofters had control – 'at the worst we could always import a Dane or a Swede, or even an Irishman, to show us how to run things' (285) – the implications are not followed through, as they are in, say, *The Drinking Well*.

The novel's title is another specific echo of Munro's work, 'The Lost Pibroch'. This story describes two pipers who come across a hidden idyll, Half Town, where they find a thriving community and also an old blind piper, Paruig Dall. As all the pipers exchange tunes and talk, the old man reveals that he knows a previously lost ancient air, supposedly the crown of all pibrochs. When the travellers request that he play it, however, he warns them:

> 'I did not tell you that the *Lost Piobaireachd* is the *piobaireachd* of good-byes. It is the tune of broken clans, that sets the men on the foray and makes cold hearth-stones.

[...] It is the tune that puts men on the open road, that makes restless lads and seeking women. Here's a Half Town of dreamers and men fattening for want of men's work. They forget the world is wide and round about their fir-trees, and I can make them crave for something they cannot name.'[34]

It is this potential for internal decay that is the psychological bulk of *The Lost Glen*. When Paruig's admirers still urge him to play, his surrender precipitates the fall of Half Town as the villagers, especially the men, gradually leave. Yet for Gunn, the problem is the other side of the emigration dilemma: what to do if one stays. *The Poaching at Grianan* introduced the reader to what was now the playground of the English, American, and Scottish middle-classes. The Highlander seemed only to have his or her identity as a function of servility. Ewan disapproves when his sister Annabel seeks a place at the American millionaire's Lodge (158-162), but he has to admit that he is himself a ghillie to comfortably-off foreigners.

Yet 'The Lost Glen', Colin's pibroch, shows that Highland culture can be vital and not simply repeat past glories. In the serial Gunn makes this explicit, especially contrasting this modern form of an old art with the mythic irrelevancies of Scotland's Tartan Charlie inheritance:

> That's why not all the Jacobite pipe rants that were ever made have a fraction of the greatness of your composition, 'The Lost Glen', because it is a miraculous expression of something very intimate that stirred your spirit. That's what the great pipe music should be; and what if our self-expression had not been arrested at the tribal stage – it might have become.[35]

Munro's stories from the shielings *are* arrested at the tribal stage. They are not the kind of self-expression to which Gunn aspires. Even so, Colin's sincerely-felt composition becomes in the novel an ambiguous creative model. The exclusion of the above quotation in the book suggests, indeed, less than a full endorsement. At one point Ewan explains that 'The Lost Glen' was based on a real glen Colin had come across, but that in the actual act of art, '"He could not leave the glen's innocence alone. He had to people it with its fancy. Poets seem fond of doing that. They can't leave an exquisite thing alone. He said, however, that it is the mood to create life and that it leaves us helpless." ' (241). Balanced against this is the tune's restorative quality. The night Colin composed it, his wife had recovered from a serious illness. Gunn suggests, in a complex story, the consequences of ignoring such an exemplar. Instead of finding hope in 'The Lost Glen', Ewan seems paralysed until chance, murder and suicide offer their exit.

As Gunn told Hodder and Stoughton, this is a novel of 'satire, or irony, or anguish' – it is not a straightforward recreation of Twilight gloom but an attack on it. In the serial version, Clare had pinpointed the dichotomy between the Twilighters' fascination with their own literary constructions and the reality on which that fascination was very loosely based. It is upon the real Highlands that Gunn would have us focus, even if *The Lost Glen* is a symbolic drama rather than a novel of realism.

> Very magical and beautiful and sad and pretty, those mod-
> ern Celtic poets. As though they were frightened to face
> their world as it really looked to them, here and now, hill
> and moor and loch and sea, in the eye. As though minds fed
> on ancient poetic imagery they were unequal to face what
> really existed, what must presumably have struck them as
> being the colossal burnt-out ruins of a dead world … But it
> wasn't dead.[36]

Clare is unfamiliar with the works of Fiona Macleod until a hotel guest from Kelvinside lends her a collection of poetry. That the Lowland middle-classes should be interested in Fiona Macleod seems rather apposite to Gunn's view of the Twilight, yet when Clare reads Macleod's 'Mo-lennav-achree', she defends it against the sneers of 'the men critics', the 'positive scientists [… who] were so sure they knew everything' (175). Her quotations from early Yeats are also highly suspect, combined with interpretations of what Ewan and his folk are actually like. 'Perhaps they were all extraordinary, these people! Had looked on the dark wind and seen the "hosting of the sidhe!"'[37] These reactions epitomise Clare's complex nature: on the one hand her educated feminism, her self-confidence and sense of her own worth as a woman, and on the other, her susceptibility, even so, to the flush of romanticisation.

The sceptical distance Clare keeps from her uncle shows that all England is not being portrayed in the Colonel, even if his enraged whipping of thistles in a field, following his attempted rape of Mary, has a clumsy national symbolism. Clare sees straightaway that Hicks has been abusing his ghillie (116), yet she also has some sympathy for her uncle as a man in desperate decline (149). When Hicks threatens to thrash Ewan for becoming too intimate with her, she makes it clear that she is utterly independent: "'You will please understand that I am accustomed to do as I please'" (306). Clearly, the English too can behave with sensitivity and integrity – a point that needed saying in a novel featuring a specifically English, brutal character. Like Forster's *Passage to India*, a deliberate attempt is made to portray opposing cultures as each fundamentally complex in themselves, with their own divisions and internal tensions and versions of their own culture.

McCulloch asserts that in matters of love and sex, Clare's thoughts fail to 'escape the confines of women's magazine writing'.[38] This is an understandable reading of Clare's sentimentalising, but an incomplete one. Clare is a much stronger character than such an analysis would suggest, and able to think positively about sex and her own sexuality. 'Sex after all meant life, came out of life. And this growing towards health and colour was warm and inviting. It made the body feel a lovely thing as if a lily had got flushed with rose' (173). This is close to Joanna's view of sex in Carswell's *Open the Door!* – 'could anything be wrong which gave such release, such harmony with the golden world and the violet heavens?'[39] Yet Clare is made vulnerable by the very things she thinks she has under control, and when Ewan's presence produces an amorous reaction she is flustered. 'The whole thing was so – coming all at once – humiliating' (203). Clare's sense of control of her own body, even as she welcomes the celebration of it, is at odds with her feelings when an allegedly more instinctual reaction takes over. In contrast to her manipulative use of sexual imagery in her letter to her boss (172-3), Clare now finds herself struggling for balance.

She seeks that balance on the night when Ewan kills Hicks. Promising herself that she will try and gain Ewan's further intimacy, she sets off, tragically, in the wrong direction. The disappointment in all the love-matches in the book is yet another example of the grand failure Gunn constructs. Even 'The Lost Glen', the sublime new composition, is used with bitterness at the end. Ewan fails its promise of rejuvenation because he is locked into a way of seeing that Gunn sympathetically rejects. As Ewan prepares for his own death, Colin's air wrongly becomes 'the piobaireachd of good-byes'.

It was Colin, at 'The Lost Glen'. Colin! He smiled, listening. On the flat space yonder, piping immortal defiance at the storm! Piping 'The Lost Glen' ... the glen that was lost ... forever lost. The old adventure was over. Eddying little wisps ... dying out ... gone. (351)

III

Morning Tide was published at the beginning of 1931.[40] A Book Society book of the month, arguably as a result of enthusiastic promotion by Faber's Frank Morley, it has lived up to its first accolade.[41] One of Gunn's most reprinted novels, it has an immediate human warmth in its affectionate depiction of childhood. It was also the first novel of Gunn's published by the culturally nationalist Porpoise Press, though they had issued his collection of short stories, *Hidden Doors*, in 1929. Porpoise was not much more than a Faber agency by this time, operating from London and with Faber's production and distribution resources until just before the War, when it folded for good.

The exquisite prose of *Morning Tide*'s opening has its hero of sorts, the boy Hugh, marvelling at the land and sea scape in which he unsteadily walks. He looks with wonder at the seaweed, is fascinated by it lying about him; he enjoys a 'faint excitement' as he pokes about among the rocks. This is a moment of independence – the 'secret water's edge' (9) is a place where the ordinary miracles of existence can be savoured, without company to enforce a blasé response. Hugh is still thinking of the social world – a shell is beautiful in itself but 'also something to "show off" ' (10) – yet most of all he is enjoying his solitude. Hugh is so enthralled, in fact, that the reader is not immediately told that he is also desperately cold – 'His body twisted and wriggled inside his clothes searching for warmth' – and that his sole purpose for being on the beach is to fetch bait for his father. Hugh's 'sense of wonder', momentarily, has overcome weather and duty.

Gunn expresses Hugh's self-absorption with a sophisticated, at times grimly funny, stream of consciousness, as in the episode of the pig butcher (11-12). In effect, Hugh is trying to reach up to the adult world of folk wisdom and its reality of violence while holding on to his own valuable sensibility. Muir makes a similar point in *An Autobiography* when he, too, describes the effect of the community's pig-killer on a young boy's imagination.[42] Gunn dramatises the slaughter but tempers it with the stress on the potency of the sensual experience – knife, neck, blood.

Hugh's self is often under attack, and he usually responds by fortifying his solitariness. His mother wants to prise an explanation from him when the blood on his jumper suggests a debacle, so he retreats out back (36); when his brother Alan has begun the one-way journey to Australia, Hugh finds a place among the birches to sob (186); and his mother's severe illness precipitates his withdrawal to the byre door to gain perspective (231). Pride in 'manliness' has much to do with this. Always not very far from tears, if only because Gunn makes the three parts of the novel describe three highly charged events in Hugh's life, Hugh is determined to 'be a man' about his crises. There is occasionally a wish among others to welcome him as a novice into the adult world and when this occurs Hugh becomes haughty with the privilege. For instance, when Alan introduces Hugh to the young pipers and they go poaching, Hugh thinks of the boys of his own age with what he thinks is adult disdain: 'What bairns they were, crying after their mothers for food!' (162).

If adults sometimes allow Hugh into their world, at other times he enters without their bidding. This is true especially for Kirsty, Grace, and Charlie, who form Hugh's initiation into the adult confusions of love. Muir, writing a month before *Morning Tide* was published, felt that in writing about childhood, matters sexual were crucial. 'The saving virtue in any description of childhood and love, both so difficult to describe without excess of sentiment, is a sense of proportion, a just evaluation of the most subtle and yet insistent realities […]'.[43] The first insistent reality for Hugh is Grace's failure to acknowledge him as her brother when he encounters her walking with Charlie. This is particularly galling to him because, having just fought with fair success a schoolyard rival, Hugh considers himself of special account. To the couple, however, 'he had not been a warrior, he had been a little fool' (32). This feeling of being unjustly ignored is clearly more important to Hugh than the fact, which we learn later, that Charlie is already amorously committed to Grace's sister, Kirsty. Hugh wants so much to establish his credibility that the discovery of the 'irregularity' in his sisters' social life is of no great concern. Only, later, when Kirsty asks if he had seen anyone while on the road, does Hugh glimpse the emotions at

stake, and the deception in which he is forced to participate
pushes him into further awareness:

> The lie remained there through the evening. He could not
> get over it. After a time, however, it gave him a quiet
> strength, as if in that still moment by the back door he had
> looked on the pale glimmer that is the ghostly face of grown
> life. (50)

Gunn reserves Grace for singular treatment. He points first to her
duplicity by dwelling on the connotations of her name. She de-
livers a 'gracious reproof' to Hugh when she is denying him (28)
and she is, again, a 'gracious woman' when offering him money to
seal his confidence (33). This expert superficiality, does have,
however, an attraction – 'what lured in the beauty was its smooth
grace' (38). Later, Gunn contrasts the simplicity of a meal's
blessing, a grace (41), with the sister's deception: 'Grace was
twenty-three years of age, and nothing that she wore suited her so
perfectly as her name' (42).

Because Hugh, being our way into the other characters' per-
sonalities, would leave Grace condemned almost unequivocally as
superficial, a two-dimensional psychology Gunn is loathe to ac-
cept, the author unusually foregrounds Grace's vulnerability from
a direct narratorial point of view:

> There came a singular, almost childlike, innocence upon
> Grace's face. The skin was pale and smooth about eyes that
> were troubled with pain, that was none the less acute for
> being indefinite. It was the face of a young woman who had
> all the instincts of beauty and yet was profoundly chaste,
> and who had inevitably reached the point of being afraid;
> not afraid of anything or anyone so much as of being
> scorched, of being burned, in her body. (106)

Grace's previous worldly manipulation is revealed as shielding a
more vulnerable sensibility. Part of the charm of *Morning Tide* is
just this divide between what Hugh is interested in, and what he is
close to without feeling the significance that we, as readers, feel.

A turning-point for Hugh occurs when he and Alan, unseen,
observe Charlie and Grace advancing towards them and, because
Alan is there, Hugh is able to assess how serious the lovers' liaison
is by watching the reaction of his elder brother. When Alan shows
a deliberate reticence Hugh begins to realise the sexual nature of
the bond between the lovers (146). The excitement of the poaching

soon diverts Hugh again, and it is not until the morning's poignant
farewells that Grace's night movements are recalled. It is then that
Hugh arrives at a more compassionate understanding, distanced
from his accusations of the night before (145). Hugh is realising
that a plurality of human problems exists outside his own imme-
diate ones, and that he has to take cognisance of them. Grace's
wordless communication with Kirsty when they are saying their
farewells redeems her in Hugh's affections, and against our first
impressions establishes Kirsty as the more emotionally resilient of
the two sisters:

> Grace kissed Kirsty, and as she did so the coat collar slipped
> from her white neck, whereon Hugh saw a thin red scar the
> length of a bite. Grace burst into tears. Kirsty's face came
> away from the embrace, her lips quivering sweetly, her blue
> eyes brimming. But her look was steady, the faintly flushed
> skin almost transparent, the eyes all light. (182)

Hugh 'turned hurriedly away', but the new understanding is
there. Grace *feels* what she has done, to herself and to her sister;
the Judas symbolism of the previous night's final family meal was,
after all, inadequate. Already Grace has been re-embraced in
Hugh's circle of love: 'He loved Grace at that vivid instant; he
loved her quite irrationally; was secretly proud of her, thrilled by
her, so that he could have wept for the something that struggled
towards impossible expression in her face' (182).

The complications of the Grace–Charlie–Kirsty triangle reveal
their intensity in Gunn's skilfully described *moments*. The kiss
between sisters bears a weight of cinematographic power, an
analogy supported by Hugh's peculiar observer role in the novel.
Perhaps the best example of this is Hugh's accidental eavesdrop-
ping when he finds himself amongst trees just fifteen feet from
Charlie and Kirsty, their delicate tense argument moving towards
more intimacy. Forced to play the spy, a prototype, perhaps, for
the arch-onlooker of Gunn's next novel, Aniel (*Sun Circle*), Hugh
witnesses his sister exhibiting uncharacteristic weakness. Her
powerlessness fluctuates – when Charlie reaches for her 'with an
explosive energy she shoved him back' (201) – but it is clear that
Charlie has the psychological advantage, and Kirsty's contempt,
which is partly a contempt for her own fragility, has in it the
bitterness exposed to the core:

> 'I know you were playing with me. Perhaps you were

playing with Grace. I don't know. I don't care. I detest you
– and I'm glad of it. I'm glad to be free of you. I hate you.'
The harsh ugly primitive elements strove for utterance in a
raucous voice. She was not magnificent: she was laid bare.
But the final basis is human, is flesh. The body speaks. It
cries. It is urgent and without grace. But in the same measure
it is potent and terrible. (204)

Kirsty is truly 'without grace'. Hers is a demeaning defeat because
she seems to be Charlie's reserve lover. In short, she is graceless
because he is Graceless.

Charlie and Kirsty are helpless within their set of cultural
archetypes; 'they were fated'. Gunn has woven the idea of Celtic
Twilight inevitability into the unassuming fabric of his love story.
Kirsty and Charlie, both personalised, exist also for a moment
within a mythological framework that fixes them as The Lovers
(Catherine Carswell felt, however, that Kirsty 'was a put up job',
and too good to be true[44]). But the 'fate' which seems to be
drawing them inexorably into intercourse is broken, without the
bathos a paraphrase suggests, when Hugh's friend Bill falls out of
his tree. The embrace, pressed by Charlie against Kirsty's will,
dissolves, and once again in Gunn's fiction we are shown the
erotic operating symbolically. 'Fate' is transformed. From less
than mutual enjoyment there arises an affectionate togetherness.

Earlier, Hugh's sense of erotic excitement had dissipated his
wish to 'save' his sister. Indeed, he had used the accident of
discovery to indulge his awakening sexuality, equipped with the
easy justification of being the sole witness (so he thinks):

A thin fire crept over Hugh. The impulse to fight for Kirsty,
that could have heaved a smashing stone at Charlie, that had
hated the degradation of his sister, that had quivered with
futile wrath, feeling weak and impotent, was now licked up
by this warmth, this trickling, tingling fire.

A strange and terrifying curiosity beset him, grew in him.
The glittering pagan look came back into his eyes. Secrecy
drew her smooth ecstatic veil about him. His lips came
adrift, his breath panting a little. (205)

For one contemporary reader, a Miss P. M. Kerr of Strathblane,
this was going too far. Spoiling 'the beauty of the story', reading
incidents of this kind was 'like coming suddenly upon something
rotten & unclean'[45]. What is special about *Morning Tide* is that

Gunn does range from truly magical moments in childhood (always, however, with a certain austerity) to intrusions of adult complexity. Here, Hugh's contrary impulses are paralysed by the erotic one.

Moments of a different timbre are to be found at *Morning Tide*'s sea edge, especially in Alan's rescue and his father's safe return. It is in this novel that Gunn establishes himself as a gifted artist of sea-scapes, whether it be the moody, irritable ebb at the beginning of the book or, later in Part 1, in the near-consuming surf beyond the break-water. *The Lost Glen* certainly introduced this aspect of Gunn's achievement – the death of Ewan's father and Ewan's enigmatic survival are not easily forgotten – but in *Morning Tide* the sea is described in a richer prose, and there is a completely new emphasis on the villagers' involvement *as a village* in the plight of the fishermen. The major contrast in the plot, of course, is that in *The Lost Glen* a father and son go to sea but only the son returns – to stagnate towards further tragedy – while in *Morning Tide* both father and son return. This is a success within the dramatic whole of Part 1 even if it is undercut by the later emigration of the son, Hugh's brother. The excitement and resolution of the sea incident provides an elegant and saga-heroic 'closure' some one hundred and fifty pages before the end of the book.

That the opening section could stand alone as a completed work of art is not too surprising: it is actually a superior expansion of a short story, 'The Sea', from four years previous.[46] Nevertheless, Gunn is clearly trying something different here. By having three parts marking three quite different events in Hugh's early life, each complete in themselves, he removes the normal continuity of the novel form. The psychological dynamics behind an individual event is the important thing.

As I have suggested, the Celtic Twilight is still a literary concern, despite the lessening of the literary self-consciousness of previous books – no Moffat, no Macleod, no Munro or Yeats. The mention of Walter Scott (108) is a wry if important aside but the values of the Twilight have been absorbed without trace of their literary excrecencies. Gunn has synthesised them within the non-intellectual lives of his characters.

The sea rescue and the events leading up to it bear witness to this. Waking in the early hours, Hugh hears Kirsty and his mother, who are obviously distraught: 'Their voices had the high sad quickening of fear. A sense of mortal loss came upon him' (62). This mood quickly gives way, however, to a greater resilience. Mrs MacBeth has 'something quiet in her voice now, like the emotion that acknowledges doom, yet is not defeated' (62). Importantly, Hugh adopts this element of endurance, speaking with 'a voice like his mother's' when Grace emerges frightened from her room. Kirsty, however, expects the worst: '"Oh, Grace, they're on the sea in that!" And in the brave cry was the note: They cannot live through it' (63). Kirsty is only 'brave' because she is expressing what Grace feels. Her mother suspends judgement – 'We cannot say. It is not in our hands' – but Kirsty's problem is that she is 'imaginative'. Here, her imagination is out of place, is ill-applied because it is alarmist. But that quality in Kirsty can manifest itself positively, as an earlier description indicates:

> For Kirsty had had the rare quality that is called imagination, and her eyes had often to remain steady in order to let her imagination go to work.
>
> And there was something, finally, in Kirsty that was like story-telling in a saga. At great moments it came into her voice. Her love had to be for someone or something outside herself. Her love for any member of her family in peril had the simple awful note of the great hero-stories. (45)

For Gunn, intimate caring has its homologue in heroic story-telling. Individuals assume a meaning at once specific to them and yet with a meaning beyond them. Amidst the storm this is reiterated, when Kirsty seems again to despair.

> 'Oh, Hugh – they'll never come home – through this.' At that moment Kirsty had for Hugh the born voice of the story-teller and the story-teller's imagination. Her tone was not mournful: it was sweet as the honey of woe; its intimacy went down through the personal to the legendary where the last strands of being quiver together. Beneath these strands there is black nothing.
>
> 'Be quiet!' said Hugh.
>
> 'I know,' agreed Kirsty; then broke the loaded silence, 'it's Alan. Mother told him not to go.' (68)

Kirsty's fatalism has the sweetness of 'the honey of woe'. Arguably, this is a peculiarly Scottish delectable: the sensibility of the 'joy of grief', as Kenneth Simpson has recently highlighted, goes back to the eighteenth century works of James (Ossian) Macpherson.[47] By characterising Kirsty sympathetically, but also as one who diverts her energies into the bliss of sorrow (albeit a genuine sorrow for her father and brother), Gunn brings the curse of sentimentality very much home. He then tempers this by having Hugh insist that such thoughts are better kept quiet, even though it is obvious he shares some of his sister's sense of foreboding.

It is Hugh who rises above such desperation, and he it is who assumes the role of leader: 'she had him for manliness and he had her to lead. So they were both comforted and encouraged' (70). This *is* a sexual discrimination: Hugh is struggling to temporarily replace 'the men of the house'. In flexing his man-child muscles, Hugh finds Kirsty too willing to suppose the worst, but this is nothing to the resignation Kirsty encounters in Morag Fraser, wife of one of the fishermen. Not bothering to rise from her bed and so involve herself in the vigil at the harbour, Morag is the true Twilight figure in the novel. That Kirsty hates her creed of defeat, delineates the two women's levels of vitality (74). Like Maggie in *The Grey Coast*, who keeps the 'murning' Mrs Hendry at arm's length, Kirsty feels compelled to literally escape from the gloom and she and Hugh go down to the harbour without Mrs Fraser.

As if in compensation for this act of faith, Morag's grim expectations prove illusory. The fishermen's safe return, though, is at numerous points shown to be by no means assured. 'The Viking', a respected veteran seaman, is as worried as Kirsty as they all look out to sea (84), but the preparedness of his fellow men for the rescue operation shows the community in general ready for the challenge. Kirsty lapses again when she sees Alan go off the edge of his boat at the treacherous shore-edge, and Twilight 'fate' momentarily reinstates itself before Hugh tells her again to hold her tongue: 'Fate will take such a man through the great danger, through the crisis, in order to kill him in a final odd moment born out of pure chance. This was the knowledge that was in Kirsty's bones' (88). This is, on the one hand, hard-headed realism, but the heroism and skill of the people on the land and on the sea conspire to triumph over such fatalism. All are saved, and the 'red ecstasy of the dawn' (101) accompanying the return of Hugh's father and his crew is an appropriate symbol for the defeat of earlier gloom.

In the second part of the book, this happy outcome is seen in the context of a previous disaster, when Hugh's oldest brother,

Duncan, had been killed in similar circumstances. The story is told by Hector, a name already used for a minor character in *The Poaching at Granan*, and who recurs with greater importance in later fiction. Here Hector is sixty years old, a fine piper, and a consummate story-teller. The drowning, like the most recent incident, had involved father and son, MacBeth at the tiller of one boat, *The Scots Rose*, and Duncan in the other, the *Fateful*. When a squall envelops them they lose sight of each other: when it clears only the father's boat remains: "'Of the *Fateful* there wasn't a trace, not a spar, not a plank, nothing. She had sailed right under.'" (150). As with Ivor's enduring *The Dawn* in *The Grey Coast* and Alan's *Morning Star* in this book, Gunn does not lose the opportunity of making his boat-names carry an extra message. Scotland via *The Scots Rose* is a stout hero and the seemingly better equipped *Fateful* proves fatefully the weaker. While this amounts to a kind of cultural fable, to Hector the story has a different message. He has told the story to remind Alan of his mother's profound fear of the sea, and thus explain her motivation for encouraging him to emigrate: "'She would rather lose you to Australia, where you will live, even though she should never see you again – rather than that you should follow your father'" Mrs MacBeth's protectiveness is to be found in several of Gunn's novels, and Hart and Pick identify a similar motivation in Gunn's own mother.[48] It is counterpointed by the father's wish for a continuity from generation to generation. As Hector explains: "'a man likes someone to come after him. [...] A man founds himself, and his race. It's not a bad old race. It's all we've known'" (151). Hector does not romanticise the hardships of remaining, but the depth of feeling he expresses seems too much for Alan who tries to circumvent it by maintaining an air of fun. Hector's pipe tune, *Chi till mi tuille* ('I shall never more return'), leaves the boys in no doubt that their leaving is no small tragedy (155).

The pibroch of goodbyes in Part 2 is succeeded in Part 3 by a hymn of joy. Despite McCulloch's view that 'Part III of the novel is on the whole superfluous',[49] there is much to praise in it. It is worth remembering that the original title of the book, 'Under the Sun' is taken from the Scripture quoted in this section (242). In the preceding sections, Mrs MacBeth is established as a character of determination, but also of benevolence. If she is over-protective of her sons, this is to some extent counterbalanced by her husband.

Hugh and Alan, like Kirsty and Grace, are also adept at keeping themselves to themselves when needs be. What happens in the third part, however, is a shock. The mother is shown to be frail. Her weakness in the heart, which we learn (perhaps a little contrivedly) has been long established, has worsened since Alan's emigration. Perhaps this is a kind of guilt response, compounded with the simple terrible loss. Kirsty had remarked, after all, that emigration was just like a death. When Hugh and later Kirsty return to the house they find their mother very ill indeed. Each feels guilty for lingering out of doors, and Hugh realises that Kirsty's guilt is exacerbated by her having been with Charlie in the intimate woods (Hugh's urgent run to contact the doctor antici-pates Finn's much longer journey to save his mother from dysentry, in *The Silver Darlings*).

Preparing for her own death, Mrs MacBeth turns to the Bible. *Morning Tide* is the first Gunn novel, in fact, to incorporate a major Christian theme. It is also the beginning of a long engage-ment with the ideas and symbols of Christianity. Character-istically, Gunn introduces Christ with the image of light, Hugh observing the red misery of sunset as once he had been exhilarated by the happiness of a red dawn: 'It was like a light he had seen in a picture of the Crucifixion' (231). Yet Hugh defies the religious significance he himself has read into the sunset. The life impulse in the individual is what counts, and one must not be carried away by the ease by which one symbolises the worst, attractive though these symbols can be. Hugh strives to keep 'this gloom, this death' at bay (234), first by initially refusing to see his mother, and then by shouting and singing (234-5), keeping the doctor in mind 'in a fugitive visual way' (235). But when the doctor finally arrives there seems no two ways about it: '"I doubt if she will see the morn-ing"' (239). The readers, too, become woeful pessimists. When Kirsty reads Ecclesiastes at her mother's side, however, a whisper of higher perspective seems to undermine the utter despair.

The presentation of Kirsty's reading is unusual. The embedded italicised quotations are accompanied by what amounts to a commentary on the relevance of the text not only to Mrs MacBeth but to the way of life of which she is a part. These words of exegesis would be out of place if spoken by Kirsty: the voice is authorial. It reworks the Preacher's message and speaks to us directly, cherishing the charitable impulse, the spiritual reconciliation of life's ordeals with a wiser happiness, and imploring us to find a profound but dynamic peace, 'under the sun'. (George Malcolm Thomson of Porpoise disliked the book's working title because it was 'misleadingly tropical' [50]) Kirsty reflects that,

> 'There was nothing ever sad or sorrowful about mother. She was never like the wifies who go about mourning at communion times. Have you ever thought of it, Hugh, that mother was never very religious. And yet –' Kirsty's low voice came with a rush of conviction – 'I would sooner have her mind than all the religions in the world!' (248)

If Kirsty's elegy goes on to strain credibility (Mrs MacBeth 'is like a great mother of great peoples' (249)), Gunn signals to us that to Hugh Kirsty is 'overwrought', and 'was overdoing it' (249). Gunn's apparent wish to make Mrs MacBeth a kind of archetype seems to be deliberately undercut via Hugh, so that we are returned to the real person of Hugh's mother. The fact that Kirsty uses the past tense when her mother is still alive seems at first another kind of Twilight gloom, but Gunn twists this, too, by adding that 'to speak of her mother, almost as of someone gone, was the beginning of an assurance that her mother would not die' (251). Mrs MacBeth recovers and the novel concludes with Hugh's undisguised ecstasy. Free now to think of his father and brother, both so far away, proposals for hunting exploits, and even a pagan-like 'offering' in the trees (256), Hugh ends the novel in emergent light, 'his bare legs twinkling across the fields of the dawn'. In the inventiveness of his prose style, his remolding of form, and in the bright poetics which underlie these things, Gunn had sent the Twilight packing.

3

Making History

Sun Circle and *Butcher's Broom*

> But it is not merely historical novels that are wanted but
> novels which, whatever their location in time and place, will
> be distinctively Scottish in the deepest sense [...] and will
> make history in a fashion that the whole tale of Scottish
> novels since *The House with the Green Shutters* has com-
> pletely failed to do.
>
> C. M. Grieve, 1926[1]

Throughout the 1920s and '30s, and well into the 1940s, Gunn's
works show him particularly fascinated and troubled by the
threatened identity of the northern Scots, especially the Gaelic
speakers. Though he could not converse in their language, a note-
book from the earlier years shows his attempts to get to grips with
it.[2] Much later, he recalled to Hart that Gaelic had been the
language of his father.[3] He could not have been an authority on
Gaelic, but Catherine Carswell appears to have accepted a selec-
tion of Gaelic poems he had chosen for her forthcoming anthol-
ogy, presumably *The Scots Week-end* (edited by Donald and
Catherine Carswell) published by Routledge in 1936.[4] In his own
writing Gaelicisms are occasionally manifest, in seemingly circui-
tous phrasing as well as a curiously sensual form of expression.[5]

'The Gael' had appeared fleetingly in his debut novel as a
cardboard racial stereotype to be challenged, and Gunn had
seemed more at home with Caithness Scots. In *The Poaching at
Grianan* Gaelic occurred only in MacDonald's last cry of defi-
ance. There is a more comprehensive treatment of life in Gaelic-
speaking Scotland in *The Lost Glen*, where the issue surfaces in the
Edinburgh debacle over 'origins' (39) and in the Colonel's furious
encounter with the blethering ghillies (265). As I have suggested,
The Lost Glen and *Morning Tide* both address much wider

cultural problems of which the Gaelic language was and is but one aspect. Though Gunn was suspicious of racial labelling, this was more to do with a distrust of generalisation that a rejection of ethnic variety. The traditions of Scottish Gaels Gunn saw as both distinct and distinctive. The fact that he had only a sketchy reading knowledge of Gaelic meant, however, that for his fictional representation of Gaelic people and culture he was relying on the few translations of Gaelic work available at that time, on his considerable but ultimately inadequate contact with Gaelic speakers over the years and on his own invention.

Throughout the 1930s his publisher and confidante George Malcolm Thomson warned him of the spurious and dangerous nature of racial romanticisation. Tinkering with ideas of race had an increasingly ominous ring when Germany was taken into account. Moreover, Thomson saw the Gaelic Idea as politically unsustainable in what was (and is) essentially a multicultural Scotland.[6]

Gunn nevertheless insisted that Scottish identity, Lowland and Highland, was expressly Celtic because it had been comprehensively so in the past.

> What, then, is Scotland's historic background? Against what natural stage setting do we comport ourselves with assurance and freedom, importing significance to the slightest gesture, the least stressed exclamation? Unquestionably it is Celtic – in that racial sense in which Celtic is not so much opposed to as set against Teutonic, Slav, etc. [...] See how excitement reveals a man's nationality, making it leap out of him! And culture is an infinitely more difficult thing to satisfy than excitement; it is, as it were, excitement become a conscious art.[7]

This reads like a rather mild version of Grieve's ambitions for Gaelic empire. Grieve had become contemptuous of Gunn's fiction by the mid-1930s, but this had very little to do with criticising his Celticism, since it was to a caricature of Celticism to which he made his most rabid appeals for a Scottish Reich. (In fact, apart from personal jealousy his dislike of Gunn was more to do with a fervently-held belief that the novel as an art form was a lesser one than poetry, and, anyway, was now most certainly on the decline.)

Scottish nationalists [...] ought to consider carefully the principle which Hitler and his National Socialists in Ger-

many oppose to Marxism. Hitler's "Nazis' wear their so-
cialism with precisely the difference which post-socialist
Scottish nationalists must adopt. Class-consciousness is
anathema to them, and in contradistinction to it they set up
the principle of race-consciousness [...]

The importance of the fact that we are a Gaelic people,
that Scottish anti-Irishness is a profound mistake, that we
ought to be anti-English, and that we ought to play our part
in a three-to-one policy of Scotland, Ireland and Wales
against England to reduce that 'predominant partner' to its
proper subordinate role in our internal and imperial affairs
and our international relationships (not to go further for the
moment and think of a Gaelic West of Europe as essential to
complement the Russian idea which has destroyed the old
European balance of north and south and produced a conti-
nental disequilibrium which is threatening European civili-
sation, and behind that, white supremacy) are among the
important practical considerations which would follow
from the acceptance of *Blutsgefuhl* in Scotland.[8]

That Grieve talks about 'imperial affairs' as well as internal ones
shows to what manic pitch his 'Gaelic blood-feeling' had excited
him. At odds with his increasingly estranged colleague's Gaelic
racism, Gunn's Celticism was at worst only implausible and sen-
timental. The 'Gaelic Idea' was to him much more the theory that
Scotland could come to exemplify a cultural alternative than that it
should be a potential powerbroker.

Lord knows there is no greater admirer of English culture
than I, but I am aware it is subtly antagonistic to the neces-
sities of the Celtic character.

English culture is showing elements of disillusionment,
tending, while it is still forceful, towards the mechanistic
aspects of life. Spiritually, it is approaching sterility.

Celtic culture on the other hand, is eager and ready to
receive at the present time a spiritual infusion which will
quicken it to full growth.[9]

Following *Sun Circle* and *Butcher's Broom*, Gunn was seen by
some as a Scottish Fascist. The communist novelist James Barke,
who had earlier written to Gunn calling *Butcher's Broom* 'far and
away your masterpiece',[10] expanded on this in an article (actually
devoted to Lewis Grassic Gibbon) in *Left Review*.

Gunn is a Gaelic culture revivalist: and it follows that, philo-
sophically, he is an Idealist. He distills from the Gaelic past
something of the quality which he believes to be the domi-
nant racial quality of the Gael: an aristocratic, individualist
quality. The survival of this quality is all-important to
Gunn. Hence his Scottish Nationalist alignment. For Scot-
tish Nationalism is largely inspired by the superior race-
theory of the Gael and the 'currency' demagogy of Major
Douglas. The identity of Gunn's Nationalist ideology with
that of the Aryan theoreticians of Hitler Fascism is not so
fortuitous as its superficial form and expression might indi-
cate.[11]

In the same article Barke pays tribute to Gunn as a 'great' writer
(whereas Gibbon was an 'important' one), so this is not quite the
condemnation it appears. Yet despite what he says about 'superior
race-theory', Barke seems to maintain that, alas, there are only
cosmetic similarities between Gunn's fiction and fascist ideology.

Clearly nettled, Gunn took exception to Barke's interpretation.
Invited to write for a special Scottish issue of *Left Review*, Gunn
delivered in one of the short-lived mouthpieces of the pre-war
British Left perhaps his most animated anti-ideological rebuttal.[12]
He denies, first of all, any knowledge of 'Aryan theory'. Stressing
the best of 'the Gaelic polity' – which he identifies in the Scottish
education system, the Scottish democratic political tradition, the
Scottish non-feudal relationship to land, and in Scottish folk mu-
sic – he calls Scottish intellectuals such as Barke to account for
being disloyal to the people they would represent. In addition the
utopianism of writerly English middle-class 'socialism' (typified
by Wells), and the ideology of organising the mass, are all rigor-
ously questioned.

Accordingly, what I fail to understand is how Scottish intel-
lectuals of any persuasion, and particularly the proletarian,
are not prepared to accept this historic past subsumed in this
country of their own and attempt therein to make a concrete
contribution to social reconstruction in the interests of the
folk. Their historical background and educational facilities –
if there is anything in the idea of dialectical materialism –
equip them for the task in a way undreamt of by the Russian
mass, and should enable them to short-circuit the more
obvious crudities of dictatorship and bloody violence.

Anyway, it is a job of work. But they fly from it and cover their desertion by calling the Scot who would like to attempt the job a Fascist. Marx knew the primary value of practice. He also strove to make it clear that in his theories he envisaged living working men, not economic abstractions. But when we avoid the concrete job in front of us in order to go theorising internationally, no wonder we become 'consumed with the vision of Cosmopolis' – that typical bourgeois vision that Wells has made all his own, and is not merely the negation of the 'aristocratic, individualist quality', but surely a conception of a beehive tyranny unspeakably repugnant to the free-thinking developing world.

In opposition to European materialism and the nightmare of New Town Europe, Gunn's thesis can be seen as every much as modernist as Lawrence's appeal to the freedom in the primitive. The history novels of the early 1930s reflect an extended presentation of the Gaelic cultural commonwealth idea as an antidote to Western materialism. Where Lawrence sought strange gods abroad (a phrase Gunn actually uses in *Sun Circle* (256)), Gunn could imaginatively invoke a past civilisation literally from his back plot. And like Lawrence, and Grieve to some extent, Gunn saw this artistic delving as resurrecting, or reconstructing, a variant consciousness of use to the world.

The dissatisfied Scot may be feeling back for a potency greater, more imperatively needed by humanity at large, than he knows of. His stirring to a a sense of receding nationality may also be an instinctive reaction against a world-wide gathering of mechanistic forces, his Celtic unconscious rebelling against the tyranny of the iron wheel.[13]

If the latest speculation in anthropological psychology could be adapted for the national cultural project, Gunn was not the man to miss the opportunity, even if he misapplies the theory to do so. This passage seems to draw on Jung's concept of 'the collective unconscious'. This is the alleged capacity of all people to mythologise in similar ways, harking back to primitive humankind's first organisation of a civilised way of life, with its archetypal figures of authority.[14] It was not meant, I think, to refer to particular racial memory, as Gunn seems to use it: he misreads Jung to appeal to a mythical sense of a shared ancient past among 'Celts'.

An activist for the National Party of Scotland in the early

1930s, Gunn had considerable experience in day-to-day politicking, and his struggle to keep the nationalist idea simple and widely appealing was a key factor in the amalgamation of the NPS with the Scottish Party to form the Scottish National Party in 1934. His nationalist propaganda was the more visible side of a highly active political life and, as one sees in his attack on Barke et al., his belief that nationalism made economic as much as cultural sense put him in the anomalous situation of appealing to an idealised view of Scotland while looking forward to realistic economic programmes.

The call for a new Scottish history had been made by Grieve in 1925 in 'The new movement in Scottish historiography',[15] and Gunn's historical novels of the early 1930s were written in this spirit. In a fundamental way, of course, they fictionalised history, but they also re-focus it. In *Butcher's Broom* a radically new historical view emerges, anticipating much later trends in Scottish social history. But in *Sun Circle* (1933), his first clearly historical novel, the dearth of evidence in Gunn's chosen era makes for a fantastic fiction which, even as it observes nuances of human psychology, and is at times violently realistic, also has a political framework.

Sun Circle is set in the days of the initial Viking raids on the north eastern seaboard. It recounts the story of Aniel, an apprentice druid under the supervision of 'the Master', the enigmatic head of a pagan clerical class whose officials live at a distance from the Pictish people, 'the Ravens', they serve. The story relates Aniel's teenage affection for two young women. Breeta is superstitious and impulsive, and she even questions the new Christian religion that has been established among the Ravens by the missionary, Molrua. Nessa, the daughter of the local chief, seems more superficial but more alluring. Though Christian, the Ravens are still inclined to the old pagan ways and when news of the advancing Vikings arrives they revert to druidic worship. This does not save them, however. Despite isolated acts of bravery and fine fighting, the Vikings massacre them. Aniel, as a druid not obliged to participate, watches the defeat.

Breeta manages to escape the pillagers with Aniel's help, but Nessa is captured. The young Viking chief, Haakon, takes her into the woods and tries to rape her, though there are suggestions of compliance. During intercourse they are captured by a band of young Picts, and Aniel is forced to decide whether to kill them or not. He stalls for time by going to seek the advice of the Master. Though Aniel wants to let Nessa and Haakon form a new Pictish-Norse leadership, and so protect the remnants of the Ravens, this soon becomes irrelevant. The fire started by the Vikings to burn down the druids' pagan grove whips across the landscape and Nessa and Haakon are incinerated. Aniel himself narrowly escapes death. The novel ends with the departure of the Vikings and Aniel walking south, accompanied by Breeta. He should be able to find and bring back the son of the dead Raven chief, currently at the royal court.

Sun Circle shows cracks in 'the Celtic psychology' akin to those weaknesses 'Fiona Macleod' had lamented and celebrated in 'The Gael'. Celts as Picts receive a heavy defeat at the hands of the Norse killing machine when they foolishly commit themselves to fighting openly, a matter of pride. Their desire for straight-forward confrontation is set against their clear inferiority in number and in standard of weapons. Even worse, the Ravens' Pictish neighbours use to Viking attack as a diversion for a violent raid on their summer encampment inland. The Ravens' relationship with other tribes is not exactly a shining example of Celtic pacificity either. The Finlags who 'trade' with the Ravens are in fact in their thrall. It hardly amounts to a vision of pan-Celtic harmony.

Aniel himself bears testament to a seeming weakness in the Pict. Though acting quickly and commandingly when he organises the Finlags in a small counterattack, he agonises over the choice of long-term direction for his people. When he hesitates and fails to escape with the disgraced Nessa at the only opportunity, he himself feels that his personal lack of resolve is a cultural trait.

> And he now knew that that was the fatal flaw in his make-up, an eternal weakness of will against the supreme moment. She, on the other hand, could have made that supreme decision of will. The Northman could have made it. As all the great figures of legend made it [...] they had that one thing, the supreme thing, that creates the ruler and the conqueror, the maker and the breaker of laws. (351)

If Gunn is acknowledging an innate shortcoming in Aniel's psyche is he not just expressing again the cult of defeat which is the aesthetic and political hallmark of the Celtic Twilight?

Why do their people need leadership? In the natural play of

their minds they are an affectionate people, desiring peace rather than strife. They are a dark intricate people, loving music and fun [...] How then can they ever lead? They cannot. At a time when a great decision has to be made, a decision to go forward, to conquer for the sake of conquering, to conquer and hold, they feel that by going forward they leave their true riches behind. And if they don't feel that, yet the instinct for that is in them and acts like a nerveless infirmity of the will. (353–4)

Astonishingly, the Twilight flaw becomes a sun-loving virtue. This vision of a hedonistic anti-heroism emphasises endurance not aggression, 'a profound persistence rather than a conquering or leading' (354). Whether this is a true account of the constructed 'Celtic psyche' is not the point: the interest is in the values themselves, and in the offering of those values as an alternative myth of virtue. Not only do they give a dignity to defeat, they question the definition of defeat itself. Weakness becomes strength because survival of the commonality goes beyond survival of leadership.

Even so, Gunn recognises the danger in praising moral victory above the actual one. He has turned the poetics behind the Twilight into something more ambiguous, but here at least, he fails to rise above that ambiguity. This is because Gunn's focus on race rather than culture admits very little room for a theory of dynamic adaption. In 'answering' the Twilight vogue he has accepted some of the premises on which it is based; he is more a revisionist than an iconoclast. The ruler

lives thus on the blood and flesh of the people, and is therefore for ever less than the people, and is for ever being consumed by them – to be needed once more, or the people themselves will be broken by a greater people under a greater ruler. (355)

Like the consuming fire the Master predicts, this passage prophesies the Clearances. The Highlanders were indeed broken by a 'greater' people under a 'greater' ruler, and the cultural and temperamental difference between two people's ways of seeing had once more risen to humiliate Gunn's not to distant ancestors. As *Butcher's Broom* shows, this was an internal problem as well as a problem of advancing European capitalism.

In *Sun Circle* the religious struggle is another manifestation of this 'innate' instability and acrimony, Aniel, as a dedicated pagan, has his loyalties confused when he hears Molrua preaching very movingly on the eve of battle. The story of Molrua's conversion to Christianity, poignantly inserted into the narrative as a flashback immediately before his murder by the Vikings, makes a particularly fine defence of a personalised vision of Christianity. His ambition to realise a 'Christian community of workers' is dealt with sympathetically (174), and it is one that Gunn explicitly endorsed some years later when he praised the recent re-establishment of the Iona community by a Govan minister and groups of the unemployed. This, he wrote, was 'a deliberate effort to revive in a small way the old Columban idea of fellowship, communal labour and ministry.'[16] Molrua's name suggests a model in the seventh century missionary who settled at Apurcrossan (Applecross) in 673, and who is celebrated in Scottish folklore as being martyred at the blades of the Vikings.[17] In all probability this is an orally-transmitted hagiographical exaggeration propagated by the Christians who came much later, since the first recorded Viking attack did not occur until 794.[18] Maelrubha, the ecclesiastical descendant of Donnan (the patron saint of the Gunn clan), consolidated the Celtic church in Ross, Sutherland, Caithness, Skye and Lewis.[19] Unlike Columba, he had no church biographer to lift him into a position of indelible significance, though he may have had considerable importance to the extreme north of Scotland. In Gunn's depiction of Molrua, therefore, there is a refinding of Scottish history.

Gunn suggests a different way of looking at Scotland's early medieval period in *Sun Circle*. This alternative perspective is suggested from the very first pages which begin looking from the cartographic north of Scotland and only travel south to come back to the novel's home, the extreme north-east. Rescanieres suggests that there is also a 'deliberate vagueness [that] exists in the historical framework of the novel.'[20] If we accept Molrua as Maelrubha, this vagueness is actually anachronism. Gunn's claim that the history was 'accurate' is palpably untrue, even if he did correct himself by saying 'the usual "realism" bores me.'[21] Drust, the name of the Ravens' chief, is the name of several Pict rulers spanning several centuries, but the issue at stake is not an identifiable historical event.. The novel is an allegorical recreation of the past. Pinning *Sun Circle* to the eighth century[22] or the ninth[23] ignores this deliberate vagueness. When Aniel heads south for the seat of power on 'the Broad River' (42), Inverness surely, he goes to 'the great chief who was now king all over the country'. Given the *general* sense of time, this can only be Kenneth mac Alpin, who united the Scots with the Picts to form Alba, around 843. By collapsing about one and a half centuries of medieval history Gunn encompasses in one story early Christian evangelism, still fairly virulent pagan worship, the coming of the Vikings, and the first unification of Scotland.

At the end of the book, then, Aniel and Breeta are walking away from the relics of faction and suffering towards the birth of a nation. In embracing the authority of the king from the relative south, however, Aniel is also bowing to the Christianity practised there. This might seem an act of self-betrayal, given Aniel's heathen credentials, but the Master persuades him rather magnanimously that the essence of spirituality will survive even so. Christianity will only falter, as the pagan polytheism had, on the earthbound issues of clerical control and authority, and then a new spirituality will replace it (116). This will contain that with which all religions began.

Obviously Gunn created in the Master a hypothetical pagan. 'Such Druidic philosophy as there may be is my own', he told Grieve.[24] The 'aristocratic individualism' Barke noted in Gunn's work surfaces in the Master's spiritual individualism which focuses in particular on solitude. Aniel is always the loner: the observer, the voyeur, the satirist, the artist. This is a result partly of his vocation, the Druids being a class set apart from the other Ravens and even set apart from each other. Partly it is because Aniel is drawn as the moody adolescent who, like all Gunn's youths, has a deliberate apartness concomitant with the emotional disturbance that usually precedes early adulthood. The Master's paganism also bears the weight of modern existentialism:

> [...] ours is not a single belief, but an intense and prolonged striving to get at the dividing of forces, with no gain and no loss, with no question of going beyond the reward of being there, therefore may we feel that it possesses human loneliness in its naked form. (117)

Here is the protection of self from the unintelligibility of vast reality, the creation of a pocket of meaning in which to rest, and from which is safe to look out.

This is not to say that the religion Gun constructs is atheistic.

For the Picts, Bel, 'the giver of light', and the sinister moor-god, Rhos, do exist. Breeta is horrified by blasphemy against the pagan faith; one man goes near insane because he believes he has been 'visited' by the sun-god, and in times of trouble human sacrifice is still a trusted method of worship. Even so, Aniel and the Master are set against the literalist Druid, Gilbrude, in their belief that the gods are not spiritually central. In this view the individual is necessarily the limiting determinant of religious or any other meaning. What exists outside the individual must be subordinated to his or her way of thinking. This is tempered, nevertheless, by the traditions of society. The acknowledgement of powers and forces outwith full comprehension places the spiritual burden on the self which in response invents a 'logic' that subdues the threat constituted by what cannot be understood. Sacrifice, ritual, and all manner of behavioural ploys are the bolsters which contribute to self-protection.

Aniel realises the secular implications of this philosophy. Bringing back Drust's Christian son is not a betrayal of his mentor's teachings. Like young Hugh denying the apocalyptic associations of the evening sky, Aniel's essential task is to keep evil and sorrow psycho-spiritually impotent by whatever means are at hand:

> There were many religions in the world and the gods had many names. The rest was loyalty. Only of one thing were we sure, that there are dark beings, malignant and cruel; that pain and terror and disease and disaster overtake us. Each man was a lonely being in that battle, he had to hold the gods and demons at bay by propitiation, by sacrifice, but even more by the strength within himself. Let him be as one in his circle. Then the gods will respect him and the demons fear him, and he will know that joy which gives the only vision [...] The earth beneath, the sun above, and we the children of their union. That is all we know, and perhaps all we need to know to find the power that has serenity at its heart. (388)

With his 'circle' of happiness, despite the deaths of Raven, Finlag, and Viking alike, Aniel provides a coda of hope. It is also the first comprehensive philosophical statement Gunn makes in his fiction, and though his arguments have become extraordinarily sophisticated by the time of *The Atom of Delight* (1956) the essence changes little over the years.

Aniel has literally been through fire to deliver it, yet the closure is not now complacent even if it is optimistic. Aniel has been an unlikely Celtic hero – lascivious, cruel, treacherous, arrogant, and abusive of his authority – but some of these attributes have been winnowed by experience. Breeta's reappearance promises a personal resolution for them both, but with that antagonism which marks out many of Gunn's most endearing couples. The last pages look towards the promise of love as they look forward to the promise of political unification of the problematic Celts, but they do not guarantee an easy fulfilment. The integration of a wide historical framework with a close observation of the 'artist as a young druid' is at times weak, but that the personal and the historical are assumed inseparable is essential Gunn.

Butcher's Broom (1934) probes much deeper into the question of Scottish historiography, this time depicting a fictional Sutherland glen, the Riasgan, within the Kildonan strath, at the beginning of the nineteenth century. The narrative focuses most closely on the life of Elie, who lives at the croft of an elderly healer-woman, Mairi. The book is divided into four parts, and the first describes the hard-working and austere way of life in the glen, but also the pleasures of the play, the arts, and the invention enjoyed by the people there. The personal centre is Elie's love for Colin, the grandson of one of the more well-to-do crofters, Angus Sutherland. The hermetic nature of the glen and the parallel relationship between the lovers are broken very quickly by the raising of Highland regiments to fight in the Napoleonic wars. Colin signs up as a soldier, answering the call made by his clan leader, and not knowing Elie is pregnant. Elie leaves the Riasgan soon afterwards, pretending to find work in the Lowlands but really in order to have their child.

Part Two features her return several years later with her little boy, named after his father. Mairi hears of the hardships of living in the south, and of the deceit and trickery Elie encountered. The Riasgan is now threatened by the *laissez-faire* economics of the south and Elie becomes to many of the Riasgan folk not only symptomatic but symbolic of the oncoming fall. The Marquis of Stafford's factor, Mr Heller, is planning the removal of most of the Highlanders tenanted throughout the Kildonan Strath, so that the land can be settled with sheep. This would be profitable given Britain's increasingly scarce food supplies, a result of her quarrel with the French. Part Three deals with the brooding months before the Clearance and Elie's uneasy marriage to the brutish but also rather vulnerable miller, Rob. The Clearances themselves close this section with an onslaught of racism and violence.

The diminished life of the Riasgan folk now transposed to the bleak Sutherland seaboard is the subject of the fourth and final part. Rob is dead and Mairi is regarded suspiciously, almost as a witch. Davie, Mairi's grandson, plans to emigrate. The Riasgan is officially out of bounds and any cattle straying back are impounded by the shepherd, who is assisted by vicious dogs. The story comes to its terrible end when the now very elderly Mairi goes back to the Riasgan apparently to search out herbs and useful plants. A flock of lambs surrounds her and then come the dogs, which attack her. She succumbs and is killed. It is at this point that the wounded veteran, Colin arrives – unaware until now of the desolation of what was once his home township. He kills one of the dogs and the shepherd retreats with the other. His son, who has gone looking for his 'Granny', appears only in time to help bear Mairi back to the shore, and there the story finishes.

For north-east Highlanders, Bliadhna an Losgaidh, the Year of the Burning (1814), was still a strong folk memory in the 1930s, but as a local minister warned Gunn, the secluded nature of the north made some of his wry references impenetrable to outsiders.[25] Gunn made the real-life factor Patrick Sellar the diabolical Heller. James Lock, the architect of the purges, is simply Mr James, and Lord Stafford's first Commissioner, William Young, becomes Elder. Previously, the centralist, elitist historiography of both the English and the Scots had rendered the whole episode a no-go area. Gunn's book was one of the first extended fictional realisations of the event ever published.

The act of eviction is introduced only after the reader has witnessed the vitality of the Riasgan community. Though Gunn's intrusive authorial voice establishes at the beginning an expectation of a tragedy whose proportions are outwith the Riasgan's comprehension, the arrogance of the conquering businessmen comes after we have been immersed in the personal affairs of Elie and her people. The sophistication of tradition, the complex emotional tensions, and the general verve of the Highlanders establish that there is no humane excuse for what is to follow. As Muir said, Gunn's 'description presumes a definite political point of view, which colours the picture, and with which the reader is indirectly urged to agree; he must take sides.'[26] Though Gunn had described a concert hall ceilidh in *The Lost Glen*, it had been very much deformed. In *Butcher's Broom* there is a greater energy: much is made of the participants' tricksy verbal interplay, eroticism bubbling beneath the surface of an explosive wit. Carmichael's *Carmina Gadelica* (1900) and Campbell's *The Grampians Desolate* (1804) informed Gunn's descriptions of the gathering and other aspects of pre-Clearances life. Mac Colla's *The Albannach* (1932), a story of self-abasement and small community narrowness, which concludes nevertheless with a symbolic regenerative ceilidh, may have been influential as well.

In the background, too, was Daniel Corkery's *The Hidden Ireland: a study of Gaelic Munster in the eighteenth century*. Gunn had read this several years earlier and based the 1928 article, 'The Hidden Heart', on it. In 1935 he was still writing about Corkery, though in phrases that constitute a little-changed rewording of the earlier essay.[27] *The Hidden Ireland* had probably been the source for MacDiarmid's use of the word 'Gairmscoile' in the poem of the same name, and it is arguably a seminal work for the Renaissance. Because is shows a cultural richness, a Gaelic literary sophistication comparable with but quite distinct from European high art, and argues that comprehension of the most intellectual poetry existed in eighteenth century Munster among the most impecunious and illiterate, *The Hidden Ireland* was strong medicine for both Grieve and Gunn's politics and art. Corkery argued that even the most balanced of historians of Ireland had been unable to recognise the Celtic heritage living behind the language barrier in the remoter Irish-speaking areas. This was a result of both the historians' Anglo-centricism and the Gaedhealtacht's resistance to self-publicity. Following Corkery's lead, Gunn set out to break the corresponding silence in Scotland. He developed his hypothesis explicitly in his book-length essay *Whisky and Scotland* (1935). In Gunn's construction, the Gaelic people are a folk who, for all their gifts of civilisation, education, high and folk art, an elevated morality, and a democratic way of seeing, have been badgered to the fringes of the world they had actually helped prosper. But the Gaelic essence remains, even it has become Englished. Indeed, at the core of the avant-garde and modernist art is 'the prose of a figure of such world importance as James

Joyce, a prose distinguished above all else by its Irish rhythm, its 'hither and thithering waters of' the Gaelic soul' (69). Though in private Gunn had some reservations about Joyce,[28] giving 'the Celts' and nationalism a modernist manifestation was part of the propaganda gift.

That *Butcher's Broom* is both a historical and polemical project is evidenced by Gunn's authorial voice being occasionally foregrounded to supply anthropological detail which could not be shown incidentally. This occurs, for example, when the author explains the strict work and activities differences between men and women (65). He implies that *Butcher's Broom* contains a history with as much right to be remembered as the French marching on Moscow (21-2). Moscow, after all, was rebuilt. 'Only this glen here, that was itself and the other glens, suffering fire as did the Kremlin, and destruction as did the battlefield, has remained into time dark and desolate and dead' (22). The phrase, the glen 'that was itself and the other glens', uses an English Gaelicism which points up the self-contained nature of the Riasgan, it was *itself*, as well as its fictional representativeness as *all* the other glens. The reference to the march on Moscow is a nod to Tolstoy's opening paragraphs of 'The French at Moscow' chapters in *War and Peace*. There Tolstoy argues for a much more complex understanding of history and history-making, and in particular for scepticism towards the kind of history that emphasises leadership skills above so many other factors.[29] There is also the suggestion, perhaps, that Russian and Celtic civilisations are two facing apices of alternative culture, looking across Europe's central civilisation. Gunn often referred to the Russian Revolution in his essays about nationalism, and in particular to its nationalist implications (though Stalin destroyed much of his faith in it). MacDiarmid had suggested this analogy some years earlier, seeing in Scotland a counterforce to the emergent Soviet Union,[30] but nothing quite so grand, or self-deluding, is offered by Gunn.

It is simply the presentation of Difference, an alternative especially to capitalism, which *Butcher's Broom* undertakes, and one aspect of that is rootedness. When Colin and the soldiers and Elie and the young women leave the Riasgan, full narration will not follow them. Some of their experiences are recounted but only through the vehicles of hearsay, unofficial news, and first-hand account (when the speaker is firmly back in the Riasgan). The journeying which is part of the Clearances story is outside the novel's central poetics of belonging to a specific home and land, and so what might have been an epic becomes an implied epic or even an anti-epic. The only immediate and detailed narration of events outside Sutherland occurs when Heller visits the Marquis of Stafford, later the Duke of Sutherland, in London. The kilted-up Highlanders at Stafford's door suggest what kind of view of 'his people' he is likely to take. Indeed, he has only gained ownership of the strath via marriage to the female head of the Sutherland clan. Westminster politicking and the pursuit of status in wealth are dealt with here succinctly enough for this to be the only exterior view the narrator thinks we need.

Back in Sutherland, Heller and his colleagues exhibits the prejudices of Corkery's Anglified Irish, the 'Ascendency'. Corkery is particularly eloquent on this theme:

> The first article in an Ascendancy's creed is, and always has been, that the natives are a lesser breed, and that anything that is theirs (except their land and their gold!) is therefore of little value. If they have had a language and a literature, it cannot have been a civilized language, cannot have been anything but a *patois* used by the hillmen among themselves, and for their literature, the less said about it the better.[31]

Samuel Johnson had similar preconceptions of the Gaelic language, or 'Earse', as he called it, though he later modified his view: 'It is the rude speech of a barbarous people, who had few thoughts to express, and were content, as they conceived grossly, to be grossly understood.'[32] Such crassness is instantly recognisable in *Butcher's Broom*, especially when the chorus-figure, Tomas the Drover, is speaking in Gaelic before Heller and his associate carpetbaggers. They contemptuously and ignorantly call the Gaelic a 'dialect' – the idea that a British language might be unconnected with Mother English is unthinkable. '"We know they are unlearned, and their dialect can have only a very few words, because the things around them are few and they live pretty much like animals"' (159–60). With the force of the law to enforce this hatred, Heller and his men proceed to raze the Riasgan. But the tragedy of the book is not the tragedy of utter extermination. It is the tragedy of surviving.

Elie typifies the grim passivity which lives on. Her acceptance of Rob's marriage proposal had been resigned – 'at last he carried her fate upon him' (280) – but she survives him to receive (presumably) Colin once more. The song she chooses to sing at her wedding is traditional, but it is also the song she had sung to Colin, unselfconsciously and at the height of their love. It is ironic, of course, that Elie should sing Colin's song at her wedding to Rob, but there is a feeling, too, that the song's story, like Elie's story, is a distillation of the Gaelic people's. Elie is 'singing this love song of tragedy out of the heart of their race.' (294). In the nature of folk singing Elie is at once intimately involved with the song and detached from it

> Here was the girl in the song comforting this unreason with humanity's final logic, tragedy. Elie knew all about that girl and gave her the dignity due so ultimate a role. Her voice could not be shamed by any sound between earth and heaven. And no personal stress or sentiment flawed its nameless power. (292–3)

Is this not, in some sense at least, Gunn's position, too? He has cast himself in the role of story-teller, yet he has very close links with his subject. As Hart and Pick show, these were very much his people.[33] It was the Gunns who had walked to the Duke's castle at Dunrobin in protest at southern snoopers (actually prospectors); it was the Gunns who had been read the Riot Act. In this way loss made into history is not only a political consciousness-raiser, it is a personal release. Perhaps it is this that makes the invocation of 'the Gaelic idea' less shrill here than Grieve's more outlandish fantasies.

As he later told the historian Agnes Mure Mackenzie, Gunn distrusted conventional history, or despaired of it.

> I must say that I have found the reading of Scots history at any time difficult. It was either dead uninteresting with no space at all given to real social conditions, the life of the folk, or if really concerned with the truth about Scotland then – it was difficult to read because of the mental complications engendered in the process![34]

The texture of life for ordinary folk, contextualised in the politics and economics of their time, is the stuff of Scottish history now, but before *Butcher's Broom* (and for a considerable time after) nothing much like it existed. Making detailed social conditions and relations the fabric of his history novel, and thus rejecting the romancing anaesthetic fabrication of history such as we see in the

worst of Scott, Gunn politicised the very bones of the history
novel. When Gunn reviewed Muir's *Scott and Scotland*, he drew
attention to what had gone wrong with Scott:

> [...] Scott himself, in a moment of moving self-realisation,
> cried out against the historical material he dealt in, calling it
> 'stuffing my head with the most nonsensical trash.' Scott
> was so great a genius that what he dealt in must have some
> reality to the mind of living men. It is not that the history
> was untrue or was inadequate subject matter for his genius;
> it was that it no longer enriched or influenced a living
> national tradition; it had not even the potency of pure leg-
> end; it was story-telling or romance set in a void; it was seen
> backwards as in the round of some time spyglass and had
> interpretive bearing neither upon a present nor a future.
> Only some such intuition from Scott's 'secret world' could
> have drawn from him in his latter years these bitter words.[35]

The argument here is that Scott was no longer writing in conso-
nance with a Scottish cultural tradition (or, indeed, any tradition),
and that consequently his work suffered from being as artistically
lifeless as it was intellectually crippled. Moreover, and here is
Gunn's point about making history speak to one's own time, Scott
is accused of dodging the problems of his day by making his
history novels have 'interpretive bearing neither upon a present
nor a future.' Though this argument is not tenable for all of Scott's
novels, notably *The Heart of Midlothian*, the implication is that
Gunn's fiction does what Scott's signally failed to do: it makes
history *matter*.

As if to emphasise this, not only is *Butcher's Broom* a reliving of
a more uncomfortable episode in Scottish history, history-tellers
themselves appear as characters in it. Notably among these are
Angus Sutherland and Tomas the Drover. Mairi, because she is so
isolated in the community perpetuates the rituals of the past
without communicating them to others, but Angus's poetry and
stories bring more than a millennium of oral literature to the
youth in the township. Tomas's speeches recall for his many
listeners a proud people jealous enough of their land and values to
defend them against the might of Roman soldiers, the parallel
between British Imperialism clearly intended (106). Angus, when
he recited the poem about the Ancient Bard, tells not only of
bygone creatures, heroes and heroines, but of the ancient way of

perceiving things. Pagan, generous and at one with the world, Angus's Bard counters the hell-fire politics of the Johnnie-come-lately Christianity preached by the churchmen at the edge of the Riasgan (57). Angus, passing on the neglected names of plants and places, and a legacy of stories, is a history-maker of Gunn's kind : a historian of 'the life of the folk'. As a reminder of Gunn's limitations, however, it is interesting to note that 'The Desire of the Ancient Bard' which he quotes in English (55) is the only poem from the 1841 anthology *Sar-Obair nam Bard Gaelach* that appears in English as well as Gaelic.

Another 'historian' in the book, Tomas, remembers Calgacus's stand before the Romans; ironically, that Calgacus was defeated is conveniently forgotten in his gusts of pride. The recent military triumphs of the Highland regiments are highlighted, too (108). This is recognition that in addition to Angus's aesthetic inherit-ance, the Gaels have a bravery of very direct relevance to their contemporary Britain. But this is also foolhardiness, as Calgacus's defeat might have warned them, and as the Ravens found out to their cost in *Sun Circle*. The Highland soldiers had been doing the dirty work abroad while Britain carved up their families and houses at home. This situation arose, the thesis of the book argues, because of something innately unsatisfactory in the society itself: in this recent case, primarily the out-dated allegiance Highlanders felt to their nominal chief (Stafford's wife). The Duchess of Sutherland had her authority taken over through marriage by a man who, it would seem, was versed in little more than an abridged version of *The Wealth of Nations.* Tomas's final speech ends, therefore, in his physical collapse, the shame of the Gaels' degradation forcing him down.

Yet, contrary to Twilight defeatism but also in a way as frightening, the people of Riasgan in general are survivors. The narrator had lamented that they could never say, as Christ had, 'it is finished' (21). It is their enduring tenacity that produces the greatest tragedy, because it is a kind of perpetual cruelty. Those that survive remember only that something better but now irre-trievable had existed. Mairi, Angus, and Tomas, all the history people except Elie, are dead or demented by the close of the novel. What is there left except to bear the dead away? Colin says to his son, as they take Mairi back to the shore, 'We'll take it in easy states, time matters no more' (429). Gunn had made time matter, but he was faced, once again, and despite himself, with a poetics of the grim, of the past. Several years would be needed before he could slough off that recurring sensibility and re-emerge with a novel that celebrated the present, and looked ahead once again, with hope.

4

Different Sources

Highland River

...man is in part divine,
A troubled stream from a pure source.
                        Lord Byron, *Prometheus*, II, 48-9

Highland River (1937) may have had its source in an idea for a light river book of more commercial success than Gunn's two previous novels which, whatever their merits, sold poorly. According to Hart and Pick, the idea emerged when several of Faber's men, Frank Morley and T. S. Eliot among them, suggested that the recently published piece, H. R. Jukes's *Loved River*, might be a model for a similar Highland book.[1] Morley and Eliot actually visited Gunn at the time, April 1935, and it was on their diverting drive back south (another visit in 1937 was to celebrate the success of *Highland River*) that Eliot encountered Rannoch Moor, the subject of his only Scottish poem.[2] Though Eliot had visited in 1933, too[3], the 1935 trip, it seems, had been precipitated by a fear that Gunn might leave Porpoise/Faber, a fear started by the publication by Routledge of *Whisky and Scotland* (1935). There was also the by now obvious deception of Porpoise claiming to be a 'Scottish' imprint while being little more than a Faber appendage. Though the whisky book was part of a clearly separate non-fiction series, and as such Routledge were not exactly competing with Porpoise, that Gunn tried Collins with *Second Sight* in 1939 shows that Faber's anxieties were justified (Gunn did stay with Faber, however).[4]

Eliot's poem, as Robert Crawford has suggested, is, among other things, a 'piece of political analysis, based partly, perhaps, on Eliot's own meetings and contacts with Scottish writers including Gunn, Muir, and MacDiarmid.'[5] Gunn's *Second Sight* (1940) shows poignantly that indeed 'here the patient stag/Breeds for the rifle', and the novels before *Highland River* show exactly the contrast between expansive northern landscape and claustrophobic psychology upon which Eliot focuses. But most of the novels including and after *Highland River* have a much more optimistic view. In *Highland River* there is a deliberate distancing from Eliot's view of the aridity of Scottish society (and indeed the failure of all 'culture'). Instead Gunn takes up the water motif which Eliot had used brilliantly but pessimistically in *The Waste Land*. He shows that there is much more than 'the sound of water only' both in Scotland and in the affairs of the world at large. Eliot's suggestion in 'Rannoch, by Glencoe' that there is a self-defeating intransigence in the Scottish character (epitomised by the poem's location near the slaughtering ground of the MacDonalds by the Campbells), will simply not do for Gunn. It has, indeed, a refined sense of the very Celtic Twilight Gunn had been struggling with for over a decade.

In *Highland River* it is almost as if Eliot's views acted as a worrying reminder to Gunn of the way Scotland appeared to outsiders. Eliot is also likely to have made Gunn think in more formally experimental terms (though, as I have earlier argued, Gunn had already been innovative). Six months after the Faber delegation to Inverness, a delay suggesting some hard thinking and mulling over of ideas, he wrote a follow-up letter to Morley:

> This idea of yours had already occurred to me and I had thought of its flowering summat in this way: the poaching (salmon) experience of three boys (one of 'em like Hugh in *Morning Tide*) on this river. Now, out of the memorable moments in their lives, I should like to create a philosophy (appalling word) of sorts. Probably I am getting to that sterile stage where I want to 'say' something. It wouldn't be a novel. It would be comparatively short. And it would be appallingly difficult to do [...] But I have the title: *Highland River*.[6]

The book was not as short as Gunn anticipated, but in the other respects this statement of intent holds good. In *Highland River* Gunn's interest in remembrance, in the relation of single events to much wider issues, and in the expression of philosophical ideas through the medium of constructed memory, is sustained. Despite its seemingly introspective theme – the recollection of a Highland childhood – there is also a more deliberate outward-looking sensibility. This confirms his more conscious ambition to '"say" something'. That Gunn did not conceive the book as a novel suggests why it is so structurally ingenious. The novel form, *per se*, was inadequate for his desired mixture of semi-biography, fiction, and thought.

At first, however, it reads like a sequel to *Morning Tide*. The letter-dedication to Gunn's brother at the beginning makes that connection explicit but it also prepares the way for what Muir called without disparagement a 'very elusive book.'[7] It is not, Gunn tells him, 'the description of our Highland river that you anticipated', but 'though there is no individual biography here, every incident may have had its double.' It is fictional biography, yet even the conventions of biography are to be avoided. Moreover, it is about the pursuit of ideas and sensations, even more than about the ideas and sensations themselves: 'if only I could get you to see the hunt as a poaching expedition to the source of delight we got from a northern river, I feel that you might not be altogether disappointed should you come back (as we have so often done in our time) with an empty bag.' This is a warning not to expect resolutions, an explanation, or an ordinary reward.

Only one sentence, some six pages from the opening, alerts the reader to the retrospective nature of what is being presented. Kenn, the central figure in the book, is utterly immersed in the bare-handed tackling of a massive salmon. That this experience is a memory is played down. '[...] of all that befell Kenn afterwards, of war and horror and love and scientific triumphs, nothing ever had quite the splendour and glory of that struggle by the Well Pool [...]' (12). This is the only indication we have that Kenn exists in the book's 'now' as Kenn, the adult. The immediacy of the water hunt overrides this one hint of remembrance and we are speedily reabsorbed into the battle. Much of *Highland River* is taken up by similar seemingly isolated occurrences – war experiences, a birth at a tenement, his walking home from the sea with his father – and if few have the exhilaration of the first encounter (one becomes accustomed to the technique, and Gunn becomes more discursive) still they seem less acts of remembrance than presentations of simultaneous existences.

In the first instance, when Gunn reminds us only fleetingly of a future that already exists he is emulating a technique beloved of Proust. Gunn admired in particular the first volume of *Remembrance of Things Past* [8], and there are strong affinities. For example, when Marcel is suffering an agony by being deprived of his mother's kiss, his mother being hostess at a dinner party downstairs, the reader is taken into the intensity of the child's feelings and then Proust informs us, almost as an aside, that as an adult Marcel learned that the man responsible for such deprivation, Swann, has a sensibility actually much akin to Marcel's. This tiny suggestion of an already realised future is exactly what Gunn gives us in the first rush of Kenn's struggle with the giant fish. Past events in Proust and Gunn retain a wholeness, a brightness of detail of their own, and for the time of remembering the future only keeks through.

A similarity, rather than an influence, is also to be found in the two writers' exquisite enjoyment of things sensual. The greased laces of Kenn's new boots, which smell of snow, and potatoes shoving themselves out of their delicious, steaming, skins – these are the matter-of-fact items and experiences which have fabulous intensity for Kenn. Proust, too, derived more than ordinary pleasure from taste, hearing, and smell, as testified, for instance, by the indulgently and extravagantly described smells of Marcel's Combray house.

Highland River is more discursive than any of the novels beforehand, and of the later novels only *The Well at the World's End* approaches it. The reflective mode, and especially the interest in childhood and psychological development, in anthropology, and in the relation of thought to spirituality and science, makes the book seem at times an extended essay. Taking account of this, Gifford suggests that Wordsworth's *The Prelude*, with its assembly of incidents bonded by retrospection, is a kindred text.[9] Certainly, *The Atom of Delight* (1956) confirms Gunn's enduring interest in Wordsworth, with Gunn quoting from *The Prelude* at length (62-3), and the formal and thematic similarity between the two Gunn books might imply shared sources, too. But most claims of intertextuality have to be treated with extreme caution. As a writer Gunn was more interested in what Saul Bellow has called 'the human essences', than in the distractions of literary allusion.[10] Gunn does mention 'I wandered lonely as a cloud', (243), and Wordsworth's 'The Green Linnet' is a productive subject for comparison, given Kenn's remembrance of the uncatchable green linnets of his childhood (82).

While Birds, and Butterflies, and flowers
Make all one Band of Paramours,
Thou, ranging up and down the bowers,
Art sole in thy employment;
A Life, a Presence like the Air,
Scattering thy gladness without care,
Too blessed with any one to pair,
Thyself thy own enjoyment.[11]

Even if the echo is not intended, and I think it may be, Wordsworth's poem is a beautiful way into *Highland River*. The flitting nature of the linnet has the elusive delight Gunn's loner so enjoys, Kenn seems to identify with the green linnet, and 'Thyself thy own enjoyment', reminds us of Kenn's childhood secrecies, and his absorbed lone adventures. The phrase also points to the Romantic interest in the nature of solitariness. The mature Kenn who emerges from a background of brotherhood, close family ties, and to some extent childhood camaraderie, is unusually alone. It is one of the few novels in Gunn's corpus which ends without the promise of romantic union, and though Kenn is to bring his friend the nurse a handful of petals from his Scottish rose, he remains a solitary figure.

Formally, too, *Highland River* is set apart from Gunn's novels. The isolation of individual incidents, an extension of the technique used in *Morning Tide*, and the presentation of these incidents in an often non-chronological rearrangement again recalls Proust. In *Remembrance of Things Past* Proust has Marcel liken his singling out of events and thoughts from a mass of reality to the 'severing' of a gush of water. It is this technique, and a version of this metaphor, that Gunn adopts.

> [...] my dreams of travel and of love were only moments – which I isolate artificially to-day as though I were cutting sections at different heights in a jet of water, iridescent but seemingly without flow or motion – in a single, undeviating, irresistible outpouring of all the forces of my life.[12]

The metaphor of sampling a potent everflowing fluidity is at the core of what is, after all, a river book. Proust's mixing of biography with fiction through an only partially distanced central character is found in *Highland River*, too. That the river stands for something more than itself is clear: it is 'the river of life' (4) for Kenn, both in the personal sense of being a formative part of his life, and in the metaphorical sense of it being like the river of humankind, an analogy he develops in his discussion of parochialism. Kenn's river-metaphor also accommodates the shared values of working men in all places in society 'as a stream that carries all sorts of queer craft and cargo and debris' (55). His war-changed brother, Angus, has a 'nerve thread of pain winding underneath', which 'was the old river in a shadowy land' (167). And immediately after describing a harrowing childbirth in a sordid city tenement, Gunn uses the river once again, this time to describe compassion and political activity: 'Kenn, who has never belonged to revolutionary political societies knows what moves them. Old as the rocks, nameless as the old woman, warm as sunshine, insinuating as the wind, is this river that flows down the straths of time' (197). Douglas Gifford gives a fuller account of the multiplicity of meaning within the river motif, a motif whose meanings, as one might expect, flow into one another, shifting and bubbling as they do so.[13] Suffice to say here, though, that the river's association with an individual childhood is coupled with a much wider significance. The river and the child life entwined with it take on, for Gunn, an anthropological ideal. As Turgenev quipped in *Rudin*, 'The whole aim of learning is to reach consciously what is given to youth for nothing.'[14] In *Highland River* this applies as much culturally as personally. Kenn inhabits a landscape which is both super-physical and storied, and which offers both sensual pleasure and entrances to the origins of his people. Similarly, Gunn's serpent motif not only evokes Kenn's cosy satisfaction but harks back to the snake emblem of Kenn's prehistoric ancestors (to which we are later introduced, p. 233).

> 'Hah-ha!' he breathed, wide-mouthed; he constricted and blinded himself with his mirth, turned in upon himself like an adder, seeking the central core of himself, so that he might burrow into that, crush his laughing mouth against it, and go blind in the last tension of fun. Then he drew back, open-mouth and listening, like a troll, and heard nothing in the world but the river. Contract and expand, systole and diastole: the river flows.
> The river! In the night of the world. Listen! (111)

In this passage there is a movement from self-absorption, 'seeking the central core of himself', to a curious leaving of self, wherein the river virtually consumes Kenn. And from the child world we are lead into a more narratorially contrived view of the stream. 'Systole and diastole' gives the river a life of its own even as it reminds us of Kenn's heartbeat in the silence of his bed. In his use of that phrase Gunn may also be alluding to a certainly very relevant essay by Jung, published in English in 1928 as 'On psychical energy.'

> From primeval times certain plant and animal species have remained at a standstill without further differentiation, and yet have continued in existence. In the some way the psychic life of men can be progressive without evolution and regressive without involution. Evolution and involution have as a matter of fact no immediate connection with progression and regression, since the latter are mere life-movements which, notwithstanding their direction, actually have a static character. They correspond to what Goethe has aptly described as systole and diastole.

In a footnote Jung adds:

> Diastole is an extraversion of libido spreading through the entire universe; systole is its contraction into the individual [...] To remain in either of these attitudes means death, hence the one type is insufficient and needs complementing by the opposite function.[15]

Jung's 'constriction into the individual' is exactly parallelled in Kenn, 'constricted and blinded ... turning in upon himself like an adder.' The opposite energy, which makes Kenn universalise his own experience and, here, makes the world listen to his home's river, is embodied in Jung's interpretation of Goethe's 'diastole'. There is also the dynamisis that Jung felt was the very essence of life, an interweaving of these forces, a continuous movement in and out of immediate being and reflection on that being, and a continual moving from enjoyment of the very personal nature of this and the relating of its significance to humankind in general; a private and social balance. As Muir put it, this is also a delicate interplay between the seeking and the thing sought: 'Kenn, pursuing the upward course of his Highland river, is really pursuing himself; he is both hunter and quarry, and is torn between the equally fatal alternatives of catching himself and letting himself go.'[16]

Jung's observation that organisms exist today that have not evolved, but are none the worse for it, would have been grist for

Gunn's watermill. The idea that underlying psychological struc-
tures can exist in stasis alongside advances in living standards and
technology would have reinforced Gunn's argument that the re-
tention in one's psyche of aspects of 'primitive' experience offers
to the modern age a re-connection with a wrongly discredited
past. Jung used the river as a metaphor for this, too:

> Although our inheritance consists of psychological path-
> ways, it was nevertheless mental processes in our ancestors
> that traced them. If they come to consciousness again in the
> individual, they can do so only in the form of other mental
> processes; and although these processes can become con-
> scious only through individual experience and consequently
> appear as individual acquisitions, they are nevertheless pre-
> existent pathways which are merely 'filled out' by individual
> experience. Probably every 'impressive' experience is just
> such a break-through into an old, previously unconscious
> river bed.[17]

With 'impressive experience' we are returned again to Gunn's
moments of delight, and are reminded that his poetics stress, in
Highland River at least, that the child is also linked to mankind's
(prehistoric) infancy, a hypothetical Golden Age, and both are
held up as psychological states of regenerative power.

Edwin Muir, especially Muir the autobiographer, is close to
Gunn in this. For both, the act of autobiography was necessarily
an act of spiritual investigation (and Muir was not averse to
fictionalising his personal history, either). Grieve is relevant here,
also. Patrick Crotty has argued that MacDiarmid's poems of the
early 1930s, to which Gunn had early access, follow a 'water of
life' metaphor with its basis in his boyhood river. While doing so
the poems express a 'rejection of childhood as an obsolete stage of
development.' This view is clearly at odds with both Gunn and
Muir's high regard for the formative years, and the metaphor is
specifically at odds with Gunn's use of his own childhood stream
in *Highland River* (Grieve's troubled childhood contrasts with
Gunn's rather happier one).

It is perhaps yet another difference in their respective world-
views responsible for their increasing disenchantment with each
other. Certainly relations between them had been strained for
several years before *Highland River*, with Grieve's dismissal of
the novel as an inferior art form: 'I am prepared to hold […] that

no fiction whatever matters a damn in relation to Scotland while any poem whatever matters a great deal.'[19]

Yet *Highland River*, especially in its excitement over scientific discoveries (Kenn is a physicist) and its confidence in discussing metaphysical topics from a Scottish groundbase, has much in common with MacDiarmid's poetry. Gunn reaches out – he finds no difficulty in measuring Kenn's salmon days alongside the aspirations and abilities of da Vinci, of Rontgen and other scientists. The old woman Kenn 'chooses' to represent humanity before God in a serious tongue-in-cheek meeting of human and Deity, is chosen against all the respected heroes and discoverers and intellectuals and artists in history because she has true humility. She'd offer God all she could – a glass of milk (80). Like MacDiarmid's dismissal of crass opinion, Kenn's saints do not have their virtue measured by the barometer of popular acclaim.

Gunn puts his theory of childhood to the test in the passages which deal with Kenn's First World War experience, and, later, in Kenn's scientific work. We are taken to the Front only twice: in Chapters Three and Fourteen. The first instance details Kenn's lucky escape from otherwise certain death, the second describes Angus's miserable death. In so far as one of Gunn's brothers, Ben, was killed in the First World War, and another, John (to whom the book is dedicated), survived a gas attack, there are resonances here that are even more personal than the other biographical touches in *Highland River*. The first episode is clearly signalled as an exemplar of childhood reserves standing up to the constant threat of death: an incident on the Somme 'still makes him smile, because in its cool river cunning, it shows so clearly the effect of his early environment' (42). In the trenches, Kenn's past recurs. Advancing Germans appear with pacific irony like 'winter hares coming in a drive over a ridge at home' (43), and his automatic energy recalls the instantaneous aliveness of his first salmon hunt. In a Leicester hospital, when Kenn wakes up from a gas attack coma, the phrase 'Leicester is famous for boots' plumbs the childhood anxieties of the class-room, when such stock phrases were the stuff of British-Scottish education. Gunn has synthesised a criticism of the rote method of education, and its cultural imperialism, into a sign of life – a characteristic example of Gunn's optimism.

In the same chapter, the description of the death of Kenn's friend, Ned, is astonishingly brief. Indeed, Gunn has to tell us Ned is his friend because it is the only appearance he makes in the novel. The effect achieved, I think is to disconcert the reader into Kenn's self-centred and euphoric point of view. By a miracle Kenn had stooped to pick up some equipment just as the fatal shell came over the ridge, killing his friend who was standing to his rear. In a non-thinking, 'instinctual' way Kenn celebrates his own survival: 'It was a perfect piece of timing and it stirred his mathematical bent to abnormal acuteness' (44). The gruesome slapstick of this is deeply disturbing: the war has forced men onto a landscape of moral irreconcilables, a lunatic as well as a lunar world.

The short chapter finished, we are returned to Kenn's river, but seeming to contradict what has just gone before, Kenn emphasises the communality of life at home. 'He started amongst people.' The river mouth and the harbour instilled a hardworking fellowship marred only by the occasional unpleasantnesses of swearing and blasphemy (51-2). This community is suspended, however, when the fishermen are ultra-individualists at sea. Gunn begins to bring this individual-community dichotomy into unity, and into unity with the 'outside' or 'modern' world. The resilience and skill of the fishermen, their Calvinist hardness, contribute to an individuality akin to those scientists who are now Kenn's peers (55). Kenn's earlier observation of the 'perfect piece of timing' with which he avoided death, and the mathematical beauty of it, is, in his own mind, at one with the spirit of his people. Instinct, tradition, and scientific 'absolutism' are merged.

In Chapter Fourteen the War is revisited. Connections between the past and the present are again numerous, but there is poison in the relationship. The narrative dwells on the changes evident in Kenn's elder brother, Angus. Angus's disposition recalls the 'white smile of fear' he had had when running the gamekeeper's gauntlet at home (160, 162). Worse than this, though, Angus seems to have turned away from his background, and is uneasy when Kenn wants to talk about the river they had once shared (169). Angus, the brother Kenn had looked up to, has become alienated, and desperately vulnerable. To Kenn, it is as if Angus's consciousness no longer relates to the more satisfactory dynamisis of the old country. He has become frozen between the energetic extremes of the quest associated with the river. He has 'the alert preoccupied movements of neither the hunter nor the hunted but of an in-between state' (171). When news of Angus's death comes through, Kenn breaks down in the knowledge that while the physical circumstances of the killing are harrowing enough, Angus's cynicism had not saved him, and the brothers had parted for the last time worse than strangers to each other. The next chapter sees Angus as a youth, boldly if boastfully preparing to jump from one tree across to another – no suspension of energy there. When he fails and knocks himself out, so that even Kenn's father suspects the worst, Gunn effects a resurrection, as indeed he has resurrected Angus's memory. Fully recovered, Angus is delighted at having been 'Clean out!', and we are reminded of the differences between the same person over time. The tragedy is acknowledged, and set in bitter contrast with Angus's previous adventurousness, but the boyhood hero is remembered fondly too: both Anguses exist in Kenn's consciousness. This, like so many other examples, is contrary, then, to McCulloch's assertion that in Gunn's philosophical works (amongst which, rightly, she includes *Highland River*) 'one is aware of the absence of any consideration of the paradox of the *interweaving* of good and evil in human existence'.[20]

In the last pages of the book, Kenn reaches the source of the river. The last two chapters revert to a chronological presentation of the story. The reader, too, is seeking the source of the river with Kenn. But while the journey itself elicits moments of bewitching beauty, when Kenn reaches the originating loch the nature of the emergent revelation, if indeed there is one, is inexpressible. 'A surge from all the ways of life behind him pressed up, unvisualised and unresolved' (254). Closer to the undisclosed moment, Kenn realises that it will provide no easy resolution or adequate satisfaction, that the soul (if that is what it is) finds significance perhaps only in the search for significance. Achievement in all areas of human experience always calls for further, higher, demands. 'Responsibility; the inexorable search for truth; the vision that came to the scientist, not of personal salvation, but of an unending spiritual drive into the unknown' (255). Kenn's 'transcendent' moment, just before it is about to arrive, is described as 'a feeling of strange intimacy. 'It is the moment in which all conflict is reconciled, in which a timeless harmony is achieved.' But we are never given access to the point of revelation, we are told only that 'it was coming upon him now' (255). In a sense, Kenn's expectation that he would find '"Nothing"' at the source (225), an expectation first raised in Gunn's dedication to his brother, has been fulfilled. As John Burns puts it: 'To ask for explicitness at the end of *Highland River* is to have missed both the experience and the meaning.'[21] Instead the book finishes with Kenn moving beyond the river's beginnings and towards the mountain ahead – the mountain, indeed, that Kenn had agreed to climb with Angus and his Canadian friend when the War finished. Very much alone now, Kenn is moving towards another anticipated moment, another step, he hopes, in understanding, – indeed in kenning – 'what lay in his heart and in his mind.' This is where his location within the universe, 'the earth as a ball turning slowly in the immense chasm of space', will be set against his position in the immediate landscape of the northern counties; a balance of the cosmic and the local. To seek and cherish personal meaning is the imperative. The full meaning of the river is beyond the river.

5

City Work and Country Play

Wild Geese Overhead and Second Sight

Wild Geese Overhead (1939) is the first novel Gunn published following his resignation as a excise officer in 1937. Like the Hebridean travelogue *Off in a Boat* (1938) and the 1940 novel *Second Sight*, it tested Gunn's ability to subsist on writing skills alone. It is also clear that *The Silver Darlings*, published in 1941, is the polished product of extended thought and research spanning several years. 'The Boat,' a short story of 1937, is recognisably the prototype for the first chapter of *The Silver Darlings*[1], and Gunn's journalism of the later 1930s displays a knowledge of the sea and the western isles that obviously informs his magnum opus. The two preceding novels are in some ways, then, artistically subsidiary. They are, nevertheless, highly readable and they serve as good introductions to the work of the war years.

Though in *Wild Geese Overhead* there is a river, in contrast to *Highland River* it is an urban one and behind high walls. A huge and ugly city broods on its banks. The glimpses of Scottish cities in novels as early as *The Poaching at Grianan* have given way here to Gunn's most comprehensive depiction of Scottish urban life. It is his only novel to ignore the Highlands, Caithness and Sutherland, and even the countryside from which the hero of the book, Will, chooses to commute is Lowland countryside. As with the dank Glasgow in the later *The Lost Chart*, in *Wild Geese Overhead* the city is never named; the word 'Glasgow' appears only once, as an epithet (25). Its relative anonymity confirms the chaos Gunn seems to associate with urban life. It is more often simply called 'the City', and it seems intended to be seen, like Muir's and Kafka's urban worlds, as a

> dark mythological city; a city of tall dark walls, a prison-city, wherein man wandered, seeking escape and yet not seeking escape, desiring it and yet afraid of it, appearing for a

moment and then disappearing in the shadows of the dark
walls, entrapped by the dark walls, trapped and forever
committed. (260)

Nevertheless, the shipyards and steamers, the football, the slums,
trams and socialism, and the history of its working-class activism
– 'Did any city in the world ever put up such a fight for workers'
rights as this city did?'(123) – and even a snatch of dialect (130), are
plain indications. Glaswegians are shown as people with dignity,
as people deserving consideration as human beings. They are
neither monstrous nor sentimentalised. While Gunn almost to-
tally ignores the spoken language of Glasgow, there is a sense, as
there is not in *The Lost Chart*, that the city here is a subject in
itself, rather than a useful context for quite another debate.

The main character, Will, is a sub-editor, journalist, and re-
viewer, primarily attached to the evening paper. He is also on a
socialist committee where he is responsible for supplying and
presenting information on the city's social conditions. It is
through this connection that he has become a friend of Joe, the
chairman, through whom Will and the reader are taken into the
heart of the slums. Tension between life in the country and life in
the city is created by Will's flitting to a countryside farm, where he
takes up lodgings on the strength of an earlier momentary sighting
of wild geese. That moment, as the title suggests, comes to mean
'more than itself'. A romantic element is important to the book,
and focuses eventually on one woman, Jenny, who also stays in
the country and works in the city.

Will comes across at times as rather patronising in his attitude
towards some of the working-class characters. His background is
comfortably middle-class and he has a tendency to offer ready
explanations for the behaviour of people he meets in the poorer
districts, as in the episode of Jamie, whose wife dies in childbirth
(143-4). In general, Joe's socialism does not blind him to the
individuals he tries to serve, as Will's psychological musings seem
occasionally to do. Middle-class characters, who are usually
English, are often treated in this way by Gunn, and one may
concur with Nan Shepherd that he always draws them unpleas-
antly[2], or perhaps just unskilfully. The way in which Will speaks
often seems unnatural, and at times it is unclear whether this is
simply poorly handled dialogue on Gunn's part, or actually 'in
Will's nature'. I think a case can be made for Gunn's being

distanced from the way Will puts forward his theories, even if he might agree with their content. This distancing certainly occurs in the novels from the late 1940s onwards, where outsider characters are deliberately dropped into situations where they act without proper sensitivity. One is reminded, too, of Clare in *The Lost Glen*, who sentimentalises the people she admires, despite her best intentions. Both Joe and Will, however, are guilty despite themselves of generalising individuals away, of seeing people as symbols and 'problems' rather than as complex beings. Will later explains why both he and Joe can't help being imperfect:

> 'When you shift the emphasis from the individual to the society, to social relations, you shift it from the vivid springing core of life to a windy, if convenient, abstraction. But, and this is the snag: it is *difficult* to be a real individual living from your feet up. It needs grit, and pride, and courage, and power to endure through despair; you need to be quick with beauty, and light, and love, and sex; you must see men, not as social units but as your individual brothers, full of this magic thing called life. And that is difficult.'(204)

This speech shows how close *Wild Geese Overhead* is to *The Green Isle of the Great Deep* in theme, and yet how distant they are from each other in presentation. Both are founded on the principle that the individual has a special sanctity, that a person has more meaning than 'the people' and the knowledge that to keep one's freedom and respect others' is a continuous and arduous struggle. Yet Will is to a large extent a solitary and a speechifier, whose paucity of human relationships makes his ideals lack the personal warmth he regards as vital. This is at variance with *The Green Isle of the Great Deep*, whose central characters exist from the start with a profound respect and affection for each other (and whose speech is much subtler, and more convincing). It is an intentional irony, perhaps, that the geese Will sees overhead, and which give the book its title, seem to him at first more powerful symbols of human delight than humans themselves.

Running alongside the descriptions of slums and hardmen's pubs, and the oppressive suggestions from Will's journalist colleagues of accumulating conflict abroad, is Will's involvement with women. The unnamed conductress on his local bus, Ivy the prostitute, the socialite Felicity, and finally Jenny – each occupy very different levels in society, and Will's reactions to them chart a

progression from more or less impersonal sex and sexual tempta-
tion to love. His banter with the conductress is merely flirtation.
He finally agrees to intercourse with Ivy, but when Joe bumps
into them with a policeman they separate. Later, Felicity, a 'free-
thinker' of some wealth, offers him sex at the party of an ac-
quaintance, Philip Manson, (235), but his loss of will does not stop
her. When he doesn't turn up at her room, Felicity visits his. It is
only the fact that he seems physically ill that puts an end to their
planned night together. When Felicity meets him in town she
plans to take him to a private summerhouse, but she has forgotten
the key and once again an opportunity is lost. Though often more
by luck than judgment, Will avoids 'unsuitable' liaison in what
becomes an allegory of temptation.

Other evidence shows that the moral plan of the novel clearly
associates the worst of the city with a twisted sexuality. This exists
at all levels of society. The shipping-firm executive Philip Manson
enjoys 'running the typist' (70), and though he is about to go on a
weekend with a lover, we see his official wife-to-be at the party. It
is significant that the one aspect he remembers of his childhood
experience of the country is a bull servicing cows (45). Will's well-
to-do Aunt Marion dislikes the Italians because they venerate
nude statues! (171). There is also the spoken 'sexual filth' (85) of
the children living in tenements; the older ones indulge in 'pre-
cocious sex' (86). Will himself has a dubious fixation on matters
sexual. In a particularly puritanical fragment of internal mono-
logue he avers (looking at his 'own thin hand') that: 'Flesh is
opaque; it lets light through. And when no light comes through,
outside flesh slithers against flesh in a dreadful promiscuity'(122).
In his chauvinist way, he assesses Jenny's involvement with Philip
as a product of fear of virginity (166). Walking behind her (before
he actually recognises who she is), 'before he could stop himself he
had the shoes off her and the stockings and the rest – but no, she
wouldn't quite straighten up from her bare heels. She merely
became uncomfortably naked. He didn't pursue the thought.'
(176). At least in this there is the late realisation of wrong. But later
he goes with Mac to 'The Blue Club', where 'Blue' presumably
refers to the 'bawdy stories and vile language' told and used there
(269). Later, rather hypocritically, he theorises that there is a
sociological connection between pornography and what he sees as
the increasing cult of the mass: 'For the most part thrilling

allurements of sex you go to the pictures, not to bed.' (283). Despite Will's being drawn to the very thing he sees as a symptom of decadence, this is an important expression of Gunn's fears. Cultural trends, he seems to suggest, now accommodate and encourage the mass *as the mass*, and in doing so threaten to devalue the individual.

In one of Will's trips into the slums, the use of sex-associated swear-words is seen as the point of unhappy departure for a tradition not without vitality:

> There were far more people about to-night, and more gaiety and boisterous fun. There would be an odd fight later on and some drunken jollity. Great leg-pulling about busted coupons. And arguments over Jimmy or Bobby, over centre forwards and inside rights and referees; with a virulent discussion going on just behind him about 'a pure bloody offside goal if ever there was one'. This opinion was equally strongly resisted. The language became more pointed. The two favourite sexual words were used with increasing directness and with a penetrating rhythm. Overwork did not dull their variety or scatter their strength. On the contrary, all other oaths were sucked into them. And to bear witness to so strange a fecundity the protagonists called upon Jesus Christ. (128-9)

Notice Gunn's use of the sexual metaphor for the description of 'sexual swearing' – 'a penetrating rhythm', and 'all other oaths were sucked into them.' The increasingly disdainful and ironic tone of the last three sentences here implies that 'bad' language is where the arguers begin to tip over from a rough camaraderie into something offensive, more powerful, and more aggressive. It is at this point that the barman intervenes and what had been 'a good-natured crowd' returns to being good-natured. Gunn is not sneering at their interest in football; when he talks about 'gaiety and boisterous fun' he is describing, if in language that shows how much he fails to catch the Glasgow idiom, a liveliness that would not be out of place in a ceilidh. It is also important that the last straw for the barman is blasphemy. It is the danger to the human spirit that Gunn is most concerned about, and as if the misuse of 'sacred' words is more an offence to the self than to God, blasphemy is often an indication in his work of something wrong in the spirit.

At a different pitch, Mac, Will's sub-editor colleague, is singled out as a nihilist also in spiritual danger. Will challenges his nihilism by quoting to him Francis Thompson's 'Hound of Heaven' (183) thus suggesting that Mac's profound cynicism is actually a form of escape from a spiritual conception of the individual, almost a fleeing from Christ and from the Devil, too. Earlier he had described Mac as being hunted out by 'the hounds of hell,' (119). Despite Mac's outburst at the suggestion of escapism, and the unresolved nature of their argument, the two part on relatively good terms. In Will's view, however, Mac's very departure echoes Thompson's 'I fled Him, down the arches of the years,' (183): Mac makes 'his solitary way down the arches of the streets,' (186).

Yet Will is not as self-confident as his accusations and analyses might imply. His moods fluctuate. He goes through depression and sleeplessness, and though he has a temporary feeling of elation brought on by the sight of the wild geese, he descends into a severe mental collapse which cannot be solely accounted for by the assault he sustains just before it. Thompson's 'labyrinthine ways' (183) provide the psycho-spiritual analogue to his vision of the city as 'A besieged, a beleaguered town, seen from above, like a Cretan maze' (114). When he emerges from the slums into theatreland he finds himself embarrassed at his relief. The theatregoers, their cars and their cosy wee night-cap thoughts (109-10), shame him. 'It's back I should go, he thought. Back there, I should live it out there, live it into and out of my system [...]' (110). When he gets home he is even 'ashamed of the wild geese incident, of the bird-singing, and of all the easy emotion that had been born of them' (111). This crisis of self-esteem, which is also a severe scrutiny of the country idyll and a precursor of his major breakdown, culminates in a vision of extreme loneliness (115). When Will wakes up the next day he looks 'like a dead man keeping watch,' (117).

Eliot's living dead in *The Waste Land* and in later poems seem to have crept into *Wild Geese Overhead*, and perhaps it is not coincidental that this is the first novel to be written after Eliot's short stay with Gunn in 1937. It also shares with Eliot's work a depiction of emotionless sex, carnality, and sexual debasement. As a reviewer fascinated by literary criticism (31), Will admires Eliot's poetry for the way its innovative technique is accompanied by a defence of tradition in his theory. 'For the interesting thing

about Mr. Eliot was that, though regarded as the most revolution-
ary force in modern poetry, yet no man in his essays put up a finer
case for orthodoxy and tradition' (41). Coming so early in the
book, this focus on the function of literature suggests that we
should pay closer attention to the relation of Eliot's theory to
Gunn's practice in the book.

In an essay written around this time, Gunn specifically singled
out the role of tradition in Eliot's thought, insisting that the
doyens of modernism were in complete agreement with his own
ideals (even extending this to nationalism).

> When T. S. Eliot, writing of James Joyce, calls him 'the most
> ethically orthodox of the more eminent writers of my time,'
> he is aware of Joyce as the product of his Irish environment.
> Indeed, tradition and orthodoxy are complementary to
> Eliot. 'I hold ... that a *tradition* is rather a way of feeling and
> acting which characterises a group throughout generations;
> and that it must largely be, or that many of the elements in its
> must be, unconscious; whereas the maintenance of *ortho-
> doxy* is a matter which calls for the exercise of all our
> conscious intelligence. The two will, therefore, considerably
> complement each other ... Tradition may be conceived as a
> by-product or right living, not to be aimed at directly. It is of
> the blood, so to speak, rather than of the brain; it is the
> means by which the vitality of the past enriches the life of the
> present. In the co-operation of both is the reconciliation of
> thought and feeling.'
>
> Tradition is not a static thing; it is a living growth. And I
> have mentioned these two writers, who have probably had a
> greater influence on modern letters than any other two one
> could readily think of in the world to-day, because they are
> popularly held out to be revolutionary and unorthodox.[4]

In *Highland River*, Gunn had shown himself a consummate mod-
ernist technician, but the important thing was to describe a con-
tinuity of tradition which, if broken or diminished, still flowed
on in the most personal of ways. The river, as in several key
modernist texts, was an important symbol. If we think of *Heart of
Darkness* or *The Waste Land*, however, we see the distance he
keeps from modern gloom. Nevertheless, in *Wild Geese Over-
head*, like Eliot in London, Gunn introduces us to a city where
life-enhancing traditions are running dry. Though to a much lesser

extent, the life of the river is used as a measure of this. For Gunn, it is not urban life itself that is the problem, it is the particular type of urban life. Despite the city's industriousness, many folk had (and indeed, still have) disgusting living conditions. Those that had work often worked in scandalously dangerous workplaces. One of the characters in the novel, Jamie, had lost his arm in an industrial accident, and at the time of his wife's death (in child-birth) his employer was trying to avoid paying compensation. Unemployment was creating a further marginalised class-within-a-class. In Gunn's city, cheap, ironically named 'Empire' wine is a treat; mixed with meths and re-named 'Red Biddy' it is the usual tipple for those who are only a penny or so better off than the down and out.

Yet when Will imagines Jamie to have drowned in the river he finds the thought all the more bitter because the river, though 'banked up, shut away' (92), still retains a measure of its industrial life-blood. It is a historied river.

> Will looked at the black water, which glittered here and there, and thought of Jamie. Beyond the dock, the river slid past. Will imagined its slow, drowning, rat-coloured swirls, its choking smoothness.
>
> Down past the building yards where carpenters and riv-eters, dockers and dredgers, worked where his comrades worked, where all the men worked whose forefathers had made the river, the river of sea-borne traffic, the wonder river, bearing Jamie's body, the one arm turning over, not in salute, not in underwater farewell, not in bitter irony, but filth and grime. Food for the eels. (93)

This is reminiscent of both the oily Thames and the drowning imagery in *The Waste Land* and of 'The River of the Suicides' in James Thomson's *City of Dreadful Night*. And while Gunn rec-ognises a tradition attached to life by the river, with its own special decency, the river bisects a hell. That hell, like the *City of Dreadful Night*, seems at times worse than Dante's.

> The bright lights of the great thoroughfares were gone. Here was only a darkling light; and presently, as they passed a street entrance on their left and Will looked down it, his heart constricted. The electric globes went into the distance, one after another, balls of bluish light, suspended in impen-etrable gloom. The balls hardly lit the air about them. No

traffic. No headlights. Involuntarily Will stopped, but went on again at once.

'I had thought I had visualized the thoroughfare to the underworld,' he said to Joe, with an effort at light irony, 'but I was wrong.'

Joe glanced at him. 'You mean?'

'The classical conception provided a certain measure of drama. That was not drama. The gloom of a terrifying nihilism, hung with balls of incandescent steel.'(84)

It is the idea of this hell on earth being no worse than the hell in the modern mind, that 'terrifying nihilism', which makes the decadent city and the decadent psyche so closely related. This in turn reinforces the suggestion that Will's increasingly disturbing experiences in the city are stations in a spiritual allegory, realistically portrayed. Nevertheless, the pomposity and unreality of Will's speech suggests that Gunn has lost grip of convincing dialogue, even if Will is a fundamentally pompous and psychologically unbalanced character.

The last chapter of *Wild Geese Overhead* presents an unashamedly personal resolution to Will's purgatorial progress through the city. Gunn has trawled him through violence, debauchery, and sorrow, with international insecurity looking increasingly dirty, and now brings him to the beginning of a love affair. The wild geese which had made a moment of private epiphany are now to be reinterpreted. They had brought Will back to the country and to his first sight of Jenny. They have turned out, then, to be symbols of much more human significance than might have first appeared, and it is this that jolted Will back into his memory when Jenny walked into his ward (340), where he is convalescing after an assault.

Jenny is referred to by Will as 'Primavera, the Lady of Spring' (16), but this reference to Botticelli's painting (in the Uffizi) is not used by Will to place Jenny on any pedestal. On the contrary, he sees her as placing herself on the plinth – as a haughty city woman playing in the country. He misjudges her. As he gradually finds out, Jenny is in fact a keen gardener and her interest in the countryside is not merely clothes-deep. That Will's recovery takes place under Jenny's aegis in the country returns us to Gunn's rural poetics. Gunn has shown in the book that though the countryside and freedom may gang together, the connection is neither exclusive nor easy. As Will tells Jenny, the working class know that their lives are hard but this is not necessarily connected with the ambience of the city: they 'don't feel that greyness as we would. To them the street noises and the grinding trams are their singing birds,' (326). Nor is Will's love of the countryside a backward-looking thing. At the end we are given a premonition of *The Silver Darlings'* House of Peace, when the would-be lovers reach a Lowland pagan place. 'The mound lay with its back in the sun, full of silence, of the past, of sleepy memories of strange rites being dreamed into the present, into the future,' (336). That emphasis on tradition growing into the present and the future makes this an earnest symbol of optimism not of escape. The mound is a pre-historic sanction (as well as a classical one), it seems, for the psychological and spiritual power-house Gunn believes is the essence of human good.

It is individual experience that is important, and it is the vigorously living people in the city with whom Will has become involved who have made him see that the country-city dichotomy is ultimately a false one. The light end of the book, then, is not quite the volte-face it seems. Gunn often presents moral fables which, while descriptively realistic, have plots whose internal ethics seem to deny realism. The allusion to Dante in this novel may be only via Eliot, but the references to Botticelli show that Gunn was thinking in terms of allegory and, interestingly, in terms of the European Renaissance (he also explicitly quotes from Walter Pater, 259). Because *Wild Geese Overhead* shows Gunn grappling with both contemporary and timeless problems, with an unusual display of literary and artistic reference integrated into the plot, it is a much more important novel in Gunn's corpus than has generally been admitted.

Second Sight (1940), a story of the well-to-do on a stag-hunting holiday, with the old division between ghillie and 'guest', would seem to have more in common with *The Poaching at Grianan* and *The Lost Glen* than with the novels immediately before or after it. As Hart and Pick show, it started out *circa* 1937 as a play.[5] This probably accounts for its largely enclosed settings, and its finishing cathartic nemesis. The date also suggests that it was one of the first things Gunn turned to after his Hebridean voyage. The plot is

lean and, in the nature of Gunn's plays, discursive dialogue rather
than action carries the theme.

A young ghillie, Alick, 'sees' a funeral procession before him,
and the pall-bearers seem familiar. At the hunting lodge the holi-
day-makers naturally become uneasy, except for one, Geoffrey,
who scoffs. A debate ensues between Geoffrey (a scientist), and
one of the sportsmen, Harry, who is more sympathetic towards
the Highlanders. In the background there is a sense of competition
between them over the killing of the most prestigious stag on the
estate, 'King Brude' (named after the great Pictish king). Towards
the end Geoffrey shoots it, but significantly he does so messily,
and his ghillie has to finish the job off. When he returns to the
lodge, Harry tries to make him leave, believing that it is Geoffrey
Alick had seen in his vision. Geoffrey refuses to go and, instead,
resolves to play a practical joke. He feigns sickness and then makes
an appearance as a shrouded ghost. Unfortunately, one of the
party attacks him, and in the scuffle he is killed. The last scene
shows Alick and his friend, Mairi, resolving to head south for the
cities, where they can find a new life.

On one level, *Second Sight* is almost a camped-up Gothic hor-
ror story (the antithesis between folk wisdom and an arrogant
scientific rationalism is a Gothic motif). From the first paragraph
we are aware of an intangible discomfort.

> With the lighting of the lamps came a slight uneasiness into
> the sitting-room of Corbreac Lodge. Upon the hollows and
> passes of the deer forest, darkness would be settling down,
> and though there was no need for anxiety, still there was
> always that odd chance of an accident of the unforeseen. (9)

The narratorial 'reassurance' has the opposite effect. It transpires
that the vaguely 'foreseen' – Alick's vision of death – is more
worrying than the unforseen. Gunn has a good measure of fun
with the nerves of his characters, and creates different frissons of
horror which all have perfectly good explanations. A curtain
touches Helen's hand (33) – it is only the wind; Harry hears
footsteps just after he has disclosed Alick's vision (40) – they are
only the women's; Joyce touches a cold hand in thick fog (109) – it
turns out to have been Harry. This teasing technique intensifies
when, towards the end of the book, the friends' discussion of the
nature of murder stories prefaces Geoffrey's death. One character
argues how unsatisfactory some of the newer stories are when

their sleuth becomes emotionally entangled in his work, rather then rationally distanced. 'But some writing johnnies clutter it up with stuff like emotion. I once read one – you won't believe this I know – but it's fact. *The detective wept!*' (299-300). This 'expounding [on] the whole construction and aesthetic of the detective novel' (300) is foremost a tension-raiser, because there is still an unsatisfied expectation of death lingering from Alick's second sight, but it is also an ironic introduction to Gunn's method of genre-bending. As we shall see in the 'detective story' of *The Key of the Chest*, and in the other 'genre novels', emotional engagement is exactly what Gunn is interested in.

If the horror story is parodied, second sight is treated with much more respect. On his recent journey around the Hebrides, Gunn had found Johnson's *Journey to the Western Islands of Scotland* an irresistible companion (in *Off in a Boat* he refers to it again and again). In his *Journey* Johnson goes to some pains to put forward arguments for and against second sight. Gunn follows a similar framework of discussion. In particular, his defence of second sight is established by Johnson when Johnson says that those who doubt second sight's existence 'presuppose more knowledge of the universal system than man has attained; and therefore depend upon principles too complicated and extensive for our comprehension [...]'.[6] Second sight, as Harry answers Geoffrey, is 'something outside natural law *as we know it*' (37). Alick proves that this is a viable idea by 'miraculously' rescuing Geoffrey in the dark. To all others the feat seems almost unbelievable, but Alick's explanation of how he achieved it shows that he was working from a complex but thorough understanding of the terrain. He had still been lucky, but his luck had not been so very out of the ordinary. The others had merely presupposed that more knowledge of the situation was needed than could be known, while Alick had seen the system in the apparent chaos. Here, perhaps, is the genesis for *The Other Landscape*'s proposition that God has a 'different system' which makes sense of the apparent meaninglessness of human existence. Alick's reluctance to disclose his experience is further corroboration of Johnson's view. 'By pretension to second sight, no profit was ever sought or gained', and 'Those who profess to feel it, do not boast of it as a privilege, nor are considered by others as advantageously distinguished.'[7] Johnson also says that in favour of the existence of second sight is 'the indistinct cry of national persuasion, which may be perhaps resolved at last into prejudice and tradition.'[8] Second sight, Johnson suggests, is in some way part of the essence of Scottish difference, and as such it is set against the refining influences destined to render it merely a 'prejudice' or a 'tradition'. In Gunn's novel small nationalist prods occur in the characters' conversations. Harry, for example, recounts the ill-fated plan to introduce English park deer into the 'noble' Highland stock (171-4) – a (rather crude) nationalist parable. While Harry literally seeks the sound of bagpipes, his colleagues are discomforted by them. Gunn pokes fun when one man says 'knowingly', 'I know what it is. It's a pibrok,' (247).

The plausibility of second sight is not left at the mercy of national interest, however, and Gunn doesn't totally rely on Johnson's argument of the basic limitation of man's understanding, either. A more modern voice is brought in to assist. Like James Leslie Mitchell's time travel novel, *Gay Hunter* (1934) *Second Sight* enlists the time hypothesis expounded by J. W. Dunne in his once very popular book, *An Experiment with Time* (1927). Dunne argued that time was 'the fourth dimension', and being such it was possible to travel, in an analogous way to normal movement, 'along' time's axis. It was possible to master the skill of 'time travel', and Dunne gave examples of how he had trained himself to predict some events. Clairvoyance, therefore, was not to be ridiculed. He 'showed' that humankind had at least a rudimentary capability to tap into the 'fourth dimension'. For Gunn, the same science that seemed to threaten the extinction of second sight could now be used to sanction its validity. Dunne, like Johnson, had been a topic for discussion on Gunn's Hebridean journey (*Off in a Boat*, 140). This had been a journey about confidence. Confidence in his marriage and confidence in his ability to be a self-sufficient writer now that he had left the Civil Service. Confidence, too, in finding and standing by the values he felt inherent in his society, especially as set against the very different ethos of the darkening 'modern' culture in Europe. Given these preoccupations, second sight should not be seen as the subject of a retrogressive fascination. *Second Sight*, like *Wild Geese Overhead*, and despite its apparently credulous subject matter, is deeply concerned with what Gunn increasingly saw as a battle between the spiritual conception of freedom and an enslaving materialism.

This theme bubbles under Harry and Geoffrey's arguments, and finally surfaces in no uncertain terms when they attend a dinner-party at the home of a church dean. Dean Cameron and his mathematician friend, Colonel Brown, are erudite and the implication is that they can offer a higher authority of knowledge in their respective fields than either Harry or Geoffrey. In defence of second sight, Colonel Brown explicitly cites Dunne, and paraphrases him at length (224-5). The conversation moves on, however, to other intangibles, to emotions, to the mysticism of the Yogis, and to love. The Dean finally draws from this the much larger debate behind the question of second sight.

> 'The strife here is between matter and mind, and mind will win through, because it is more important, more stupendous in its significance, than matter. A boy whistling a tune is a more wonderful phenomenon than the largest inert sun in all the universe, and we know it, and the materialist admits it. At times, matter will predominate and we become estranged from the things of the mind, by excessive toil, by material greed, by all sorts of sensual cravings and excitements, by intrigues, by tyranny, by lust for power, and by the conjunction of all these in war. Not only does the mystic tell you that, not only the Christian, but even the so-called anti-Christian, anti-mystic, like the communist or socialist, tells you the same thing. Everyone who is for the freedom of the spirit, for its integrity and need for development, must tell you the same thing, and must damn and want to destroy all that which thwarts it and keeps it from its high adventure. Now the spirit will never be defeated. [...] The materialist, the scoffer, the sceptic, may try to destroy that spirit. He can never succeed. In the struggle it is not the spirit that he will destroy, *it will be himself.*' (235)

Here Gunn is ably exploiting the two-fold nature of the book. The Dean's warning that the materialist is on a collision course with suicide is, first of all, a prophecy. Geoffrey, who has all along been cast in the mould of narrow scientific rationalist, is indicated as a marked man, within the conventions of the supernatural thriller. But the Dean's warning is of a much wider application. Second sight has become one of the lingering signs of 'a spirit in decline' (237), but the implication is that the scientism now in ascent will be a dangerous force (ultimately, indeed, dangerous to itself), if it can see only an unspiritual world.

The antithesis between Geoffrey and Harry, which epitomises the conflict the Dean has been describing, is reinforced by their respective behaviour when hunting. Geoffrey's maiming of King Brude is a particular example of the lust of the materialist at work – Geoffrey 'unsportsmanly' shoots when there is a high risk of failure and, therefore, of unnecessary cruelty. Harry, on the other hand, is much more relaxed. He had let King Brude go rather than risk causing it a lingering death. When he does shoot a stag without killing it, Gunn's description of its paralysis, and Harry's shock and distress before Alick quickly kills it, suggest where the sympathies of both author and character lie. Yet Gunn seems to endorse the principle of hunting – he only objects to unnecessary cruelty. Muir's observation on *Highland River* seems as true for *Second Sight*: 'by some ancestral hocus-pocus the trapper is generally a lover of freedom, and the huntsman unconsciously identifies himself with the creature he hunts.'[9]

Harry's friend, Helen, sees the hunt in terms of maleness, a perspective that characterises Gunn's polarised view of gender:

> Running deer, lovely running deer. Her sympathies were with the deer and not with the hunters. This was like a betrayal, a betrayal of Harry, of all her men, the hunting men, the hunters that came over horizon after primeval horizon, through dark ages and medieval ages, into the September sun of this day she was live in.
>
> As she shifted her stance, she glanced at Donald [her ghillie]. His eyes never left a certain point in the hills. He had the keen concentrated expression of the hunter, the eyebrows gathered a little over far-sighted eyes. Ruthless, she thought.
>
> And all at once she was struck by something terrifying in the aspect of man, something she had never experienced before, that separated man from her, some dark force of the spirit, that could grip male flesh.
>
> The moment's sensation carried within it its own visual image – an aspect of man, a man's questing head, potent and mythological. Deep in her it would remain for ever.
>
> For here was Helen, Helen Marway, in the bright sun, running with the invisible deer, running beyond men, in the light. (199)

Helen sees herself as set apart from men, and in particular the potential brutality of men, yet of course she is in love with Harry, too. While Gunn may idealise women, he nevertheless attempts to show men and women as complex in themselves and in their relation to each other.

What is so uncomfortable about *Second Sight*, however, is that very serious ideas of this nature are presented in a world where many of the personalities, especially the token English, are simply and deliberately caricatures. This is knotted up with the comic portrayal of the richer middle class and the melodrama of the plot. Does the subversion of genre and the movement back and forth between parody and obvious seriousness create an instability in almost all the viewpoints represented in the book? The end, or rather Geoffrey's end, goes over the top, an effect O. H. Mavor warned of when he read *Second Sight* as a play.[10] Of course the lighting and sound effects and his 'walking corpse' are the absurd exaggerations of the horror film, designed as such by Geoffrey to expose the ridiculous in his colleagues. But George's fatal assault on the 'ghost' is preposterous, and all the more so because Gunn had earlier contrived to make him say (unaware, as it were, of what was to come), that if he saw a ghost he'd punch it. Given that this is part of the dramatic build-up, one might expect Geoffrey's death to be the end of the book, but it is not.

The final pages are left to Alick and his decision to clear out with Mairi. This is structurally weak because the novel has not developed Alick's character fully enough to give their exodus much impact on the reader. Yet perhaps in his playing down of Alick's role in the novel and the camping up of the middle classes, Gunn is being rather more subtle. As Alick puts it, he can't stop the outsiders 'playing their little tricks,' (315). The Highlanders are peripheral in their own home, and *Second Sight*'s presentation of them is faithful to that marginalisation. The switch to Alick and Mairi at the very end of the book reminds us that we as readers have been led to be more interested in the goings-on of the pleasure set than in the existence of those whom, to varying degrees, the pleasure set exploit. This refocusing to a 'minor' romantic sub-plot is, then, deliberately disconcerting. It asks us in a bitter postscript to consider the people who to some extent have been only exotic background to the 'main plot'.

6

Progress and Progression

The Silver Darlings

The Silver Darlings (1941) resumes the unofficial history project Gunn had started with *Sun Circle* and *Butcher's Broom*. Even more than *Butcher's Broom*, it is the product of considerable research. Hart and Pick note also the personal encouragement of Peter Anson.[1] The chapter on 'Religion and Superstition' in Anson's *Fishing Boats and Fisher Folk on the East Coast of Scotland* (1930) seems to inform Gunn's depiction of folklore in the book (the saying of 'cold iron' to correct blasphemy at sea, the avoidance of the word 'salmon', and the ability to whistle up a wind). Frazer's *The Golden Bough*, too, was a favourite book and a source. Gunn probably had a good idea beforehand of many of the customs in the book, not least because his father, to whom the book is dedicated, was a fisherman. Like *Butcher's Broom*, *Silver Darlings* grew partly from very personal connections with the subject matter. Anson's technical help on the fishing of the past, and his affecting line drawings both of the desolate harbours of contemporary Dunbeath, Lybster, and Staxigoe, and of barrel-laden Wick at the furious height of the fishing boom, collectively contributed significantly to the book's sense of historical authenticity. In addition, Gunn's long and at times frightening sailing holiday in 1937, and his subsequent experiences on the sea, appear to have surfaced in beautifully observed sea sequences.

A novel of the post-Clearances herring fishers of the Caithness sea-board, the plot is basically the biography of its central character, Finn. Finn's mother, Catrine, loses her husband, Tormad, to a Royal Navy press-gang who actually kill him, but she does not know this for sure for over twenty years. Pregnant with Finn, she leaves her home in Sutherland and travels to 'Dunster' in Caithness, where she settles at the home of Kirsty, a friend of her mother. On the day that she arrives she meets Roddie, who is about to become Dunster's first sea-fishing skipper. The novel follows Finn's development from infancy to young man, a maturing process marked by his increasing involvement in the precarious business of open-boat herring fishing. Understandably, Catrine hates the sea, and she is over-protective of Finn. Their relationship is worsened by her growing entanglement with Roddie, whom she eventually marries. Meantime, the fishing takes Finn as far afield as the Flannan Isles, and his adventures give him among his own people an heroic quality. More self-consciously, this lends an epic flavour to the novel itself. Finn's emerging maturity helps resolve his disturbed relations with Roddie and Catrine, and the novel ends on the evening before his wedding to a fish-gutter, Una. He is in 'The House of Peace', the old missionary area of the hill associated in local lore with an early Christian 'evangelist'. It is a place he has visited many times over the years, and this latest visit seems to symbolise a finally attained harmony.

The question of why Gunn chose this particular point of history for what would be his last and greatest historical novel is a vital one for our understanding of his work in general. Isobel Murray and Bob Tait suggest that Gunn's 'beliefs and hopes about *living* traditions of individuality and community [were] rooted in the history of his part of the world,' and that the period of *The Silver Darlings* 'could legitimately be regarded as a period that gave him something to celebrate.'[2] Several critics have pointed to Gunn's alleged belief in the existence of a primitive but harmonious 'Golden Age' of humankind, and at first sight it would seem that here Gunn found one not so very far away. Murray and Tait are also right, however, to question this.[3] Such a view would suggest a naïvety scarcely credible given Gunn's knowledge of the era. He knew that the fishing industry had experienced a disastrous decline towards the end of the nineteenth century. He himself may have became a civil servant because there was not enough trade for any of the Gunn brothers to follow in their father's bootsteps. Gunn uses the term 'Golden Age' to describe at least two quite different things, which he occasionally conflates (a sign that even to himself the subject was a nebulous one). Firstly, there is the idea of a prehistoric Golden Age when primitive man allegedly existed in a purely instinctual state of being. Secondly there is the rather different sense of there having been a Golden

Age of arts and culture, especially Gaelic culture. In *Whisky and Scotland*, for example, Gunn postulated with a chuckle that the Golden Age saw the birth of whisky.

On the relatively few occasions Gunn uses the term, the Golden Age of either definition is usually accompanied by authorial distancing or doubt. The first kind is usually defended, cautiously, as an idea plausible to 'modern anthropologists', an appeal to an authority which also attempts to make the assertion impersonal. Even then, it is used not foremost as an ideal for society but as an ideal for individual psychology. As we have seen, for Kenn the 'golden age' had been the time of the 'hunters'. These epitomised the dynamic *individual* (124). This Age could not be recreated in any meaningful sense in the modern world, but the lessons of the self were important. In his assessment of James Leslie Mitchell's achievement, Gunn described a slightly different version again of the pre-civilisation golden Age, but here too it is obvious that he is concerned with an individual *sensibility* not any concretely realised social structure.

> [...] Mitchell believed, in common with a modern school devoted to scientific research in anthropology, that before civilization came to ride us, there did exist on earth what the poets have called a Golden Age. The belief was at the back of his mind giving it poise and philosophy, impetus and wrath. And whether (as with his Cosmopolis and racial judgements) it is right or wrong again does not greatly matter to our purpose, for man has in him to this day a positive intuition of that far-back primordial goodness. Mitchell knew it not only scientifically but in the marrow of the bone.[3]

Though here again are appeals to sanctioning authorities – poets and scientists – that 'right or wrong' shows how unwilling Gunn was to be drawn. Hart and Pick discuss his conception of a Golden Age and they, too, show him being very cagey.[5] As to the Gaelic-related definition, in his 1930 essay 'New Golden Age for Scots Letters'[6] Gunn uses the term simply to refer to 'a new age, possibly a golden age, in Scottish letters.' He compares the Scottish Renaissance with a by-gone Gaelic culture 'which was in its most perfect flower centuries before even the beginnings of English Literature.' In doing so, he is primarily colluding with MacDiarmid's cultural line *vis-à-vis* the 'Gaelic Idea'.

The Silver Darlings, then, has very little to do with the 'Golden Age'. Rather it celebrates a society not only coping with great change, but positively thriving on it. To Gunn it symbolised a synthesis of individualism, community values, tradition, and the challenge of the modern. The subsequent and continuing decline was not forgotten, however. Gunn's angry journalism of the late 1930s again and again criticises the way the London Government was undermining the Scottish fishermen. But in the book a discussion between three curers shows that even in the nineteenth century the Government, to conserve stock, was moving to restrict the activities of all herring fishers because the curers, especially those with many other interests beyond the herring, were too greedy to regulate themselves. The victims then were the small-scale west coast fisher-crofters as well as, presumably, the less successful Finns and Roddies. Gunn tells us (in a rare, glancing narratorial intervention) that this indeed turned out to be the case (352). The small businessmen (and, worse, the diversifying businessman) inevitably squeezed out the more modest exponents of the fisher-class. Towards the end of the book, there are intimations of the worsening herring stocks – Finn says to Roddie that 'the West is going to get worse before it gets better' (560) – and when Catrine says to Finn, '"Take the sweetness of life, Finn, while still you have it,"' (581), her sentiment of *carpe diem* seems to expect harder times in more than personal terms. But for the most part, here, just a hundred years ago, was a time when self-sufficiency existed once more in Scotland. Though the very individualism Gunn celebrates was to get out of hand, and in fact contributed to the fishing demise, the period still had considerable exemplary resources.

A tireless, tough, and God-fearing people, taking their lives in their hands, on these treacherous coasts, in their small open boats – and sending their tens of thousands of barrels of herring deep into Germany, into the Baltic Sea, and far into Russia.

I cannot pursue the story here and tell how boats got bigger, got decked, until finally the steam drifter took over and concentrated the herring fishing in a few large ports. Many of the smaller creeks, which once knew such a surge of warm life, are now quite derelict. But the men and women of that time – for nearly a whole century – did something remarkable, with more wonder of achievement in it, than any story of mine could ever adequately tell.[7]

This, then, sets the context of *The Silver Darlings*. And as with so many other of Gunn's books, within the novel itself there is an emphasis on re-telling one's history and traditions. Kirsty is a chronicle-maker who knows and enjoys explaining the genealogies of people from miles around. Roddie's crewman, Rob, is famed for his stories and his adherence to old customs. But the greatest story-teller turns out to be Finn himself. Because he retells the stories Gunn has necessarily told us, there is a strong connection between Finn's telling role and the author's. Finn's ability to transform his living story into a fiction is obviously akin to the author's ability to fictionalise the real events of the herring folk. Both make reality break free from the time by which it is pinioned. This is given a further dimension when Finn is lightly compared to the Celtic hero, Finn MacCoul, and by no less than an old drover from the days before the Clearances (449) (could this be the arch-history-teller, Tomas, strayed in from *Butcher's Broom?*).

The allusion to Finn MacCoul is a small example of the technique which Gunn uses throughout the book, which might be called 'progressive repetitition'. By this I mean the process of attaching cumulative associations to single motifs threaded through the novel. He had experimented with this in *Highland River*. The little pellet of earth which Kenn had seen move when he was a boy at the snaring, is repeated when a bullet displaces earth in the trenches at the Front. The later incident shows Kenn perceiving his survival in the war in terms of protecting his earlier hunting self. In *The Silver Darlings*, the rowan berries and the 'grey fool' butterfly are perhaps two of the best examples.

At the beginning, Catrine has a nightmare in which Tormad is taken away from her by a kelpie. The landscape's 'tallest trees were rowans, heavy with clustered berries of a menacing blood-red, the clusters leaning slightly towards them, as watching faces might lean' (35). Because we have already been told of Tormad's bloody struggle with the press-gang, though chronologically after Catrine's dream, the blood association has a strengthened sense of the second sight. Catrine remembers the rowan berries five or so years later when she receives a letter from Tormad's best friend, Ronnie, who assumes that she knows about Tormad's death, though Catrine does not. Indeed she does not learn directly for many years to come. However, time is slightly altered again in a way that emphasises her preoccupation with the berries' link with death, and also reinforces their association with prevision. The berries are textually a prelude to Ronnie's letter, even though chronologically it was clearly the letter that made Catrine think of the berries.

> Tormad in the woods. Tormad – with mind and body thrilled to an unbearable stillness, until she felt she would dissolve, fly into bits, unless... ah, the crush of his arms, crushing all the bits back into shape, and the relief of it, the unutterable, divine relief, and the sudden exquisite lack of care, of caring no more, of letting go... Tormad – and the red berries... Blood-red magic.
>
> The letter had been written by a man for Ronnie in the West Indies last year. (153-4)

Gunn also connects Finn's birth with the berries, recounting his nativity only at this point, long after we have seen him as a little boy. He has been a counterbalance for his mother's darker loneliness – 'loveliest of all had been these last few years with Finn' (156).

The next time the rowan berries appear, they are part of a chilling coincidence which brings Catrine's Sutherland past into collision with her increasingly complicated 'new' life in Dunster. When Finn goes on a visit to relatives in Helmsdale (Sutherland) he meets Ronnie, who has finally left the Navy. As they walk up the strath, Ronnie talks of his fondness for Catrine and, unwittingly, he draws Finn's attention to some rowans. He then tells how Tormad died.

> 'I used to think about her often when I was away.' His tone was clear and frank and transcended Finn's embarrassment. 'The autumn is on us,' he said in the same tone, lifting his face. 'The rowan berries are red.' Finn looked at the mountain-ash with its load of berries, blood-red berries over green leaves in the September sun. Their stillness and silence touched him, as if they were waiting or listening.
>
> 'We'll sit in the shadow for a little,' said Ronnie, 'for I'm feeling a bit tired.'
>
> The moment had now come, Finn knew, when Ronnie would tell about the death of his father. (453)

The rowan berries' animate quality plunges us back into Catrine's dream. As in that dream, Tormad's death follows quickly – this time Ronnie 're-lives' the death when he tells it to Finn. Ronnie suggests that Finn take a sprig of rowan home to his mother: the two men occupy a meaning-laden landscape they cannot fully comprehend. The reader too does not know the implications of Ronnie's comments about autumn's arrival until in the next chapter Catrine remembers his earlier remark about its 'being too late' for them to try to get together (461).

> She would never get away from the past with Ronnie. He was its ghost. The strath, the outline of the hills, Tormad, the red berries – with the life that ran through them, the flame of youth, quickening, terrible, enchanting. Ronnie would lead her back there, remind her. It could not be borne. (461)

The 'progressive' aspect of this repetition is that the berries now symbolise much more than they had at first. To Catrine they represent a whole desolate past as well as a youthful love literally murdered. And they are now attached to Ronnie, a brutalised reminder of that past. For in fact it is not autumn for Catrine, it is not too late for her. In fact it is only the beginning for her second life – with Roddie.

While Finn has been away, she and Roddie have finally united. She seems at last to have put Sutherland behind her in having rejected Ronnie, and she has accepted Roddie's advances. He carries her in an embrace 'over to the stall with the straw, where Finn had been born' (478), a detail which, as well as recalling the Nativity, looks back to the earlier balancing of the berries with Finn's birth. When Finn returns he is upset to realise that they have crossed the barrier between being friends and being lovers but, later, when Catrine is on their own, he innocently offers her the sprig.

> Her eyes were on the berries, her face death-pale, her lips apart, her fingers against her breast like claws. She collapsed so suddenly that she fell her length before he could stir a foot to save her. She hit the floor with a solid thump, and lay with the crown of her head a couple of inches from the sharp edge of the hearthstone. (482)

Round the berries, then, Gunn has gradually clustered a range of Catrine's problems. Finn's return with the berries is a reminder that he, too, is attached to her past, and that her wish to be extricated from it is just not achievable. Yet she is restored to a happier balance, once the relationship between Roddie and Finn improves, the two working together to try to save some fishermen whose boat has been wrecked at the sea-edge. Progressive repetition occurs here, too, because the chapter of Tormad's death, 'The Derelict Boat' is translated into 'The Wreck', the chapter that reunites Tormad's son with Catrine's new husband (and Finn's new 'father').

For Finn, too, apparently small things have symbolic resonance. Young Finn's fascination with the toy trumpet at a fair is narratorially connected to the trumpets of Jericho in the lesson taught by Sandy Ware (whose name, incidentally, echoes the name of the nineteenth-century evangelist Sandy Gair). The trumpets merge in Finn's dream when his trumpet, which is also the curved horn of Finn MacCoul, blows down the wall at the bottom of the croft. This, with the previous chapter's title, 'Finn Blows his own Trumpet', emphasises that even at this early stage he is coming to an understanding of his independent self. Finn's early encounter with a butterfly shows another sophisticated and lasting layering of meaning. It is significant that the first time he appears in the novel he gleans a sense of the division between right and wrong, an understanding of morality and of how it can be changed by the surfaces of language. It is also the first time he visits the House of Peace and, importantly, also his first separation from his mother. Chasing the butterfly known as 'the grey fool', he finally catches up with it and kills it. But later when Roddie finds him, he is told that the grey fool is also known as 'God's fool'. (This distinction is probably derived from *Carmina Gadelica*, where it is also noted that 'Amadan-De' is 'sometimes applied to giddy, foolish children'.[8]) Finn is distraught at the different light the changed name sheds on things. The 'reassurance' that God's fools never harm anyone does not help at all and so Roddie promises him an introduction to the sea to cheer him up. Catrine's extreme reaction to this promise makes the butterfly chase resound with one of the main tensions of the book, namely Catrine's hatred of the sea and her corresponding over-protectivness. 'Her lips trembled. The meanings had started to take her son away from her. Already the terrible knowledge of good and evil was in him. He had killed the butterfly' (100). The impression that Finn has experienced in some way a 'Fall' is especially poignant because it is Catrine who sees his separation most unequivocally in these terms. It is only she who wants to compel him to remain firmly in a hermetic Eden. But Finn, though regretting killing one of God's meek creatures, has experienced a near-autonomous self, and Roddie has promised more of the same. For Gunn any such Fall is actually a step up.

Much later, on the idyllic isle of North Uist, Finn comes across the butterfly again in a story told during a ceilidh (543). The frisson of recognition is immediately followed by a girl's lullaby. Again meanings resonate. The ancient song describes a mother losing her child forever, a theme that draws us back to Catrine's fear of losing Finn both on the specific occasion of his butterfly chase, and more generally. But the lullaby is also the very same one Finn remembers hearing as a boy. For the first time, he begins to appreciate his mother's fears. The need for detachment, yet the awful need to be needed, to connect, to be cherished, seem caught at last.

The motif which is developed alongside Finn's developing relationship with Catrine is the House of Peace. As I have noted earlier, the 'spiritual mound' exists in largely undeveloped form in Gunn's earlier fiction. He greatly admired Gibbon's *Sunset Song* (1932), and it was partly the Stone Circle there that showed him how a much more important role could be given to the mound. A person and the earth itself, Gibbon showed, could be seen to symbolically intersect in the highest expression of a sense of place. The history (even the pre-history) of one's people could be redivined by the individual who sought the mound's psychological shelter. Even so, the circle in *Sunset Song* is very different from the House of Peace (which is a Christian site, and certainly does not hark back to any Golden Age). While the Druid Circle gives Gibbon's main protagonist, Chris, literally space to think, and to ask questions about self and identity, Chris's conclusions are diametrically at variance with Finn's. Although Chris and Finn both take stock in places shunned by their respective communities, Chris is much more of a solitary, defiant of and aloof from her community in a way that Finn is not. Gifford rightly contrasts the two when he says that the House of Peace has a 'radiating influence for Good and spiritual revival', while the Druid Stones have a 'more desolate and elegiac influence.'[9] Gibbon offers no culminating vision of Chris in harmony with history, her people, or with her more personal circle of relationships. Yet the fusion of all these things is exactly what is presented in *The Silver Darlings*.

Gibbon's Druid Stones are fixed in suicidal futility to a past world, while the future is given to Ewan and his communism at the end of the book, but the House of Peace invests Gunn's vigorous optimism in the resources of the people themselves, not in Gibbon's merely geologically perfect version of Communism.

There are at least two real-life precedents for the House of Peace. 'The Hill of Peace', Hart and Pick point out, was actually a place of play in Gunn's childhood in Dunbeath.[10] While this is the clearest source, there is another site which may have been influential. When Gunn stayed as an adolescent in St John's Town of Dalry in Galloway, it is likely that he would have been aware of the one-time existence of Candida Casa, the religious centre near Wigtown established by the first Christian missionary in Scotland, Ninian. Candida Casa translates as 'The House of Purity' or 'The House of Whiteness'. Gunn draws on both his personal experience (always important to him) but also on the resonances of early Christianity in Scotland, the echo of *Sun Circle's* Molrua in *The Silver Darlings* (189) making this all the more clear. He makes a specific reference to Candida Casa in *Off in a Boat* (145), where his journey has overtones of a pilgrimage. In addition, the House of Peace motif is perhaps associated with the twenty-third Psalm, repeated through the book: 'Surely goodness and mercy shall follow me all the days of my life: and I will dwell in the house of the Lord for ever.'

Though Gunn clearly intends the House of Peace to have historical and religious depth, admitting Finn to an (authorially-constructed) spiritual tradition, this is only one of its aspects. For the most part, it is used to signpost different important moments in Finn's growing up. The first appearance of the House of Peace takes place when Catrine is pregnant and has just arrived in Dunster after crossing the Ord; she is introduced to it by Roddie, who has volunteered to take her to Kirsty's house. Catrine takes immediate comfort from it: 'the name had been like a benediction sounded softly in her mind' (61). The House, then, is there at the very beginning of the long courtship between Roddie and Catrine, a temporary salve to her anguish, introducing a special intimacy of understanding between them. The House of Peace is a 'protagonist' in Catrine's life, as well as Finn's, and, as we shall see, plays a key role in her relationship with Roddie.

After Finn's first encounter with the House (the butterfly

incident), the next recorded visit is when he is a young teenager. This, like the accentuated selections of life in *Morning Tide* and *Highland River*, is partly Proustian, but it is also in keeping with Gunn's poetics of the self. For Gunn, the capacity of the self to construct or extract significance from selected individual experiences is literally of the greatest moment. With his friend Donnie, Finn has trapped a rabbit in a cairn up on the hillside. Because Catrine has forbidden him to go down to the sea-edge, he uses the rabbit as an alibi. He lets Kirsty think that he's going to hunt rabbits at Donnie's, knowing that the rabbit has already been killed and will therefore 'corroborate' his story later. In this way the House of Peace allows Finn, as it had earlier, to exert his independence from his mother. It also allows him communion with the sea, where the serpent-like eel he hooks (but which escapes him) reiterates the earlier Edenic suggestion of the human need to re-experience 'sin'. In this way Gunn shares MacDiarmid's interest in questioning and realigning the symbols of Christianity and their implications, the most obvious comparison being to the serpent focus in *To Circumjack Cencrastus* (1930). In this instance, Finn acts foolishly, and while he is fishing the tide strands him on rocks. In the condemning look he receives from Roddie, who rescues him as Catrine looks on (169), there is an early example of the conflict of emotions which Roddie and Finn experience in their relations with Catrine and to each other.

Perhaps the most dramatic House of Peace episode is Finn's encounter with the tall priest-like figure there. This occurs when cholera has taken hold of the north-eastern seaboard. While the epidemic is harrowing and harrowingly drawn, the opening lines in Chapter 10, 'The Coming of the Plague', suggest that it also represented a release for Finn, into the freedom of the sea (193). The severity of the situation becomes clear when, near the House of Peace, Roddie advises Finn to stay away from home, as Kirsty is ill. After a strained talk with Catrine (separated by a stream for safety), Finn, crying, makes his way to the childhood sanctuary. He finds some solace there. Falling into a state of near-sleep, he sees the 'tall figure of an old man in a white cape.'

> [...] The face did not speak to him or move: it just looked, the body standing still in a natural way. But the look was extraordinarily full of understanding, and somewhere in it there was a faint humour, the humour that knows and

appreciates and yet would not smile to hurt, yet the smile
was there. (214)

The shaved head of the ghost identifies him as the early missionary
which, we had heard earlier, legend associated with the mound.
Finn's sleepiness, his anxiety, and the previously-known folklore,
suggest a psychological interpretation of the apparition, but there
is a hint that he is plumbing a genuinely supernatural continuity
with the history of the place. Gifford remarks that Gunn 'creates a
"take-it-or-leave-it suggestion, because he himself is both tradi-
tional Gael and modern rationalist, aware of complexities of psy-
chology."'[11] The important point is that Finn's virtual prayer is
answered with a benign vision, and that even in the most desperate
of times the warmth of humanity is illuminating. This is also an
important stage in Finn's development of an understanding for
others. He is beginning to realise that personal well-being, in a
profound sense, is derived from the mediation between the self
and the lives of others. Catrine's ordeal has meant a similar thing.
On her death-bed, Kirsty warns her that Finn will be damaged for
life if he is never allowed to go to sea (239). Catrine's reluctant
recognition of this precipitates Finn's release, and the plague is
therefore shown to be a liberating force. Once again, disaster leads
to the release and re-channelling of constructive energies.

'Finn in the Heart of the Circle' is the title of the last chapter.
He is at the heart of a very densely-packed circle. Lying within the
round ruins of the Christian cell, he finds the pagan circle of self,
'curled up like an adder that had accidentally stung itself' (582).
He has become a hero and a story-teller, like Roddie. There is
expected the endless spiral of 'children and children's children'
(583) and the look to the future when he seems himself like 'the
white-haired man he had once imagined here,' (583-4). Both are
visions he laughs at, but he seems to be in certain consonance with
them, too. In effect there is almost a transcendence of history by
his identification with what is timeless. Furthermore, there is the
place he has earned within the larger circle of the community, and
within the small circle of close family. There is also that special
intimate 'ring of silence' (583) he and Una share in their soon-to-
be-wedded togetherness. And because Finn's circle is not as im-
pervious as he had liked to hope, there are also his encircling men-
friends who, shaking the trees in pursuit of the stag of their stag
night, are closing in. Like *Highland River*, the novel ends by

moving on from the central image of the book, having finally absorbed its meaning.

7

The War at Home: Innocence and Experience

I WAR-TALK AND IDEOLOGIES

[...] a curious thing is happening to the individual in these days. So drawn together are we in fatality that when the individual breaks free from the concerns of the mass, even for a moment, he is affected by something like a sense of guilt. To turn to Nature is to turn away from the dread realities that encompass us, is to escape, and in the act we suspect a weakness, a selfish trifling, which is highly reprehensible and of which we are openly or secretly ashamed. [...]

The war is not altogether responsible for this attitude. It has emphasised it, brought it actively into consciousness, but the whole trend of our age was already shaping that way. [...] For a man to be concerned with his own soul, even with his own reactions, is inept, incredible, laughable. There is not time for all that any more, no time for falling leaves in a world falling in ruins. The big business man feels the same way, for his business has got linked up with the business of the State into a mystical wholeness in which all individuals must pull as one; no trouble, no sectional claims, only one united endeavour.[1]

The three novels that are solidly of the war years, both in publication and preparation, are *Young Art and Old Hector* (1942), *The Serpent* (1943), and *The Green Isle of the Great Deep* (1944). The war, however, hardly seems to encroach on the fictional world of any. Even in the last of the three, where tyranny surfaces in a most sinister fashion, the tyranny seems more a nightmare of socialism than Nazi terror. In the war years Gunn was painfully aware, however, of the general disjunction between text and exterior world. Only months after *The Serpent* was published, he was half apologising for it:

> Frankly, I naturally felt it was quite the wrong time for work
> of that kind, with its seeming old-fashioned divorce from
> time and place and mood. But then again I wanted to put
> over certain value's, which I think are for all time, and if we
> are going to be governed in these matters by what is no more
> than a passing public aptitude in such matters, how are these
> values going to survive? In these matters it is surely up to us
> to choose the field of action![2]

Only half apologising because Gunn is, of course, defending
himself. His emphasis on the moral imperative of art, as against
pseudo-democratic crassness, 'a passing public aptitude' shows
him appealing to a 'higher' ethics which does not so much obviate
the Second World War in his work as encompass it. McCulloch's
comparison of *Young Art and Old Hector* with 'The Ecchoing
Green' is highly appropriate.[3] In both works there are children at
play while benevolent elders look on; with Blake, Gunn believes
'The Child's Toys & the Old Man's Reasons / are the Fruits of the
Two seasons'. They are both works of seemingly guileless charm
conceived in times of extreme turbulence, and, like Blake, Gunn
does more than first appears.

In his regular column for *The Scots Magazine* in this period,
'Memories of the Months', Gunn fondly describes the beauties of
the land and the sea, and the problems and small triumphs of the
people who live and work there. Unlike the novels, however, it
refers directly to contemporary events. Gunn describes the air-
raid siren that, thankfully, proves a false alarm, the harbours that
cannot be named because of their strategic importance, and the
farms that would look so much like little factories from the air...
The piece quoted at the head of this chapter is particularly appo-
site in considering what Gunn saw as perhaps the greatest danger
inherent in the forces behind the war: the bureaucratisation of
power. It is taken from an article rounding up a year of 'Memories
of the Months'. Gunn takes this opportunity to focus on what he
identifies as the general modern malaise. The whole article is
devoted to the plight of individual freedom in the face of a world
trend towards orchestration of the mass. Gunn argues that this is a
specifically modern manifestation, 'the whole trend of our age',
which cannot be seen solely in terms of Nazism, and it is this much
wider political interpretation that underlies the war novels.

Naomi Mitchison's chiding of Gunn for, firstly, producing
what she saw as the sentimental *Young Art and Old Hector*, and,
secondly, for producing an anti-communist text in the sequel, *The
Green Isle of the Great Deep*, misconstrues both Gunn's intention
and his practice.[4] The real target in both books is the dehumanis-
ing centralised bureaucracy which manages the mass as if 'the
mass' were more important than the individuals of which it is
constituted. In such a society, colourlessness and mediocrity, the
lowest common denominator, are the typical traits, and there is no
room for intellect, art, or the 'deviations' of alternative traditions
or identities. It is humanity conceived as an insect brood, a per-
fectible beehive.

Gunn had been reading the work of left-wing critics of Stalin-
ism, in particular Herbert Read and Arthur Koestler[5] who both
saw the equivalences between the Russian experiment and the
society forged by Hitler. Koestler's *Darkness at Noon* (1940) and
Arrival and Departure (1943) are crucial forbears of *The Green
Isle*. The earlier novel details the last days of a Bolshevik revolu-
tionary imprisoned in one of Stalin's prisons. The two different
approaches to torture and interrogation that the victim experi-
ences, one more psychological, one more physical, are also anti-
thetical methods favoured by Merk and Axle, the Questioner's
assistants in *The Green Isle*. In *Darkness at Noon* Stalin and Hitler
each become simply 'No. 1', and in *Arrival and Departure* the
protagonist has escaped to the mythical country Neutralia. In
neither book are the Soviet Union and Germany actually named,
though they are quite clearly the two forces at war: thus Koestler
both condemns specific powers and offers a more general critique
of the nature of ideology. Gunn's *Green Isle*, with its sinister
'Administrators' and 'Coastwatcher', and its bureaucratically
numbered 'Regions', uses a similar technique. In its concern with
the individual in conflict with the sophisticated social condition-
ing methods of the super-state, *The Green Isle* anticipates, and
compares favourably with, Orwell's masterpiece, *1984*.

In Koestler's *Arrival and Departure*, the fascist Bernard pro-
poses that the 'city-states' of African white ants are the exempli-
fying apotheoses of a 'collective consciousness in the full bio-
logical sense of the term'.[6] Gunn was already aware and concerned
that moderate British thinkers also aspired to this kind of utopia,
albeit in the cause of world peace. In particular Gunn singled out

H. G. Wells, who had much earlier used the ant-hill metaphor in
The World of William Clissold:

> I do not regard the organisation of all mankind into one
> terrestial anthill, into Cosmopolis, the greater Athens, the
> Rome and Paris and London of space and time, as a Utopian
> dream, as something that fantastically might be. I regard it as
> the necessary, the only possible continuation of human his-
> tory. To fail to take that road will mean a fraying-out and a
> finish to that history, a relapse through barbarism to sav-
> agery, to the hard chances of animal life for a creature too
> scarce and long-lived to be readily adaptable, and so at last
> surely to extinction.[7]

This could not be further from Gunn's view, and Wells's 'influ-
ence' on the thinking and the imagery of *The Green Isle of the
Great Deep* has so far been underestimated. In a review of an
anthology of philosophical opinions, *I Believe*, he derides Wells's
goal of a world state and the scapegoat of nationalism:

> Here we are at system-building and world-building again.
> But I have never been able to follow Mr Wells into his higher
> social-speculative regions. Most of us seem to him like bees
> who refuse to run our hive with the efficiency of real bees,
> though he demonstrates, complete with flower-seed pack-
> ets, the only way to do it (even if his demonstrations change
> with the years). Jettisoning the immortal soul of the indi-
> vidual, he, however, believes in 'the immortal soul of the
> race'. 'Naturally my ideas of politics is [sic] an open con-
> spiracy to hurry these tiresome, wasteful, evil things – na-
> tionality and war – out of existence.' He does not define the
> evil that resides in nationality. Is it implied that nationality is
> the sole cause of war? But later on he says: 'All war is not
> nationalist.' In fact in another moment he finds the war
> danger arising from a 'great release of human energy and a
> rapid dissolution of social classes, through the ever-in-
> creasing efficiency of economic organisation and the utili-
> sation of mechanical power.' The terrific internal war in
> Russia was not nationalist, and if wholesome progressive
> countries like Norway and Denmark and Holland had had
> their wish they would have had less than nothing to do with
> this war.

Gunn perceived the tension between nationalism and utopianism long before the outbreak of war. In an article of 1931, Wells again appears:

> [...] it would be almost as reasonable to suggest that we could get rid of the unwelcome noise of our machine age by first of all abolishing musical scales and musical instruments as it would be to suggest that we could get rid of jingoism by first of all abolishing patriotism. There is no philosophic basis here, and the reasoning is of the kind that has been prolific of so much action or rather restriction, in recent world legislation. What interferes with our national love of country to-day may regulate our drink to-morrow, our clothes the day after, and our conjugal relations next year. Patriotism may yet keep us from being slaves – if only of the Wellsian aseptic city-honeycombs.[9]

The belief that one form of patriotism countered the war impulse as another form fired it up attains a prophetic significance for our own times. Gunn argues that the complexity of a many-nationed world is not only the guaranteur of its diverse collective cultural wealth, but of its collective peace, too: 'Internationalism carried to its logical conclusion of a single centralisation of all power – arms, finance, law-making – could result in the greatest tyranny the mind of man is capable of conceiving.'[10] In the war years the association of nationalism with the unleashing of ferocious Germanic energies made any loyalty to Scotland, rather than Churchill's England ('Britain'), an uncomfortable one to maintain in public: 'No trouble, no sectional claims, only one united endeavour.' It is clear that Gunn saw in attachment to a sense of Scottishness just the positive individualism he so wished to defend. Indeed, what Scottish nationalism represented to him, paradoxically, went beyond devotion to Scotland.

Withdrawing from direct involvement in the affairs of the SNP from 1939 onwards, Gunn's belief in Scotland did not dwindle, but wider (connected) issues had been emerging on the world scene for some time which seemed to redefine his locus of concern. In a letter to the Party's Secretary John MacCormick he describes why this was an issue of fundamental human liberty, not one of Little Scotlander politics. He also explains why the pacifist stance then popular among many in the SNP was unacceptable to him.

Personally, my attitude to this war business includes motives beyond the immediate issues of self-government. For a long time I have been troubled and uncertain about Russia, but recent events have satisfied me that Stalin and Company have got bitten by the lust for power. Communists in this country seem still to confuse Stalin with communism as many a simple wife does an errant Moderator of the Wee Free Kirk with Christianity. The forces of the world seem slowly to be aligning themselves into two groups: those who wish to retain man's freedom to express whatever integrity may be in him and those who don't. This freedom of expression is to me supremely important, and I am prepared to align myself accordingly. Scotland's national historic attitude, before and after the Declaration of Arbroath, shows her as one of the earliest and finest champions of this freedom and it is inconceivable to me that she adopt any other attitude now. On this issue I am prepared to take a stand for or against any country, my own included.

And meantime my belief in the need for realising our Party's aim is, if that were possible, growing stronger. The position therefore to me is that we must press as strongly as possible and by all means to realise our aims, but not in such a manner as to dissociate ourselves implicitly or explicitly, from such forces as may be fighting to retain individual expression of opinion. There is no division here, for this very freedom is, as I say, implicit in the Scottish tradition, and any declaration by the Party should make this grand old historical fact clear.[11]

The Declaration of Arbroath of 1320 was a letter from a group of Scottish Barons to Pope John XXII, in which they swore their support for Robert Bruce so long as he remained true to freedom and true to Scottish independence. The placing of 'freedom' and Scotland above the sovereign was interpreted by Gunn as a major characteristic of the Scottish constitution, and therefore of the Scottish personality. It is vital to see that Gunn's conception of nationality was bound up in his conception of the freedom of the individual, a view that was perhaps the chief characteristic of the 1989 East European revolutions.

Gunn's defence of nationalism is complicated, however, by his ties with Germany prior to the war. In 1938 he had met four German 'tourists' at the house of his friend and nationalist colleague, Sir Alexander MacEwen.[12] The Germans had in fact travelled to Scotland to encourage among nationalists the idea of a Fascist-based Scottish separatism, a message later propagated during the war by the Germans' broadcasting station, *Radio Caledonia*.[13] *Morning Tide*, *Butcher's Broom*, and *Highland River* had been published in Germany before the war, and Gunn had German friends. He visited Germany twice, in May 1938 and in February 1939, and in two essays, 'As drunk as a Bavarian', and 'How the German sees the Scot',[14] he described his reactions to the Germans, and their reactions to him. McCleery, in his introduction to *Landscape and Light*, sees these as brave but easily misunderstood pieces which attempted to show 'that Germans are people sharing in a common humanity'.[15] There is no attempt to describe Hitler, favourably or otherwise, and it is almost as if, temporarily, the emphasis Gunn put on individual psychology, on good-naturedness and the personal, masked even to himself the brutal impersonal powers of Nazism. In his journal entry for 3 September 1939 he notes: 'No special hatred against the German people. In fact, no hatred at all – whatever the knowledge, the belief, that the Nazi governing body must be destroyed.'[16] Hart and Pick suggest that 'It can safely be said that at the time [Gunn] failed to realise what monsters moved beneath the surface life of cafes, streets and the Europa Hotel [Munich]'.[17] His fiction of the time echoes his essays on Germany, in its almost perverse avoidance of mentioning the war. Perhaps Gunn's experience of the First World War, in which two of his brothers were killed, made the thought of another war like it inconceivable. Perhaps he simply could not match his limited knowledge of Germany and his friendship with Germans with the terrors of the Gestapo. Certainly, as the letter to MacCormick and the journal quoted above show, Gunn was not party to the pacifism of some Scottish nationalists when war finally broke out.

Unlike MacDiarmid and Pound, Gunn did not flirt with Fascism; at least as early as 1936 he categorically distanced himself from it. The theoreticians of the left who simplistically confused nationalism with fascism had failed to understand the nature of the nation itself.

> That a violin may be made to produce the most excruciating noises, that strychnine may be used for murder, explosives for war, are hardly in themselves sufficient cause for the

abolition of music, medicine, and mining engineering. That a
nation may be used by capitalism, Fascism, or Socialism,
hardly implies the need for abolishing the nation. If the
nation is the actual instrument by which the proletarian
theory is being put into practice in the world to-day (as it is
– and the only one), then to deny the instrument out of some
vague zeal for its international manifestation would seem to
me an act of desertion and cowardice in the proletarian
struggle. Scottish Naitonalism explicitly has nothing to do
with Communism any more than it has anything to do with
Fascism. Its fundamental aim is to reintegrate the people of
Scotland into a nation so that they may then according to
their lights, work out their own destiny and assist in work-
ing out the destiny of the world. For them not to do this is to
abdicate in the human struggle, and represents incidentally
an acquiescence in national self-destruction without parallel
in the history of the world.[18]

It is in this context, then, that we should see read the 'timeless'
novels of the war years. For the most part, these books are deliber-
ately stripped of contemporary reference. They deal with the
fundamentals of human life. When they do become involved in
wider social influences and constrictions – religiosity in *The Ser-
pent*, totalitarianism in *The Green Isle* – they do so in a way that
takes measure of what Gunn saw as the much deeper causes of the
war. By concentrating on what these causes actually threatened,
and thereby throwing the war and Stalinism into relief, he finally
produced in *The Green Isle of the Great Deep* a work of far-
reaching political and artistic importance. Refining the idea of
belonging to a nation, he celebrates the things endangered by
mass-ism. In doing so, he offers his work as both antidote to and
critique of the underlying sociological and spiritual reasons for the
modern upheaval.

II IDOLS OF THE TRIBE

Though it was published a year later, *The Serpent* (1943) seems to
have been written at the same time as, or just before, *Young Art
and Old Hector*.[19] They are linked by a concentration on home
life, and (loosely) the difference between youthful understanding

and mature wisdom, but in detail the novels differ considerably in scope and tone. It may be that *Young Art* began as a creative diversion while Gunn was involved in the occasional darknesses of the greater work.

The Serpent is the story of a Highlander, Tom, who leaves his home to work in Glasgow towards the end of the last century. Introduced to socialism there, his growing interest in politics and Glasgow is curtailed when his father becomes ill, and he feels compelled to go back and stay with his parents. His new-found atheism alienates him from his father, whose heart finally gives out after a confrontation over religion. Tom's involvement with a girl from the village, Janet, also goes wrong when Janet has secret liaisons with the local minister's son, and in fact she dies in premature labour. From this broken life, Tom manages nevertheless to find in time empathy with his mother, and a lasting and final serenity which carries him through to being the old man we meet on the first page. At the very start of the book we are told that this is Tom's last day alive, and so much of the book is a series of flashbacks.

On the face of it, *The Serpent* continues a tradition in Scottish literature: the rural youth striking out for success in the city, and finding conflict between urban society and country life. Gunn had already written in the 'lad o' pairts' genre with *The Lost Glen*, and in that sense (only) *Highland River* is charting similar ground. *The Serpent* is substantially different from the conventions of the mode. Firstly, Tom does not go south for a university education: he is an intelligent shop assistant then an apprentice 'mechanic', not an undergraduate. And secondly, his life is taken to its end, long after the characteristic return to the countryside, while Tom intermittently comments on his own life events. This latter technique, as Muir noted, gives the novel a reflectiveness in the general that over-rides the individual instances of extreme upset.[20]

Tom's Glasgow days, lasting only two years and taking up less than an eighth of the entire book, nevertheless dominate the novel. They establish the ambiguous innocence of the brand carrying youth whose left-wing atheism, provoked into hysteria, has the secular righteousness whose hollowness the novel seeks to expose. Even while Tom is in Glasgow, we see his insensitivity, the destructiveness of the rationalist. Gunn had been reading Joseph Freeman's *An American Testament*,[21] a book by a naturalised

American originally from Russia. This tells of Freeman's uprooting from his village, where as a Jewish infant he had lived in continual fear of pogroms, and describes his attraction to socialism as a youth growing up in urban America. Finally, Freeman describes the discrepancy between left-wing ideals and left-wing practice. Gunn's experience as a youth in London may have been resurrected by his reading of Freeman. Both describe the conflict between emotional response and intellectual analysis.[22] Tom is not so case-hardened as he thinks, however. When he encounters a prostitute and the chilling but obscure menace of a man pursuing her, he is revealed as more vulnerable to emotion than he might have wished to confess. Only as he looks back on the incident does Tom realise that within him had been a 'serpent head' of contorted sexual desire (19), a phrase which introduces the central but semantically shifting motif in the book.

Similarly, and ironically, the Covenanting rhetoric of the emergent Labour movement makes its mark on the impressionable Tom. At each meeting there is the 'feeling of being at some dark-figured conventicle' (23). He is affected by the biblical parodying of 'in the beginning', and he feels 'Like one converted to a new religion' (28). This, it should be said, is an accurate portrayal of the techniques used by the early Scottish socialists. As Christopher Smout in *A Century of the Scottish People* recognises, the connection between the tradition and public practice of religious dissent and the rise of Scottish socialism was a strong one.[23] While in Glasgow, Tom is introduced to the theory of 'The Idols of the Tribe'. This, stemming from Francis Bacon's *Novum Organum* (13), but renovated in the socialist theory Tom absorbs, refers to the carrot and stick of Christian theology: the Devil and God (14). Tom is persuaded that these are concepts which are used by those in power specifically to subdue the commonality and to maintain the hierarchical status quo. The illness of his father terminates Tom's sojourn in Glasgow, and the undeveloped influences of the city are packed up for the return home. In particular, his raw, city-acquired atheism is primed to explode amid the tight Presbyterianism of his homeland.

The father-son relationship is often a main concern in Scottish fiction, and is usually dwelt on with a brooding anger. *The Serpent*, unusually for Gunn, partly conforms to this pattern. Tom and his father fall out, their relationship becomes increasingly

distant, and it cumulates in a terrible conflict in
Mathieson dies and Tom goes near insane. We find
between 'freethinking' and deeply-felt religious
pressed as a father-son conflict in Freeman's ac
childhood.[24] Where Gunn departs from the Scottish conve...
fatherly intransigence is in the understanding that Tom's father is
not himself for the duration of the conflict, suffering as he is from
the after-effects of a stroke. Tom, too, at their fatal personal
denouement, is unusually agitated. Tortured by the infidelity of
his girlfriend, Janet, and agitated to fever pitch by the sanctimo-
nious provocations of his father's friend, the church elder William
Bulbreac, it is little wonder he pursues his atheist arguments with
such fervour. Indeed, Tom's psychological state is revealed by his
conspicuous concentration on examples of sexual perversion and
unfaithfulness throughout the Bible, and also his rather shallow
cynicism as to the strict accuracy of certain biblical texts. Towards
the end of the increasingly heated exchange, Tom raises the
question of Eden. He argues that it is right that mankind should be
able to choose between good and evil, that the myth of Adam and
Eve should be seen as an Ascent not a Fall, and that humanity
derives its very identity from its ability to act morally. In this
Gunn would concur but, as Dostoyevsky points out in the
Brothers Karamazov's tale of the Grand Inquisitor, 'a tranquil
mind and even death is clearer to man than the free choice in the
knowledge of good and evil'.[25] What Tom has not realised is that
he, like Bulbreac, has abandoned free choice. By pinning his faith
on a narrow rationalism he has surrendered his own conscience. It
is at this juncture that, using the power of the Idols of the Tribe,
Bulbreac declares: '[…] I see the serpent in you…' (151). The
biblical motif complements what had earlier been a primarily
psychological metaphor, firstly during Tom's meeting with the
Glasgow prostitute, and secondly when Tom had first found
himself doubting Janet: 'Words and intonations moved in him like
serpents' (134). In the village he has now become 'The Serpent', a
title he will not lose until the village comes to accept him in
different terms, and when the alternative, 'The Philosopher', un-
derlines the special place he eventually acquires.

The father-son conflict is clearly more an accident of a peculiar,
exterior gathering storm acting on already weakened personal
relationships than the result of a specific religious disagreement

distant, and it cumulates in a terrible conflict in which Mr Mathieson dies and Tom goes near insane. We find the conflict between 'freethinking' and deeply-felt religious tradition expressed as a father-son conflict in Freeman's account of his childhood.[24] Where Gunn departs from the Scottish convention of fatherly intransigence is in the understanding that Tom's father is not himself for the duration of the conflict, suffering as he is from the after-effects of a stroke. Tom, too, at their fatal personal denouement, is unusually agitated. Tortured by the infidelity of his girlfriend, Janet, and agitated to fever pitch by the sanctimonious provocations of his father's friend, the church elder William Bulbreac, it is little wonder he pursues his atheist arguments with such fervour. Indeed, Tom's psychological state is revealed by his conspicuous concentration on examples of sexual perversion and unfaithfulness throughout the Bible, and also his rather shallow cynicism as to the strict accuracy of certain biblical texts. Towards the end of the increasingly heated exchange, Tom raises the question of Eden. He argues that it is right that mankind should be able to choose between good and evil, that the myth of Adam and Eve should be seen as an Ascent not a Fall, and that humanity derives its very identity from its ability to act morally. In this Gunn would concur but, as Dostoyevsky points out in the *Brothers Karamazov's* tale of the Grand Inquisitor, 'a tranquil mind and even death is clearer to man than the free choice in the knowledge of good and evil'.[25] What Tom has not realised is that he, like Bulbreac, has abandoned free choice. By pinning his faith on a narrow rationalism he has surrendered his own conscience. It is at this juncture that, using the power of the Idols of the Tribe, Bulbreac declares: '[…] I see the serpent in you…' (151). The biblical motif complements what had earlier been a primarily psychological metaphor, firstly during Tom's meeting with the Glasgow prostitute, and secondly when Tom had first found himself doubting Janet: 'Words and intonations moved in him like serpents' (134). In the village he has now become 'The Serpent', a title he will not lose until the village comes to accept him in different terms, and when the alternative, 'The Philosopher', underlines the special place he eventually acquires.

The father-son conflict is clearly more an accident of a peculiar, exterior gathering storm acting on already weakened personal relationships than the result of a specific religious disagreement *per se*. Like William Blake, Gunn saw the vulnerable corruptible self in interaction with established social evils and personal failure as the source of constricting social observances. Mr Mathieson's death occurs when two mental tyrannies fuelled by personal inadequacies collide. Tom's mental decline after his father's death shows us the crack-up behind the intellectual aridity. The breakdown's intensity is conveyed both convincingly and disturbingly. At first the senses of taste and smell, characteristically celebrated by Gunn, are affected. Greater psychotic problems ensue, and when evidence of Janet's betrayal becomes conclusive (162), his bitterness reaches new depths. Hallucinations follow, at first without focus, but finally Tom sees his father's ghost (171-2). After a terrifying account, Gunn reassures the reader. The narrative quickly switches to the mature Philosopher who discusses, among other topics, the socio-political justification for a community-based anarchism, as well as his realisation that his own anti-religion had been as damaging as Bulbreac's Calvinism. The reader is also reminded by this diversion that Tom made it through his illness; he is alive and thinking. Bringing us out the other side of this comforting maturity of vision, Gunn drops us back into Tom's psychosis and his terrible rejection of his mother, and in so doing he prompts the question: 'How did Tom's thought evolve from such a breakdown to reach such benevolent wisdom?'. The answer unfolds slowly.

Central to the recovery is Tom's relationship with his mother. This becomes the focus of the novel, developing the empathy the two had shared when Tom's father had been alive and sick. 'He clung to her like a child wakening out of nightmare, conscious of her body as a shield against the convoluting hell behind him' (186). Mrs Mathieson is one of Gunn's enduring mother-figures: we have seen her like in *Morning Tide*, *Butcher's Broom*, and *Highland River*, and will see her again in the child-bereft Mary of *The Green Isle of the Great Deep*. In later fiction, there seems to be a shift from mother-figure to wife/lover as the central female character (*The Shadow*, *The Lost Chart*, *The Well at the World's End*, *The Other Landscape*). Gunn's affectionate characterisation of women however, always runs the risk of a dangerous if well-meaning sentimentalisation. In *The Serpent* Mrs Mathieson's commonsensical manner saves her from Gunn's excesses, helped by Tom's short-tempered recognition of her seeming clumsiness.

The suggestion of her self-torture over the rumours of Tom's sexual intercourse with Janet (195-196), and her dogged support for him even when he is at his most curt, illustrates representatively Gunn's view of women as potentially the saviours of mankind.

For Gunn, the modern era tested and threatened women in an unprecedentedly ferocious fashion. Two days before the outbreak of War he wrote in his journal:

> [...] While writing these words out of a mind strangely numb, I had a quite involuntary vision of a woman, over thirty, sitting down on a kitchen stool in a Highland cottage, with a slow movement of the body, a weary drawn-out movement, the tragic side-face & clear bone of the jaw, turning away from me, from the outside world, towards the awful despondency in her mind. [...]
>
> She is a woman of an earlier age, of the clan days when fighting was not uncommon. Her husband has just answered the summons of his chief to war. [...] And the woman is left. And this how she feels about it.
>
> And this is how she has always felt about it.
>
> [...] That melting sickness of the heart in the breast, the slumping of the vital forces, the numbing of the brain, the gathering sickness in the stomach, until the soul itself can say no more, can ask no more, no more, nothing in the world more, O God, but that he may come back, come back to me. There are women who are not like that woman.
>
> When that woman no longer prevails the world will go slowly to its end.
>
> She is love, out of which creation arises. When there is no love, only a knowledge, then creation will cease, & humanity will move slowly to its death.[26]

Mrs Mathieson epitomises this ideal, but it is a misreading to see her portrayal as the author's shedding of male responsibility. Gunn focuses on male pride, male abuse of women, and sees the female lot as one of victimisation but of resilience, too. Women, in Gunn's view, think and behave quite differently from men, and have different ethical priorities. For Gunn, the difference lies partly in an alleged innate female self-protectiveness – paradoxically a reaching out to loved ones, spontaneous and concentrated – and, especially, an instinctive 'logic' that at times extends to the irrational and amoral.

Before Tom realises his mother's strength, he has to cope with Janet's duplicity. Only much later does he realise that Janet, too, has a 'higher' morality:

> Within her realm of actual experience these acts that to him appeared deceitful were to her a feminine manner of releasing herself from what had become to her unreal in order that she bring herself into contact with the real. And he saw now how vivid a woman's apprehension of the real was. A man could cloud his apprehension with all sorts of rules, categories, principles, theories. Not so a woman. She saw what she wanted, the inner kernel, the thing-in-itself, and went, by some law of her feminine being, unerringly for that. When she did this lightly, without appearing to care in the least for her 'deceit', man called her a wanton. (240)

This apologia for women shows more clearly the way Gunn deals with issues of gender. Man's construct of virtue is often inappropriate to the female sensibility, indeed serves to demean women aching within their own, more instinctual, ethical framework. Though Janet's infidelity makes her an uncharacteristic figure in Gunn's fiction (Hart and Pick refer to a biographical motivation for her inclusion,)[27] the single-minded integrity of her unfaithfulness reunites her with Gunn's other women (for example, Catrine, in her wrong-headed but understandable determination never to let Finn go to sea).

Tom's spiritual reunion with his mother occurs just before her death. Gunn is particularly fascinated by the moments leading up to death – Mrs MacBeth's tender escape is another example, and Kirsty's demise as Catrine looks on. Mother and child come together over Tom's late affirmation of human joy above the power-broking, damnation-peddling message of her minister and those like him. Here is one of Gunn's few references to the outside world; coming at such a crucial part of the novel, it carries considerable charge:

> '[...] But the trouble with a lot of these men, like William Bulbreac, is that they're so full of themselves and so sure they're right. They are only happy when they make you feel like a sinner. Is it St. Paul who says that joy is next to godliness? But to them joy is a sin. And if you dare question them, they grow angry and threaten you with the bad place.

[...] And in Europe to-day, not in religion now but in politics, the same old hideous thing is working away. So it's no good being upset about it, Mother. Men who have power are like that. [...]' (243)

This is a reference to the events leading up to the First World War – the Philosopher doesn't live long enough to see in the Second. Yet it is clear that this momentary focus on outside events should be taken as a deliberate analogue with the Second World War and its underlying causes. Tom's emphasis on happiness, 'joy', is exactly akin to the civilised hedonism Gunn feared had been endangered by the political movements on the continent. Tom realises that the Idols of the Tribe have not been dissolved by events abroad: the religious Idols have been superseded by secular ones. He is also quite clear that it is a male-conceived social structure which has been responsible for this. It is *men* who have power who are like that.

Tom, still very much the atheist, has transferred his concern with the inconsistencies and hypocrisies of received religion to a more humane interest in people themselves. His warm and selective reading of the Bible measures his mother of god's compassion, and reintroduces Tom to the joy of a generosity of spirit, with or without God (244-5). Following his mother's death, Tom's life stabilises in bachelordom – Gunn deals with it in a few pages, noting Tom's kindness to Janet's friend Tina and her family, and his interest in philosophy as related to literature and especially the individual. The narrative turns to the old Philosopher in his immediate surroundings, enjoying bird and flower and stream, finding peace yet still inquisitive. In this like his father, his weak heart is his demise – the sight and the touch of the snake which comes upon him are enough to kill him – but there is such a tranquility in the description of the scene that a sense of the rightness of things, of dignity, overrides the tragedy. When the shepherd sees 'a profound and nameless gentleness' on Tom's face, that feeling of serenity is confirmed (256). The snake has met the Serpent in a strangely positive communion. Tom's wisdom, the mature knowledge of good and evil informed by a love of humanity, has revised the meaning of the Christian myth. The shepherd who finds Tom's corpse puts this philosophy of benevolence into practice when he promises Tom 'a Christian burial by the old church' (256) – that the atheist is reunited with his community is the important thing; the religious qualms no longer apply. 'I'll see you *home*' the good shepherd says, and the book is finished.

III FABLES

Young Art and Old Hector (1942) and *The Green Isle of the Great Deep* (1944) deserve consideration together not only because they share the same characters, and are the only two novels in Gunn's rich corpus to do so, but because the latter so clearly develops the themes and ideas of its predecessor. Nevertheless, *Young Art* should be discussed first in its own right, since Gunn conceived of it, to begin with, as self-contained.

Young Art begins with a little boy, Art, fighting back his tears and rage, as the elderly man, Hector, tries to placate and divert him. Hector tells him about Finn MacCoul, the Gaelic hero who acquires wisdom by inadvertently tasting a salmon, itself raised on 'the hazelnuts of knowledge'. It is this myth that is richly employed in the novel's sequel. Here, Art's frustration has been caused by his brother's refusal to let him accompany him on a salmon-poaching expedition. Poaching is a serious crime, but like the whisky-making he inadvertently stumbles upon later in the book, for Art it is one of the secret and traditional practices of grown-ups. By being excluded, Art is reminded that he is just a little eight-year-old boy. As the novel progresses, Art gradually gleans more and more of his community's adult world, and gains more recognition from it. By the end of the novel he has proven not only that he understands the value of the cultural heritage of his community, but that he is willing to defend that heritage. For this, Hector promises him a trip to the River. Art cannot believe his good fortune. Since the first chapter he has yearned to see the River, indeed has increasingly felt it unattainable. The book closes with boy and old man setting off.

The fact that a large number of the chapters appeared singly in two different magazines prior to consolidated publication as *Young Art and Old Hector*,[28] illustrates the separate nature of each. Gunn seems to have conceived the novel in episodes virtually self-contained in themselves. Several chapter headings home in on items and ideas which are at the core of Art's learning experience, indicating that the novel is intentionally didactic. They are fables contributing to the overall fable. Indeed, the hazelnuts of knowledge tale which Hector tells at the beginning, and which laces itself through both the Young Art novels, under-lines the impression that these stories are not only *about* the ac-quisition of wisdom, they are wisdom itself.

> Here was the permanent, changeless as Old Hector's whiskers.
>
> So much for his own world. Beyond its known rim there was, however, the other world, the world outside. Folk talked sometimes in solemn voices of great changes taking place in it, and now and then they would shake their heads in wonder. Still, it was the world outside, and though men like his father or Duncan [his eldest brother] might go away into it, they always come back, as the peewits and other birds came back to build their nests and lay their eggs, to cry in the darkening or whistle in the daylight. Art knew why the peewits came back. They came back because they liked this place best. And even if they cried and swooped and grew angry, it was no more than he himself did often. And if there had been any doubt in his mind, Old Hector had settled it. 'Why do they come back?' he had asked. And Old Hector had answered: 'Because they feel at home here.' (218–9)

In this passage we have a concentrated expression of Gunn's conservatism, a belief in an evolved wisdom winnowed on the one hand through centuries of tradition, and on the other by the life-span of the individual. To belong somewhere is precious, and that feeling is under threat. Indeed, Hector is challenged elsewhere in the book as to why his generation had hardly resisted the Clear-ances. He answers to the effect that the destruction of home was the inevitable result of the conflict between two previously sepa-rated moral schemes, the aggressive forces of a steely capitalist ethic and the passive bemusement of a small pre-feudal society. It was an issue of submission and endurance: is it better to fight and be extinguished, or surrender and survive in sub-existence? Is the swift kill better than extended cruelty? If the Clearances de-stroyed Hector's first home, his second was threatened by that slower but equally brutal force, emigration. And the move south of Art's other brother, Donul, shows, as Gunn knew well, that migration was the main symptomatic problem in the late

nineteenth-century Highlands, as it still is. Later, when Art inno-
cently repeats the teenager's well-worn phrase, 'there's nothing
for a fellow here', he prompts Hector's more explicit defence of
the value of a tradition-honoured home:

> 'Well, if I had gone away, I wouldn't have been here walking
> with you, for one thing. And for another, I like to be here.
> You see, I know every corner of this land, every little burn
> and stream, and even the boulders in the stream. And I know
> the moors and every lochan on them. And I know the hills,
> and the passes, and the ruins, and I know of things that
> happened here on our land long long ago, and men who are
> long dead I knew, and women. I knew them all. They are
> part of me. And more than that I can never know now.' (250)

Here again is the theme of acquiring knowledge – the alleged long
memory of the so-called Celtic psyche, its reverence for peopled
and storied places, and the indivisibility of home environment and
individual psychology. The individual, Gunn warns, is special, is
at risk – in the same way that the most 'parochial' of places is
endangered. Art, in this reading, is therefore not only acquiring
adult knowledge, he is acquiring the rich knowledge of what
makes up his specific cultural attachment and personal psychol-
ogy.

Unlike *The Serpent*, which has a rather more definite sense of
period, *Young Art* is chronologically vague. We know only that
Hector was born just before the Clearances (62). Placing the
Clearances around the Napoleonic wars, this would suggest a date
between just before or just after the turn of the nineteenth cen-
tury. Rightly, however, *Young Art and Old Hector* is never seen
as an historical novel. The core of the book, the relationship
between old man and boy, with Art's progressive discoveries
reflected against Hector's knowingness, is fundamentally
ahistorical. We are reading a fable, naturalistically realised but a
fable nevertheless. This is why no one to my knowledge has
noticed the absurdity in the novel's sequel of introducing a sur-
vivor of the Clearances to the upheavals of the 1940s. Hector
would have to be in the region of 125 years old, at least, to have
lived until the Second World War. This is stretching the whole-
some country idyll myth a little too far! The important thing is
that the first book, deliberately 'timeless', establishes the ethical
basis that the sequel, explicitly aware of its contemporaneity, puts

to the test. Again like *Songs of Innocence* and *Songs of Experience*, the two novels taken together counter cynicism with idealism, the squalid expediency of authoritarianism with the natural spirituality of the child.

An example of this occurs in the first book, when Art, eager for Hector's trust in remembering his homeland's names and places, suddenly remembers how he had nearly betrayed him over the business of whisky-making. Caught off guard by a school rival, Art had literally fought to try to remedy his mistake. But later, Hector reassures him by affirming the importance of defending trust. What most people fight for, Hector tells Art, is nothing so worthy:

> '[They fight] To gain possessions and to have great power [...] And then people are set upon and driven from their homes, and they die, in want and in suffering. At the core of that fighting there is only one thing, and its name is cruelty. Of all human sins, it is the worst.' (252)

Hector is to repeat this assertion in *The Green Isle of the Great Deep* (149) when his loyalties are more slyly challenged. There it is Hector's very humanity that fails him. Persuaded that to protect Art from seeming omnipotent authorities would actually increase the cruelty to those who are helping to shield him, Hector finally submits. Modern skills of interrogation confront the complex ethics of Highland society, and they appear briefly to win. One recalls Gunn's letter to George Blake about *The Serpent*, when he had asked, 'how are these values going to survive?' Then, Gunn seemed to be placing that question in the precise context of the war. Gunn is trying to answer exactly the same question in *Young Art*. If reference is being made specifically to the brutality of the Clearances, then that merely goes to strengthen Gunn's argument about the immoral basic assumptions of the capitalist creed. The *real* primitivism of capitalist impulses is quite distinct from the *civilised* society of Gunn's ancient communal exemplars.

It is no coincidence that the two folk-tales Gunn inserts in his narrative, 'The Girl and the Dead Man', and the story within 'What is Good Conduct?', are of a specifically idealistic moral nature. In the first, the sister who shares freely what she has prospers while the sisters who are selfish suffer. In the second, the brother who judges only in terms of material wealth is correctly shown up as the thief. Gunn is using all the devices at his disposal to emphasise an ethical approach quite at odds with the dehumanisation he identifies in the modern outlook; 'the bloody world and all its robotisations and beehives and capitalistic greeds'.[29] That Art is keen to take up the ways and shibboleths of Old Hector points to the resumption of an enlightened tradition, Gunn would say, not just precious in itself but precious in its assertion of alternative philosophy. By showing the child, especially, being introduced to this way of living Gunn exhibits his profound belief in the sanctity of childhood. It should be noted that many of the novels concentrate on the mental state of the developing infant and youth, a fascination perhaps made all the more poignant by the Gunns' failure to have children.[30] Gunn felt, too, that the refined social structures and observances of northern Scotland could offer a window both back into mankind's own early existence, and, more importantly, a way forward out of the impersonaltiy and brutishness of the twentieth century.

All this sounds disproportionately heavyweight; we should not lose sight of the humour and humanity of the novel – indeed, our ability to enjoy the ordinary but rich happinesses of the novel makes Gunn's argument all the more cogent. As Gunn said elsewhere, 'it is precisely the same things, the all-important, simple, enduring things, that we tend to forget; and in forgetting them, to lose the simple but profound emotions they arouse, such as affection.'[31] Like *Morning Tide*, this novel's extraordinarily accomplished characterisation of children treats us to the happy disjunction between childish credulity and the other reality of the adult world. Mannerisms and the delicate sensibility behind them are captured in an understated fashion. Art is seldom too good to be true: his blustering but short-lived selfishness is not neglected. And like Hugh, he is progressing towards the grown-up world. At first shielded from the adult dangers of salmon poaching, he moves into the community of his elders as he comes upon storytelling, the division of gender manifest in the women's gathering at the time of his mother's labour, and whisky distilling. The ultimate adult secret – the River where one can land the salmon – never materialises, however. The goal remains in the future; closure, as with *Highland River* and *The Silver Darlings* is aspirational, openended. Instead, Gunn leaves us with challenge – the flux of life confirmed in its uncertainty but in its delicious potential for advancement, too.

The Green Isle of the Great Deep (1944) begins with Art once again having failed to reach the River. This time he and Hector were diverted by, of all things, a cow with a turnip stuck in its throat. More and more folk gather at Hector's croft, ostensibly to inquire after the health of the unfortunate beast. Primarily, they are there to have a friendly blether. Though the cow is fine it is clear that events in the wider world are not. Talk of concentration camps and the torture there makes what should have been a happy evening an uncomfortable one. When Hector's daughter says 'God will call them to a terrible judgement for it,' there is a feeling among some present that nemesis might not be so inevitable (11). The mention of God's name in this way is also an unobtrusive hint at what is to come: the appearance of God as a character in the book. This anticipation is reiterated when the talk turns to the psychological manipulation being used in the war. As Hector says, 'The mind is all we have finally. If they take that from us – if they change that – then we will not be ourselves, and all meaning goes from us, here – and hereafter' (13). The ceilidh dissolves in unease. The next day Hector and Art set off once more for the 'fabled River'. When they reach it, Art is disappointed by its small size but rallies with the thought of possible adventures. He is encouraged to pick hazelnuts growing nearby, and manages to secure thirteen enormous ones. Hector declares 'They look to me like the nuts of knowledge themselves' (21), a reminder to Art of the tale Hector had told him at the beginning of *Young Art*. When the two turn their attentions to poaching salmon, Art falls in and Hector jumps in to try and save him. When they come to, they are in a green but unpleasant land – the 'hereafter'.

What is so disconcerting about Paradise, or rather, the Green Isle, is that the place seems vaguely familiar (25). It is a place of breathtaking beauty, but the inhabitants seem unfriendly. When Hector talks with any of them he is dealt with rudely; even saying nothing, he and Art are ridiculed. Art instinctively disobeys the instructions they receive from the brusque 'Coastwatcher' and instead of staying at the village inn they sleep out in the open. As we learn later this means that they do not taste the processed and poisoned food which is provided at each inn. Instead, they eat the delicious fruit which seems to grow everywhere. They do proceed as instructed towards the 'Seat on the Rock', the administrative centre of the region they have happened upon.

It is here that Art begins his series of spontaneous rebellions. Disconcerted and frightened by the city, and even more so by the impersonal officialdom with which they are received, Art escapes. Hector, wearied for the same reasons, but feeling humble before what he believes is soon to be his Judgement, is more co-operative. As Andrew Noble argues, the contrast between the behaviour of Art and the behaviour of Hector establishes the tensional form of the novel, and the political and spiritual debate.

> Art unremittingly struggles against his oppressors and their plans for him to the point of making three successful escapes from them, while Old Hector is increasingly undermined by the persistence of his questioners' probing analysis into his nature and motives. The dramatic structure of the book is, therefore, created by Art's escapes and development in his freedom, Mary and Tom's involvement in his rebellion, and the assaults made on Old Hector to betray Art to them so that the general good will be restored.[32]

Mary, who has found a remedy against the dehumanising effects of Green Isle food, proves Art's strongest human ally against the 'general good'. This is in reality a rigidly circumscribed economic system in which the individual, forfeiting self-awareness and self-expression, is guaranteed a status quo of mere biological satisfaction. Mary instinctively protects Art, even when she is summoned for a gruelling interrogation. She exhibits the quality Gunn so admired as a particularly female trait: a moral, creative and dynamic endurance that exists in opposition to the fixing quality of male systemization. But even Mary seems finally helpless before the controlling Administration, increasingly irritated by Art's evasions. Finally it mounts a full-scale Hunt to root him out. By this time, however, Hector has been brought to the end of his tether by the interrogations of the chief psychologist, the Questioner. In a state of exhaustion he asks to see God, the one request the Questioner is unable to refuse. God's appearance marks the beginning of the end for the old Administration.

The analysts of the Administration are so keen on examining in psychological detail the behaviour and social being of each new inhabitant, and especially such unusually social creatures as Art and Hector, that they fail to see the wider emotional and spiritual imperatives. This is to cost them dear when, finally, God sets things right once more, and when He begins asking *them* some difficult questions. Before this, so confident are the Administrators of the rightness of their analytical method, and of their omnipotence within the solid economic system built upon it, that they make major false assumptions about the behaviour of the more human of their victims. In this way, the Questioner, though skilled in psychological interrogation, is unable to unravel the illegal activities of Art, Hector, Mary, and Robert. Art's very spontaneity, which had led in the first place to the eating of the fruit and the avoidance of the poisoned food (a reversal of the morality of the Eden myth), is unthinkable and unthought of in the 'sophisticated' minds of the controlling bureaucracy. The Questioner and the other Administrators seem fastened with good reason to a generalising intellect – the poisoning of the fruit makes each individual who tastes it act identically and malleably, and universal consumption of the poisoned fruit seems a 'given' – but they have underestimated mankind's spirituality simply because they have underestimated mankind's humanity.

If the references to the concentration camps at the beginning of the fable were not enough, Gunn reminds us while we are inside the 'phantasy' that the Administration's behaviour has a very real grounding in the reality of contemporary political experience. As the Questioner explains, the philosophy behind this social conditioning is a development of terrestial politics:

'We now simply have to construct our parallel in the realm of mind to what happened on earth in the realm of economics. Just as we saw a corporate social state being achieved, with its individuals part of it, and the whole representing a great human advance, so we now have to consider the creation and evolution *of a corporate mind.*' (197)

Psychological cohesion to this extent, in Gunn's view, is not only the modern powermonger's ideal, it is also, unfortunately, the misplaced wish of many who genuinely seek a better way of life for all. This is where the political spectrum reveals its circularity. The national selfishness of Nazism, alluded to in the pre-Isle moments of the book, surfaces on the Isle in the use of the same skills ensuring uniform behaviour that were practised by Communists, even though the latter ideology springs from a nobler aspiration. This is why the book begins being appalled at Fascism but spends more time castigating a form of government whose centralisation and dehumanisation seem more akin to our perception of hard-line Communism. On the Green Isle, a 'higher' good has replaced the 'lower' good of individual free will. Each person has only what is necessary for survival. This is as near perfection as the Administration will allow; the notion of compassion, theoretically, is unnecessary. Mary's partner Robert irritably upbraids Hector, therefore, for thanking him for his kindness: 'Kind! Surely you need to be kind only where things are not perfect. Where all is perfect, kindness is no more needed. Can't you see that?' (74). But as Robert knows too well, the lack of compassion or indeed of any of the deeper human feelings is more to do with a corporate sickness than a divine benevolence. The individual has to be allowed feeling and expression, and if social planning suppresses or bypasses such basic human dignities, even for the 'common good', then it is a bad form of government.

> It is an implicit denial of the freedom of the adventuring individual spirit; ideally it is an effort, in time of great difficulty and danger, amid a destructive welter of conflicting ideas, to round man up and drive him back into a state of stable security, such as the security of the beehive, with its perfect economic efficiency and corporate consciousness.[33]

The security of the beehive as the symbol of a real-life hell haunts Gunn, and the insect metaphor recurs in *The Green Isle of the Great Deep* when God descends and begins asking questions:

> Lift the top off a hive, poke the ant-heap with a stick. Such was life in the corporate City on the Rock.
>
> For by corporate instinct it got known that there was something wrong at the focal point, the generating centre. The scouts were aware of this, equally with the workers. Something was amiss with the brood chamber. (228-9)

This probably picks up on Dostoyevsky's Grand Inquisitor who remarks to Christ on man's desire 'to unite all in a common, harmonious, and incontestable ant-hill,'[34] but Gunn's continuing argument with H. G. Wells's concept of a harmonious world order is a more immediate target. 'Wellsian aseptic city-honeycombs' are implicated here, and in particular the passage from Wells's Utopian novel quoted above (p. 106). Gunn, having reacted against both the image and the ideal at least a decade earlier would have recognised them in Koestler's *Arrival and Departure*. There the communist hero, Peter, argues with the fascist, Bernard, who believes in the 'perfect working model' of 'the city-states of the African white ant.'³⁵ Bernard's colossus is realised, in Gunn's book, in Heaven.

Like Koestler, Gunn is also working in the dystopian genre. In this form of the novel, a comprehensively envisaged 'utopia' is offered as essentially a nightmare version of a projected political viewpoint: examples are George Orwell's *Animal Farm* and *1984* and Aldous Huxley's *Brave New World*. Bacon's utopian *New Atlantis*, in which a scientific rationalism works hand-in-hand with a hermetic Christian theocracy, is a possible source, too. Gunn wrote that 'my knowledge of Utopian literature is very slight.'³⁶ Even so, Edwin Muir was his usual perceptive self when he described Gunn's work as drawing on both modern texts, such as Huxley, and proto-modern texts, such as Dostoyevsky's *Brothers Karamazov*. In 1944 he wrote that *The Green Isle* was a variant on Dostoyevsky's 'Grand Inquisitor' and Mr Huxley's *Brave New World*, with a special twist of Mr Gunn's own which makes it extraordinarily interesting.'³⁷ Muir is right to see Gunn contributing something unique to the canon. Gunn's fiction arises from an erudite literary, political, and philosophical awareness, and is not the product of a mind isolated in Highland reverie from either the tradition or the innovations of European thought. Gunn comes from northern Scotland, but his direction, almost without exception, is ever upwards and outwards.

As Hart has put it, the novel is more an 'anti-antiutopia' than a mere exercise in debunking.³⁸ Gunn rejects the limited view of perfection implicit in the macro-state vision, yet seems fond of perfection. Following God's intervention, a reconstruction of society takes place which leaves us in no doubt that Gunn was not evading Wells's challenge of improvement. The utopia Gunn posits attempts to resolve the eternal problem between individual freedom and state control. A checks and balances form of government in which a panel of the best thinkers will review the proposals of the new Administration before they are enacted, is to be set up. 'The mathematician knew the direction; the saint knew the way' (245). And the ordinary good-hearted folk know: Hector is asked to be a part of the learned Council, too. Though hardly a feminist ideal, when Hector says that his wife would put him right on such matters (246) Gunn is surely acknowledging man's reliance on women. This is the model, if you like, of the pragmatic idealist.

The Council of the wise men (245) is politically naïve, but we should not expect a full-blown Constitution in an ostensible fable. It is likely that Gunn's qualified faith in committee government arose from his observations of the independent and generally beneficial work of the war-time Secretary of State for Scotland, Labour MP Tom Johnston. Gunn was later to ask a dismissive Ian Grimble: 'In our time can you mention – just to give one instance – any Highlander who has done a fraction of what Lowland Tom Johnston has done for the Highlands? And I mean *done*.'[39] Gunn's appointment to Johnston's Post-War Hospital Commission in early 1941[40] meant that as he was writing *The Green Isle*, he was himself on a Council of wise men. Arguably, the Commission helped establish the fundamental tenets of the single most important achievement in our countries this century, the National Health Service. Writing in *The Daily Record* at the close of 1944, Gunn wrote passionately on the lessons of Johnston's era:

> Now I am not impressed by the mere forming of Councils or Committees. They are advisory bodies, appointed in arbitrary ways, with no power. By their very existence they proclaim that there is no real democratic power or government within Scotland capable of dealing directly and finally with our domestic issues. The utmost they can do is to beg that any scheme or plan they have formulated may be sanctioned by an authority outside their country.
>
> But I am impressed by the amount of constructive work they have accomplished within the last mere three or four years and in circumstances of unparalleled difficulty.
> [...]
> Having reached this point, I find it difficult not to take one further step in thought and ask: If so much can be accomplished by so few, gathered together in arbitrary ways and using utterly inadequate means, how much more could be accomplished were the Scottish people to appoint their representatives to Edinburgh in democratic fashion, with power and authority to re-create and build in their own country, and with the dignity that does not require forever to go begging beyond the Border?[41]

Through this experience, among others, Gunn had first-hand knowledge that devolution of power away from the executive and towards experts in their field could work very well indeed: the pseudo-humanist Wellsian World State, with chessboard Regional squares and a reductive belief in economics, only concealed the inhumanity of ultra-control. It is significant, then, that God's Council of wise men is specifically lacking in powers of compulsion: 'For well [Hector] knew that a wise man will give the best he can distil with the finest grace when he gives freely and without reward' (245). Carrot-and-stick psychology, the manifestation of a purely materialistic view of the human condition, has no place in Heaven, and is of little use here on earth. For this reason those of the old Administration are punished only by losing their particular positions. More severe punishment and condemnation of the Administration, God tells Hector, would miss the point. The Administration, He says, had been what the mass had allowed it to be, much as the mass had been what they had been directed to be.

> 'It is bad, but we cannot blame them. And we cannot blame them because we leave things to them, you and me. We forget that they live in their heads, where the knowledge of power gives to a good intention the edge of a sword.' (241)

This difficult realisation is what Witting was referring to when he said that *The Green Isle* 'has a dispassionate clarity that one would hardly have believed possible in a novel written during the Second World War'[42] It asks embarrassing questions fundamental to our ideas of justice and government, many of direct relevance today. Freedom, in Gunn's terms, can only be conceived of dynamically, as a process, one that requires involvement for its health and vigilance for its protection.

This brings us, finally, to consider the symbolism of freedom in *The Green Isle*. Art and Hector are introduced to the Isle by poaching. This is a radical act: the prohibiting of fishing had removed a once universal freedom, and had done so with the dubious authority of landownership harking back only to the late eighteenth century, an inconsiderable time in the context of Highland history. Art and Hector owe their appearance on the Green Isle, therefore, to their anti-authoritarianism. We know from the novel's predecessor that the justice of their actions is recognised by all the community, even if some, like Hector's daughter, disapprove of their practice because of the risk of criminal proceedings they may incur. Hector and Art enter Heaven, therefore, in the spirit of righteous disobedience, a principle Art, at least, never relinquishes.

It is significant, too, that pagan legend is involved in this. The salmon and the hazelnuts of knowledge (fruit which, we are told, does not grow in Paradise), are from the story of Finn MacCoul, a tale Hector told Art at the beginning of the earlier book. Then, Art had been diverted by Hector's story from accompanying his brother on a poaching foray. The tale itself recounts the Celtic hero's acquisition of wisdom by catching and accidentally tasting the 'salmon of wisdom' as he cooks it for a druid. Art had so fully identified with Finn that Hector had predicted, correctly, that he would burn his finger in emulation. The second book draws from the first in this identification with Finn. For example, when Hector is attempting to bring Art back to the Seat, he tries to humour him by saying, as if to Mary, 'once he ate of the salmon of wisdom without hardly burning his fingers' (88). Other legendary associations include Art's miraculous running speed, the eye-witness accounts which make him much older than he actually is (both traits of Finn), his use of the magic hazelnuts, and his association with the dogs, whose names allude to Celtic legend. Like Gunn's use of the Finn myth in *The Silver Darlings*, the idea of (Celtic) legendariness is more important than reference to specific legends. It is noticeable, too, that *The Green Isle* is void of the kind of stories told by characters in *Young Art and Old Hector*. This is a very obvious result of the Administration's policy of suppression. When Hector had tried to comfort Art with a story (32), Art had not been calmed. The horror of the Isle does not allow a comforting tale to work. Art restores this by becoming a militant story himself, and hence the unusual formal break when the narrator explains that it is 'the legend of Art' which excites people's interest. It is Art's legend, too, which defies the received 'wisdom' of the Administration: it becomes apparent that someone, at least, can safely taste the island's fruit raw. Myth, which to Hector in the first book had been a useful device for diverting Art's attention, as well as one for gently introducing him to the values and traditions of his home, becomes in the second book the very means by which major social change is executed. And we are reminded, too, that we are ourselves responding to a larger 'instructive' legend, since Gunn's own book is manifestly working at a mythic level.

In Hector, Art and Mary, Gunn constructs a triad of freedom-fighters who each respond to the regime in a very different way. Hector trusts, finally, to God, but not in a passive sense. His

Calvinist upbringing makes it is his greatest fear to come face to face with his Creator, but he overcomes this in order to see Divine Justice done. Art represents hope, indeed he is 'the personification of a legendary hope' (133), because of his youth, his energy, and his determined stand against seemingly hopelessly powerful forces. To complete the deliberate trinity from Corinthians, Mary acts from an enlightened sense of caring. '"Charity' was the word used in the Bible. But [Hector] had heard it expounded that the word in the original tongue could also be translated "love"' (204). Faith, hope, and charity become in Gunn's hands the kernel of a Christianity which is neither dictatorial nor passive.

Because of this dynamic view of Christian virtues the portrayal of *The Green Isle*'s God is, I would argue, a difficult task well done. Gunn certainly doesn't present us with a conventional portrait of God. Instead he suggests that, as much as Man was made in God's image, God makes Himself in Man's image. To Hector He speaks Gaelic and is vaguely familiar (258). Gunn does not show us His appearance when He calls the Administration to justify their ways – He is only a 'Voice'. And He appears to Art via a Joycean pun as the 'Starter of the Race' (the 'human race'; 175), a character we had met but briefly in the earlier book. God in the Green Isle is only a 'starter' – He is not the constantly overseeing and manipulating God some, usually atheists, expect a Christian God to be. One of the Highlanders at the beginning of the book had said, 'The trouble seems to be that, for some reason, He does not always interfere when wrong-doing is going on' (11). On the Isle, God has allowed man to orchestrate society, and He interferes only (in dream-Heaven) when that plan spiritually fails, and a legend informs Him so. Even then, He delegates authority to the Council of wise men, the implication being that humanity must govern itself, and not shrug off its own responsibilities. Freedom means self-determination on a spiritual level, too, not deferring to a power which is either non-existent or seemingly uninvolved.

This is why the fruit are at the spiritual centre of the book. It is the fruit, from the tree of knowledge of good and evil, which are the symbol of the right to make decisions for oneself. Because this is Heaven, the fruit are also the actual means by which to make decisions. Robert and Mary, who live on the fruit, are the only ones who are aware of their moral selves. Gunn, it is clear, takes the view that humankind should discern evil from good, rather

than live in a society where ethics are taken out of the individual's
sphere of concern by the State: a wish that is not as universal as it
seems. A majority of the Islanders wanted the Administration to
take away their responsibilities and cares. Happily, a minority
preserve the old ways. Mary's herbalism, which is a product of her
Gaelic ancestry, is a Celtic restorative. Her folk remedy remedies
the folk. It reintroduces them to *knowledge* and from that, one
hopes, the attainment of wisdom.

Knowledge is indeed a word much used. When Art is scared
and offended by the islanders' rude welcome, he stutters, 'P-
erhaps they k-know no better.' (29). This, ironically, is exactly the
case because the inhabitants do exist in a controlled state of
awareness. Later, it is only because Hector knows that he can ask
to speak to God that he does so: if Robert hadn't let him know,
like other newcomers he would otherwise have gone to the Seat in
less than blissful ignorance. 'It's little you know', Art says to God
when He asks why eating the fruit should be wrong (177). Indeed
it is little He knows, for by hoarding knowledge the Administra-
tion have kept God's justice separate from their social organisa-
tion. And so used are they to this technique that, though God has
become by then a little more enlightened, they continue to try to
prevent Him from finding them out.

The miracle Hector, Art, and Mary enact is a fable, with all that
that means. As Gunn later said:

> In actual life we know perfectly well what would have
> happened; the two simple country folk would have been
> physically liquidated. But my concern here was not for the
> physical but for the mental, for that state of mind which
> produces the physical manifestation. The fundamental con-
> flict is between states of mind. In essence my problem was
> spiritual not physical.[43]

Having faith in one's self, and one's community and traditions,
and looking to self-cure for one's cultural, political and economic
ailments, is, Gunn argues, the most viable way forward. He re-
turns Hector and Art to their home, and the hefty salmon they
have inadvertently landed is 'silver invaded by gold, as knowledge
might be invaded by wisdom' (255). Here is a last Highland
reminder to us of Art, Hector and Mary's fantastic and hard-won
triumph. By stressing the many-levelled concept of self-determi-
nation, with its precious simplicities and its difficult justifications,

Gunn has not only confronted the critics who judged him paro-
chial, but, more importantly, he has constructed and established
more firmly than ever before the positive and universal value of
the Scot's psychological attachment to his or her local culture.
J. M. Reid in *Modern Scottish Literature* asserted in 1945 that in
The Green Isle Gunn was the first Scottish author to directly
express the 'very Scottish respect for individual courage and loy-
alty,' and that he was also the first to demand 'contempt and
hatred for every sort of totalitarianism, [and to insist] on the value
of individuality, and on the need for the triumph of love and
understanding over force and a moral intellectualism'[44]. In this I
would agree, with the qualification that what is explicit in *The
Green Isle of the Great Deep* was actually implicit in *The Serpent*
and *Young Art and Old Hector*. The war novels come to us as
highly pertinent projections of the cataclysm in which they were
written. Indeed, by approaching his subject in an often abstract
and detached way, Gunn has written three novels of profound
relevance for our times.

8

The Good Shepherd

The Key of the Chest and The Drinking Well

How think ye? if a man have an hundred sheep, and one of
them be gone astray, doth he not leave the ninety and nine,
and goeth into the mountains, and seeketh that which is
gone astray?'

Matthew 18.12

Gunn's fiction often inhabits the body of a recognisable genre. We
have already seen the grand historical novel, the supernatural
suspense story, the dystopia, and the modernist flux-flow-stream-
of-consciousness-river-book. The Key of the Chest illustrates en-
richment of a different form: the murder mystery (that we eventu-
ally realise no murder has taken place after all illustrates Gunn's
subversion of the genre). Nor should we expect this to be Gunn's
last formal permutation. Still to come are the epistolary novel, the
spy thriller, the picaresque and the psychological thriller.

In The Key of the Chest, the setting is in and around the hamlet
of 'Cruime' (from the Gaelic for 'Crookedness'). The two broth-
ers at the centre of the book Charlie and Dougald, live several
miles away in a remote cottage at Sgeir ('Skerry'), on a dangerous
part of the coast. The opening chapters establish Dougald's social
distance from the folk of Cruime. He is gruff, clumsy in company
and either diffident or just bloody-minded. Most of the villagers
feel uncomfortable with him and even the open-hearted Smeorach
has to concede that 'There was something graceless in the man that
couldn't be got over' (16). When Dougald reappears in Cruime soon
after one of his highly infrequent visits, the feeling that something is
very much awry is compounded by this established knowledge of his
rather brusque behaviour. News that Charlie has a dead seaman on
his hands confirms the unease, especially as Gunn is keen to point out
'crime was almost unknown in this part of the world' (17).

Material crime may be scarce, but crimes of a rarer cruelty become increasingly evident. Despite signs of strangulation on the seaman's neck, the Procurator Fiscal knows that a murderer does not usually haul his victim up a high and precipitous cliff for the benefit of the police, especially when the sea would have gladly taken and transformed any incriminating marks into the apparent bruises of the drowning. Yet the brothers seem to be pushed further and further away from the folk at Cruime. In particular, the minister attempts to alienate the brothers from his flock. His lesson at the funeral is the subtlest expression of condemnation. Using the story of Cain and Abel ostensibly to mark the death of a brother-in-mankind he reminds the congregation, as *we* only realise later (in the manner of the thriller/detective novel), that several years earlier Charlie had 'betrayed' them all by terminating his divinity studies at Edinburgh. Charlie is the man who 'betrayed his brother, mocking the word of God [...]' (73). This was a betrayal because Dougald and the minister as well as others in Cruime had helped finance Charlie. That the minister's daughter, Flora, became emotionally involved with Charlie at the time of his fall from grace, points to the minister's more personal reasons for such vindictiveness.

Brotherhood, both in its specific sense *vis-à-vis* Charlie and Dougald, and in the wider sense of the brotherhood of humanity, is the principal theme of *The Key of the Chest*. It is a challenge for the individual-within-the-community, a problem that engages our attention on numerous levels. Gunn extends the meaning of being one's brother's keeper by setting up oppositions not only between the actual brothers but between Dougald and Charlie on the one hand and the people of Cruime on the other He also introduces a similar kind of intellectualisation to that found in *Highland River, Wild Geese Overhead*, and *The Serpent*. The educated and sophisticated, and those working intimately with the elements and with each other are brought into dramatic contrast. These two groups, Gunn suggests, have brotherly responsibilities to one another as well.

The intellectuals are Michael Sandeman, a rich young man living at the Ros Lodge and the landlord of large tracts of the surrounding land, and Gwynn, an ex-actor with a philosophical interest in the 'primitive'. Though the local doctor tries to mediate between local attitudes and the thoughts of Gwynn and Michael,

Gunn seems keen to emphasise the limitations of the educated southerners' arguments in a way that previous novels have not always made so clear. Hart has seen the like-sounding name of Gwynn as an indication of Gunn's self-parody, reminding us, perhaps, of Aniel in *Sun Circle*. Gwynn's theories are certainly close to the anthropological interests of the author, but they lack Gunn's experiential vigour.[1] Taking up the *political* implications of the self-assured intellectualism rendered so alarmingly well in *The Green Isle of the Great Deep*, this novel begins an attack on arid intellectuality in a more *social* personal context. Gunn is compassionate as well as critical, however. Nemesis for the Administrators of the Green Isle was first of all satirical humiliation and then simple relocation to a different type of work. There was always the understanding, too, that the corrupt had begun their project altruistically. In the same way, Michael's rather insensitive speculation about the various personal relationships within the community, as well as his intrusive photography, are shown eventually to be the past-times of a psychological casualty.

Perhaps because Gunn had recently been involved in writing the screenplay for the film of *The Silver Darlings*, photography is a central metaphor.[2] Michael's camera intensifies the emotional weight of those it captures – the dead seaman becomes disturbingly Christ-like (65), and the brothers each seem fixed in their over-riding characteristics, Dougald with a 'weird transparent vagueness' (67), Charlie starkly 'isolated in an extraordinary stillness' (68). The photographs of Charlie's love, Flora, taken on the cynical pretence of photographing her dog (170), show her at the extremes of emotion. One 'touched the heart with something perilously like pathos', in another 'She was alive absolutely as in life' – so much so that the doctor 'actually felt the gloom, the tiredness of spirit, falling from him' (171). While all these pictures are unusually successful in that they seem to epitomise the psychological undercurrents of those characters they portray, the doctor is upset that Michael should have taken them. He is unwilling to respond to their recognised quality because to do so would be to sanction the intrusion. Privacy, as Dermot in *The Lost Chart* is is to find out, is one of the sacrosanct qualities most threatened by technology ascending at a greater pace than humankind's behaviour. It is clear to the doctor, though, that Michael is psychologically unstable – has a 'sheer mental unbalance' (173) – and the doctor and Gwynn seem willing to humour him, to make allowances. Towards the end of the novel, however, Michael seems finally to realise the inadequacy of his pictures, a state of understanding brought about by his physical involvement with those in what he had cynically called his 'human comedy'. This (via Balzac) is Gunn's own attack on the modern literary canon, obsessed with city life and the middle class. A Highland cast of characters is 'provincial' to those interested in 'Grand Literature' (138, 175). Michael's attempt to rescue Charlie and Flora when they try to escape from Cruime, the villagers' rescue of them all when he fails, and the villagers' earlier assistance when he had fallen from a cliff-edge, bring him from artifice into the actuality of working mankind. After we have seen his gallery of pictures, Michael rejects it and heads out on to the shore, 'disturbing sea-birds that screeched shrilly, and from his throat harshly he answered them, crying "Simulacra! Simulacra!" An intense feeling of exhilaration began to well up in him' (239). This upsetting of the birds recalls Michael's stilling of them photo-graphically, especially the disconcertingly intense picture of the sea-gull (63). Their movement accompanies his rediscovery of his mental vitality, his moving beyond the semblances and the bitter-amused nihilism of which they had been a symptom. His cry of 'Simulacra!' is also Gunn's. The author, we realise, has presented us for much of the novel with only surfaces, with ill-focused insinuations and suspicions, frissons of terror and scandal. What had increasingly appeared to be at worst a callous murder, at best a callous robbery, is revealed in the end to have been an incident whose psychological ramifications, the love and tension between two brothers, far outweighs any 'criminal' technicalities of man-slaughter or robbery.

The expected exposure of the truth, and especially of the 'vil-lain', a must in the murder mystery, does not occur in the com-pany of suspects or a public court, but privately, between the killer, the accidental killer that is, and the sympathetic and confi-dential doctor. The doctor, now placed in the role of judge, chooses to keep the knowledge to himself. Nor has there been any clever-clever sleuth work – Charlie just speaks out – the focus, instead, is on the humanity of the brothers as *victims*. Their feeling of rejection, intensified by the minister, whose second sermon had further fixed the inappropriate Cain and Abel myth on to them, had already crystallised, we learn, when Dougald had taken the key from the emptied chest and thrown it into the sea. Charlie and Dougald, prevented from a fatal fight by Dougald's suddenly realising he had the key in his hand, had hardened against Cruime with an uneasy solidarity. It is only towards the end of the novel that Dougald is reappraised. Giving shelter and hospitality to the boys lost on the moor (194), and emerging as intuitively protective of Charlie, Dougald reverses the Cain and Abel parable by being shown to be his brother's keeper indeed.

Though the key is the specific object that concentrates the brothers defiance against the village, it seems also to refer to the experience/spirituality Gwynn and Michael are looking for, the 'key pattern' (259). From Charlie's point of view, the key is arguably his rediscovered love for Flora, a love both put to the test in their defiance of Flora's father. When Flora escapes with Charlie to the turbulent sea, the flight from the twisted father has all the makings of folk tragedy. Yet after their miraculous rescue there is the expectation that they will emigrate. The resolution seems surprisingly flat, even gloomy (despite what has been a critical overestimation of the unqualified nature of the 'optimism' of earlier books). As Pick has argued, the tone of the closure is not wholly negative.[3] In particular, the doctor understands that Flora's father, chastened by her near loss, will have finally given her his blessing. Even with the loss of Charlie, people like Norman and Dougald can see Cruime into modernisation and undestructive self-sufficiency. This is not to underestimate the unhappiness of Charlie's position, but rather to see it in a wider perspective. The doctor, who seems to have the author's sympathy, reasons that the doubt surrounding Charlie's behaviour will always remain among the Cruime folk simply in the way of village life and received ethics. To sustain Charlie and Flora's story is 'an instinct protecting the community' (256). Reminiscent of the Idols of the Tribe discussion in *The Serpent*, this seems to argue that in some sense society sacrifices the few for the many. Nevertheless, this is not a capitulation to the massism Gunn so vehemently opposed, rather it is an understanding of a dynamic sense of community, in which irreconcilables continue to arise – and continue to produce uneasy solutions. The community itself can adapt, can evolve. And in Charlie's case, the loss of his community is part corrected at a personal level by Flora, who is that 'something deeper, older, than that compelling vision of morality' (257).

Gunn occasionally plays with his reader, and his portrayal of Flora provides a good example. When she is walking in the direction of Loch Geal early on in the book, he flirts with a suggestion of impending doom: she remembers Loch Geal's association with an old legend of lovers and murder (82). From what we know already, 'murder' and lovers are expected to be the main strands of the novel's plot, but this further anticipation of 'A Terrible Tragedy' is to be disappointed. The final implication is that a sense of reality is more important than the caricature of high feeling. Flora and Charlie really are lovers, they are not The Lovers, and Charlie really did kill a man. Another deliberate 'deflation' which confirms this occurs when Sandeman hears supernatural music near Loch Geal. Accompanying him to the site, the intellectuals witness the extraordinary scene of Flora moving across the light of the moon to the sound of what turns out to be Charlie's chanter. Already established as a place of myth, here Flora and Charlie come together as legend-in-the-life revealing human reality to be as stirring as any past folklore, or, rather, recreating folk archetypes 'in body'. The music is real, and all the more precious for being so.

The contrast of Gwynn and Michael's behaviour and the doctor's as they look out on to the moor contributes further to Gunn's debunking of romanticisation and shows that the issue at stake is much more important than literary self-consciousness. The doctor is referred to only once by name in the novel: the emphasis on his healing profession is borne out in the mental realm by his careful, mediating discretion and his sensitive ability to empathise with all levels of society at Sgeir and Cruime. At the moor, his appreciation of local behaviour has already meant his correct expectation of Charlie's being the 'mystery' piper. The effect of the music on him when he finally hears it cuts him to the quick, so clearly does he understand it:

> There is a defeat that is bitter in the mouth beyond all bitterness of the bitterest herb; a sadness that has agony and the breaking of the heart in one's own hands. This is the music the doctor heard, and his mind was charged with a dreadful unknowable foreknowledge. (134–5)

The doctor is able to receive the culture-specific shiver, the coded message. Despite the 'sophistication' of the arid intellectualism that Michael and Gwynn are striving to release themselves from, the message is that there is an understood meaning beyond the precision of any message! The doctor's companions are excluded from the fuller experience. This, unfortunately, is the very kind of experience they seek.

Previously Gwynn's haunting quotation of 'Kubla Khan' and Michael's insistence that the apparition he had experienced was a murderer had created a dramatic atmosphere, again with the touch of gothic in which Gunn occasionally delights. Even with the suggestion of Celtic Twilight – 'a sadness that has agony and the breaking of the heart in one's own hands' – the staginess is pierced with raw feeling. For the reality is Charlie's desolation – his hopeless loneliness – and the love, unreturned as yet, he still feels for Flora. It is only the doctor who is able to properly interpret the way the piping expresses the scale of this emotion, and Michael's wish to 'charge' on the piper shows how distanced he is from the sensitively tuned manner of his Scottish friend. Music once more with Gunn goes beyond normal language. Later moved to the core because the music had been so foreign (paradoxically, the doctor had been moved because it was so recognisable), Gwynn and Michael begin to realise the implications of what they have heard. This becomes a paradigm for their relationship with the people whom they have tended only to analyse. It is reality that is the most miraculous thing. Gunn's 'mysticism' is, of course, nothing of the sort. His gentle poking of fun at southerners hunting the humbly archaic and supernatural has beneath it the consciousness of a northern culture far more interesting and energised than the primitivism Gwynn and Michael theorise about. When the intellectuals begin to see reality – not only the reality of 'northern culture' but more precisely of individual people — they at least *approach* the sense of spirituality they seek. As far as class, education, and sensibility will allow (and Gunn is realistic if conservative in his recognition of these limitations), a reconciliation of two widely differing traditions is drawing closer. This sensibility of salvage, rather than unequivocal resolution, is what marks out *The Key of the Chest* as another of Gunn's 'philosophical' novels, novels in which ideas of justice and personal commitment make challenging but rewarding reading.

In some ways *The Drinking Well* (1947) is a throwback to the fiction of the 1920s and 1930s, and this perhaps is why it appears so out of place amongst the much more sophisticated work of the 1940s. The story sounds familiar: a young man leaves his rural home for an education in a Scottish city, but returns prematurely and in disgrace; he finds himself increasingly isolated within the community ... Not only is this reminiscent of *The Lost Glen*, but the delivery has the same, sealed, drama-like quality, too. Unlike the other 'disgraced teenager' books, *The Serpent* and *The Key of the Chest*, the main thrust of the book is about Highland and Scottish problems alone; the issues of a wider bearing seem more coincidental than we might expect. These other books do not have quite the linearity and focus of *The Drinking Well*, either. *The Serpent* is a series of flashbacks. In *The Key of the Chest* the centre of consciousness is diffused. The main 'protagonist', the doctor, is outside most of the action in the novel.

The Drinking Well has a straightforward chronology and a clear hero. Its plot is simple. It begins with Iain Cattanach, the eighteen-year-old son of a sheep-farmer, getting ready for school. His mother is haggard and tense even in these moments of dawn. Her fear that Iain will find no work except with his father's flock, a job with little prospect, has been grinding at the bone. She has found employment for her other two sons and daughter (they all live outside Scotland as a result), but Iain is still a worry. This introduces the main dilemma of the book. Recognising that depopulation is a social and economic evil, but also that young Scots want, like everyone else, a decent way of life, what can be done for the revitalisation of rural Scotland? Moreover, is thè crisis in the countryside a paradigm of a universal problem in Scotland?

Mrs Cattanach secures Iain a clerk's job in an Edinburgh law firm by lobbying the local factor, Major Grant. Iain's love of working on the land is reluctantly put aside; his mother dies just before he goes south. In the city Iain impresses his employer with his knowledge of sheep husbandry, especially apposite to the firm's landowning clients. He complements his knowledge by reading technical reports and research. Outside the office, the politics of street speechifiers affects him, and he is drawn to the economic sense in nationalism. In particular he sees an affinity between a national confidence and a personal and communal self-confidence, especially with regard to his own experience *vis-à-vis* sheepfarming. Unfortunately he falls out with one of his superiors, Smeaton, who sneers at crofters and smallholders like his father. Finally, when Iain realises that Smeaton is deliberately concealing information of substantial benefit to a crofter whom Iain, coincidentally, knows personally, he hits him, sending him through a glass door.

Iain goes back home. He intends to tell his father why he has left the job, but he is stopped from doing so. The people at home presume he is back only to convalesce from the strain of city life. Mr Cattanach, meanwhile, hears about the office incident from Major Grant, who already holds a grudge against Iain for his suspected involvement in a poaching incident. This had occurred before Iain's brief Edinburgh days when he and his friends had been disturbed while netting a salmon, and the Major had accidentally been entangled in the mesh in the river. In fact Iain had *helped* the Major, though no one but the poachers could have realised it. Torturous father-son relations are calmed, however, when Mr Cattanach also nearly drowns, this time when the water is wintry cold. Confined to bed, Cattanach can only offer scraps of advice to his son, who takes on the responsibility of the lambing. Iain does a fine job of it, and the two grow closer once more. This is only a respite, however. Cattanach learns that Iain had been among those who had 'nearly murdered' the Major: he strikes out and Iain leaves the house … stumbling into an oncoming car.

Iain is not hurt seriously, though he is confined to bed for several days. The car belongs to the landlord, Henderson. Iain has suffered beneficial concussion, because Henderson is a progressive who wants to begin land reform. Henderson also discovers the truth about Smeaton and about the poaching incident. Calling the chief tenants around him, Cattanach among them, he openly exonerates Iain, and announces a plan for revitalising the local economy. The most important part of this is his gifting to Iain of a tract of land and a flock of sheep with which to experiment. When the time comes to tell Iain, he has gone. The plot veering dangerously close to melodrama once more, the crofters fear the worst. But Iain has neither emigrated nor killed himself. Instead he has gone to visit Mad Mairag, an old woman living on the margins of the community. Mairag had told him before he left for Edinburgh that he'd come back to the land, and despite his scorn then, he now realises she was right. When Mary, the young woman he is in love with, turns up, the novel is ready to close. This it does, rather sentimentally, with the lovers walking hand in hand back into the community.

The ending, like some events before it, seem contrived, and the closure raises an important question about the nature of the entire novel. McCulloch sees 'the collapse of a novel which, in its first two parts and in much of the third, had promised so much.' She suggests that the novel's affinity with *The Lost Glen*, and its derivation from the claustrophobic work of that time, may account for the unease with which the accidental happy ending sits.[4] Certainly the increasing melodrama seems to owe much to the atmosphere of the one-act study 'The Man who came back', and the expended version, *Back Home* (revived for radio in Gaelic in 1947).[5] In these predecessors Iain's days south are referred to but not dramatised. Instead his dissatisfaction with the desolation and self-defeat in his home-community are dealt with in lengthy speeches, as well as briefly symbolised by his unwillingness to play his fiddle – a gesture we find in the novel too. There is no resolution, however. Iain runs out of his father's house with Mary crying for him to come back, and that is where the curtain falls.

In the intervening years, Gunn constructed around the play's plot (the skeleton of the third section of the book) a much denser fiction. He also found a corrective finish. These works of the late 1920s and early 1930s are tragedies whose form is pervaded with all the expectations of tragedy, and this makes them difficult to transmute into a deliberately optimistic book. In *The Drinking Well* a residue of the original narrative pattern supplies a dilemma we are, I think, aesthetically conditioned to accept as tragic. The happy ending, one feels, has no place here. Henderson literally bumping into Iain, the manner in which Iain is discovered to be blameless, and finally Henderson's generous land reform proposals, seem too good to be true (and this leaves aside the question, earlier, of a stag literally falling out of the air into, so to speak, Iain's starving hypothermic mouth). Against the dramatic form from which the novel derives, and perhaps, against the implied politics of independence, the landlord provides the author with a *deus ex machina*.

Gunn's seemingly heavy-handed insertion of beneficent,

specific economic remedies, and the weight they carry as exem-
plars of national possibility, is unpalatable in immediate terms
because the novel has proceeded with a stripped realism in de-
scription and plot. In this respect, Scott's *The Heart of Midlothian*
comes to mind. It too has a seemingly clumsy conclusion, and
shares the same desire to construct grandly in fiction what does
not exist in reality. Scott's goal was to fabricate the feeling of safe
and prosperous independence within the Union. This was estab-
lished by settling his honest-hearted heroine Jeanie Deans on an
'island', Roseneath, where Highlands and Lowlands meet, cour-
tesy of the Royalist Duke of Argyle. Gunn, on the other hand, sets
up business for his hero with more fidelity to the meaning of
independence. Can Gifford's argument for Scott – that 'symboli-
cally at least the Roseneath section has its place',[6] – be applied in
respect to the final part of Gunn's novel?

This is the alternative interpretation: that the novel eschews the
realist novel's convention and illusion of 'likeliness' usually
manifest in a pessimistic ending and enters instead an area which
requires and stimulates a different approach. Hart seems to be
suggesting just this when he argues for a continuity of personal
ahistoricism set against a wider and vaguely realised sense of
period. Like McCulloch, he notes the marked artificiality of the
closure and the other incidents which strain credulity, but he
recognises an overall movement:

> The 'historic' dimension reminds us that Neil had always
> been sceptical of history. The novel's historic particularity
> has little imaginative relevance to its timeless issues of spirit,
> land, and well. Characters belong to a historic typology;
> what finally matters about the hero is that he is a 'certain
> type' of young man. The plot depends on accidents: saving
> the factor, the office fight, the auto accident. The story
> problems to be solved are accidents, and the solutions are
> accidental, reflecting a fundamental disbelief in the logics of
> history.[7]

Truly, the self-defeat in *The Lost Glen* is here inverted.
McCulloch and Hart are both right to stress, respectively, the
genesis in drama and the arbitrariness of the later stages of the
novel, but both underestimate Gunn's use of specific contempo-
rary source material. I would also suggest that the closure brings
with it a multiplicity of restorative implications which exceeds the

immediate social and economic rehabilitation.

At first, the ambitiousness of Gunn's claim that in *The Drinking Well*, 'I did want to do for hill sheep farming what I tried to do for sea-fishing in *The Silver Darlings*'[8] seem misplaced. *The Silver Darlings*' rich use of mythic resonance, its subtle, almost organic construction, and its intricate detailing of relationships within the broken family, mark it out as considerably more than a 'sea-fishing' book. But these attributes, except perhaps the last, also make it very unlike *The Drinking Well*. When Gunn made that statement was he just flattering a past friend, the dedicatee (who came from a sheep farming family), or was he expressing a genuine feeling about the *scope* of his new novel? The techniques in the two books are on the whole quite different, and obviously so. Did Gunn mean only that this novel would document the life of the hill sheep-farmers, so bringing an isolated and forgotten industry to a wider audience as, whatever else, *The Silver Darlings* had?

One way into discussing what the book is saying, and how it is saying it, is to ask what exactly is solved and initiated by Henderson's intervention. Here is Gunn's account of it to Naomi Mitchison:

> [...] In the end you see a young fellow with plenty of guts and ideas and knowledge prepared to put up a fight, backed by a dear old landlord! How easy to arrange for young fellows forming a kind of glen soviet and all that kind of sweet unreality. But I'm afraid, Naomi, whatever my writing may look like, I'm just a hard bitten realist. [...] *The Green Isle* rather shook some of my communist friends ! (think of me introducing GOD), but now, trafficking with a landlord in order to find a way out of defeatism![9]

The spectre of Celtic Twilight pessimism still haunts Gunn, recurring perhaps with his re-use of the older material. Emigration, an economic component of the Twilight, is still a problem and is still to be dealt with; Iain is on the verge of leaving several times in the book. But a later theme – the difference between theory and application of a political creed – has also become a concern. Gunn seems to be having it both ways in ridiculing the idea of a socialist 'glen soviet' yet describing beneficial change coming from a class his acute and sensitive sense of history, we might assume, made him distrust and even despise. That a landlord should resolve the book *is* extraordinary, and suggests that it is an important part of the symbolic schema.

Gunn's suggestion that the book made him rethink his (long-held) socialist perspective is born out by the arguments he presents in the central section of the book, 'In Edinburgh'. In fact his criticisms of Communism go much further back, as I have discussed. Here politics come under scrutiny through the vehicle of street orators near the Mound. Left-wing nationalists and Labourites are shown in contention. Iain, though seeing the justice of the socialist argument, is drawn to the nationalist point of view by one speaker's ability to talk an economic sense grounded in a detailed grasp of fact. The nationalist also has a winning practical outlook, which challenges the socialists with its here-and-now pragmatism (148–9). It is this down-to earth attitude that attracts Iain and, importantly, is the quality Henderson so admires in Iain and his like. The Edinburgh sequence emphasises the historic tragedy of Scotland, and, to some extent, its own culpability. The debate throughout this section ranges from grass-roots economics to literary concerns, and during Iain's illness culminates in his bitter and disconcerting dream. In his sleep Iain witnesses what at first seems a celebration, an explosion of streamers accompanying a mounting musical allegro (199–200). But associations anticipate revelation: the streamers are like fiddle gut (reminding us of his own violin skill), then they are like the bureaucratic red tape he has so often used at work (certainly not sheep gut). Finally, he knows what they are: human gut. Edinburgh becomes Latrinetown, Perversetown, Deadtown – not because it is a city (Iain soon assimilates and hold his own in city life), but because it is the capital city of a country in limbo.

Gunn welds this nationalist argument on to the continuing focus of the novel – Iain's personal love of and frustration with sheep-farming. Wary of his friend's romantic nationalism, Iain argues for action, for results. Landlords, he says, do not hold the key to Scotland's future, Scotland does (236). Iain's wish to see politics actually work also tells us that, in the fiction's terms, the economic recovery of hill sheep-farming is potentially a paradigm for national self-belief and self-help. It should be noted that in the mid-1940s Gunn's essays were reasserting the Scottish claim of right: 'Scotland Moves', 'And after the War', 'Questions for Scots', 'Awakening of a Nation', 'Scotland Isn't a "Region"', and 'Belief in Ourselves'.[10] The last recounts Gunn's visit to a successful Government-initiated sheep scheme, a project he cites as just one example of what can be done to correct the *national* lack of confidence.[11]

In *The Drinking Well*, Iain's conversation with Henderson towards the end of the book again includes the question of government involvement. Henderson is sensitive to Iain's suspicions of landowners, but is also attuned to modern landlords' problems. Planning to run for Parliament on the basis of his success as a landlord, he is not being wholly altruistic in offering Iain a new start. He is setting up what amounts to a pilot project. Like Lord Napier in the 1880s, who was the first to establish (via the Crofters' Commission) the right of crofters to be tenants, Henderson is an ex-colonial administrator with considerable experience of getting different cultures to co-operate. The very fact that landlord and tenant are being reunited for the first time since the betrayal that began in the eighteenth century is a remarkable proposal for harmony in itself, for Scot working with Scot regardless of class. Gunn's use of the achievements of Tom Johnston's Scottish Office further underline the nationalist implications of the sheep farming model. Hill sheep farming, which had been running down since the First World War, was in crisis – at a time when profitable use of marginal land for food production suddenly became rather important. The agriculturalist J. A. Symon, writing in 1959, summarised the problems:

> It was on the hills that many of the store sheep and cattle required by the low ground farmers for breeding or fattening were reared and so, under conditions when food production was a major objective, adequate stocking of the hill lands was imperative. But no hill sheep farmer could be expected to run his enterprise at a loss and for many years before the war hill sheep farming had been depressed. Low prices for sheep and wool, coupled with the ever-increasing costs of, and difficulty in obtaining grass wintering, since more low ground farmers were themselves keeping sheep, had made the hill farming industry largely unremunerative. There were instances of landlords being unable to let hill sheep farms, and as they could not be run except at a loss the landlords were obliged to dispose of the sheep. In consequence such farms were left ungrazed. The war worsened the position.[12]

Iain's discussions with the head of the law firm, and with the people gathered at his friend's, show that Gunn understood in technical detail what had gone wrong with Scottish hill sheep farming. Iain's analysis correlates with, and even expands, Symon's.

By placing the novel in the inter-war years, Gunn also took advantage of the war-time developments instigated by Tom Johnston, who set up a special committee to look into the problem of hill sheep farming. The conclusions it reached are the conclusions which Iain comes to, even down to his gripe that the local gamekeeper is inhibiting sheep production by refusing to burn the estate's heather.[13] Once again, Tom Johnston, in Gunn's view, had come up trumps (though not all of Johnston's activities met with Gunn's approval, notably his Herring Board policy). Iain's definition of nationalism – the state providing the opportunity for work once more – had been realised. By setting his novel in the years before the Second World War Gunn was able to use the Committee's findings, published just before Gunn began writing *The Drinking Well*, as if they were the ideas of his brilliant young hero.[14] Henderson's plan, with Iain's knowledge and commitment behind it, would indeed have been an exemplary model to the members of Johnston's committee, whose activities were broadly nationalist. It is right, then, to read this work as the most overtly nationalist novel Gunn was ever to write, indeed its triteness is a product of its propagandising nature. Its roots in his work of the 1920s and 1930s, enhanced by the Hill Sheep Committee findings makes it, as it were, the novel he didn't write for the Scottish Renaissance.

This wider interpretation, that the ending is laden with multi-level success, is compounded with the very personal meaning of Henderson's offer. Iain's family history is at stake. When the landlord announces his innocence in the Smeaton and Major Grant affairs, Cattanach is ready to take his son back into the fold. Henderson then goes on to offer Iain a whole stretch of land, Torglas; Cattanach is overwhelmed not only by the generosity but by the personal associations of the lease. In an episode reminiscent of Hardy's *Far from the Madding Crowd*, three hundred of Cattanach's sheep had perished in a snowstorm at Torglas, years before. Because extra money was needed to give Iain's elder brothers a university education, and ultimately to establish them abroad, Torglas had to be given up. Cattanach is profoundly moved, therefore, at the offer: 'Should it so happen that my son would make a success of Torglas, where I failed, that would lighten the end of my days' (450). Torglas restores a family continuity, and its association with sending children away from the home is reversed.

Turning to the other component of the finish, Iain's return to Mad Mairag's, we find the same reference back to events recounted throughout the novel. That Iain returns at all is, once again, remarkable: previously he had treated Mairag as if she was indeed 'Quite mad' (100). Iain is nevertheless fulfilling Mairag's early prophecy that he would return (99). When Mairag had told Mary and Iain, 'It's a handsome young couple you are' (101) she had been jumping to conclusions, but the ending proves her right. These events both confirm Mairag's powerful if obliquely expressed intuition and invest the novel with the narrative momentum of a prophecy, though the dramatic emphasis is light. The symbolism of Mairag's drinking well, which she mentions with a rather obscure remark (97), is not worked through, and the novel seems rather inappropriately titled, even though Mairag later calls her spring 'the well of life' (463). *The Well at the World's End* recalls the metaphor with more gusto.

The final 'success' of the book is Iain and Mary's mutual realisation of love. This has been hard-won because despite the friendship they shared from the very beginning, Iain (increasingly less convincingly) tries to deny to himself that there was anything more than friendship between them (e.g. 170, 386). This irony is of the same kind used in *The Silver Darlings,* when Finn had boyishly maintained to himself that he was aloof from the likes of Una, who ends up his bride. In *The Drinking Well* there is the added contrast of Iain's rather more free relations with the Edinburgh girl, Morna, who is given a guilt-ridden brush-off only when Iain sees Mary in his mind (219). Mary's presence in the novel is continued even when she is not physically there not only by Iain's thinking of her but by the music he plays: *Mairi Bhann.* The relationship becomes more concrete when the romantic conclusion is *the* conclusion. This final union is the last aspect of the unity for which the novel has strived. This, however, is the last time Gunn delivers a myth for specifically Highland and Scottish rejuvenation.

9

God's Fools

The Shadow, The Silver Bough, The Lost Chart, and *The Well at the World's End*

The Shadow was finished by the end of 1946,[1] but not published until 1948, the year of *The Silver Bough*'s publication. This lapse between completion and issue may give the impression that Gunn had been writing the novel at a critical distance from the War. In fact, he seems to have started on it by the autumn of 1944, when what became the novel's opening pages were published in *The Scots Magazine*.[2] The short story which he assimilates into the narrative, 'Snow in March', had appeared in 1938.[3] Despite being chronologically close to the war novels already discussed, *The Shadow* is a substantial departure from them both in formal terms and thematically, not least because it represents Gunn's most extensive depiction of a female consciousness.

The Shadow is divided into three sections, 'Convalescence', 'Relapse', and 'Recovery', which delineate the mental health of the principal character, Nan. The setting is a northern Scottish farm owned by Nan's down-to-earth aunt, Phemie. Nan is suffering a nervous breakdown which had occurred while she was living and working in war-time London. There she had been part of an intellectual clique, a kind of late Bloomsbury group (the echoes of Bloomsbury being important). One member of the group, who Nan calls 'Know-all', had been particularly antagonistic and seems to haunt Nan's waking dreams. The set's dubious blend of fast cars, 'liberated' sexuality, and hard-line Communism are the political backdrop to the assault.

'Convalescence' consists in letters from Nan to her one-time London boyfriend, Ranald, though in fact Nan does not send most of them. A sub-plot is the ruthless murder of a crofter in a nearby house, a crime which in Nan's words has cast a 'shadow' over the neighbourhood. Though Nan suspects at first a local poet, Adam, it turns out that the murderer is a deranged veteran of the First World War, a man who had in fact been a friend of the victim. When Nan agrees to go for a walk with Adam to trace the nearby river to its source, what had been a philosophical journey for Kenn in *Highland River* becomes for Nan a living nightmare. As we only learn in 'Relapse', the two come across the body of the murderer, bloated in the water, a suicide. Nan descends into a state of intensified mental illness.

'Relapse' returns to the third-person narrative more usual in Gunn, and begins with Ranald's arrival at the farm. Aunt Phemie, expecting a more conventional lover, had telegraphed Ranald to come north, but she is surprised to find him cool and arrogantly aloof. Ranald begins to thaw when he reacts quickly to the suggestion that Adam may have attacked Nan as they were walking. He seeks him out and they have a fight, Adam falling over the edge of a river bluff and into the water. Exhilarated by the tussle and not overly concerned at its moral implications, Ranald gains an aura of vitality which is outwardly noticeable. He soon leaves, however, for London. Phemie is shocked to realise that Ranald's sudden change in appearance had been a result of what was almost murder – Adam turns up in hospital some time later.

'Recovery' sees Nan up and about once more. Adam is well on the road to recovery, too, and Phemie decides she rather likes him. Nan takes part in the farm's harvest and then decides to go back to London, in essence to try and save Ranald from himself, and in particular from his destructive ultra-rationalism. She persuades Phemie to accompany her to the croft of the murdered old man where, to the unease of Phemie, she walks round the house, 'putting a circle' around it as if in some magic cleansing ritual. The book ends as they walk back home.

The Shadow's epistolary first section presents several problems, the first being narratorial reliability. How are we to believe someone who in the first paragraph admits she has recently suffered a mental breakdown, who asks 'why shouldn't I be allowed some small licence in conjuring up hallucinations and all inconsequence?' (7), and who does just that in a style which is at times particularly gushy? Another problem for some critics is this: if we finally find it in our hearts to believe the principal character, could we ever actually *like* her? Margery McCulloch finds Gunn's portrayal both unrealistic and condescending to women. In her view Nan 'glorifies the little woman's instinct beloved by writers of romance'; and her letters are 'half-educated and pretentious'. Finally, 'there is, it seems to me, a sentimentalised and ultimately demeaning view of women and their (supposed) interests and qualities in this book.'[4] Nan's style is rather studied. She uses a metaphoric language which at times seems clumsy. Here, for example, she is describing the thoughts in the letter she had just written (in itself a sign of self-consciousness):

> Well, after all that labour I can see I have produced a very small and obvious mouse. But it's done me good. I never thought I'd enjoy playing with a mouse before. Don't you think he's rather a darling? These small dark eyes, quick and cute, and he's full of the most engaging ways. Ranald, he's stopped. He's gone quite still. He's swelling. He's turned into a rat!
>
> There's a terrible number of rats about the farm. (14)

Nan ranges from association to association like this throughout the letters. Nan imagining her thought to be a 'small and obvious mouse' is similar to Woolf in *A Room of One's Own* imagining hers to be a fish: 'Alas, laid on the grass how small, how insignificant this thought of mine looked; the sort of fish that a good fisherman puts back into the water so that it may grow fatter and be one day worth cooking and eating.'[5] Though this may not be a specific echoing here, Gunn and Nan seem aware of Woolf's legacy. Nan tells Ranald that the only place she can write to him is in her bedroom: 'This is a room of my own.' (34)

Nan's images are often disturbing, especially when she twists one object into another, as she does here and when, for example, the grey thistles she sees become the sinister grey eyes of a policeman. These hardly seem sentimental. In the passage above Nan is referring to the increase in farm vermin encouraged by the chronic home labour shortage, but when she then says 'War breeds rats,' (14) one realises she is also writing on a metaphorical level. Of course, Nan's liberal use of words like 'darling', 'awfully', and 'dear' (noun and adjective) can grate, but they are examples of the vocabulary used by many of the middle-class women and men portrayed in the books and films of the 1940s. It is interesting in itself that Gunn chose letters as the means of expression for Nan. For many women, even today, the letter and the diary may be the only media available for extended communication and, therefore, creativity. Questioned many years after about this aspect of the book, Gunn said, 'I rather think that a woman needs, more than a man, to communicate – particularly in such circumstances as Nan's.'⁶ Nan, rid now of the sneers of the men she had associated with in London, finally finds room for her own voice. Though she begins writing her letters to Ranald she soon withholds them, keeping them, she says, for a more appropriate time. By the end of the sequence even this intention seems to have dissolved since Ranald is no longer addressed directly. 'Anyone reading this would think I was quite mad. Even Ranald wouldn't see that it is the madness of the world.'

The letters are increasingly a personal testament, but this is not to say that they are ingenuous. Nan is continually suggesting that she may be writing fiction. The first page's reference to 'conjuring up hallucinations and all inconsequence' (7) is followed by her admission that the thistle vision is 'a little literary', and she asks, 'I wonder if there is an instinct in us to dramatise?' (12). Is she making it all up, or is she really experiencing hallucination? Is it a ploy, at first, to bring Ranald up north?

> [...] I always come up here to write to you. I could not do it anywhere else.
>
> This is a room of my own. And another astonishing thing about writing you is this. Most times the writing just flows from me. Thoughts teem in my head, each one touching off a hundred others, and if I could get them down fast enough it would be a spate. This is bewildering to me at times, in a wild sort of amazing way, because I once tried to write, seriously, to make a living, as you know. Then I laboured. How I laboured! And what came was dead. I had bits, but when I got them together they were dead. I perfectly understood why editors returned the poor things. The made-up toys that won't go. Children are impatient with them – except maybe the odd child who thinks they look sad. You'll always find the odd one. Perhaps he's the saviour. (34)

The allusion to Woolf, and the fact that Nan is here trying to control a stream of consciousness, suggest that she is inhabiting, or reacting against, a literary world. She is thinking literature. Literature, in fact, recurs throughout. There are explicit references to Lawrence, Yeats, Barrie, Ibsen, De Quincey, and that most literary of 'scientific' writers, Freud. Gunn is presenting a complex text. He is giving us literature, his latest book, yet compelling his narrator to deny that it is literature. To be deliberately unliterary, however, requires a knowledge of literature. Nan's narration is not so innocent as it might seem. Certainly Nan orders the events she has been through with literary form in mind. This fact emerges when she describes her first encounter with Adam. 'I warn you it's a dreadful end,' she says (28). It is not until eleven pages later that we realise what the dreadful end is. In fact at one point she apologetically breaks her story because she is too overcome by it – 'To muff such an opportunity of a dramatic finish, too!' (32). What was the finish? After the encounter with Adam, Nan had encountered the local policeman who had asked her if she had seen anyone around. She had said no. When she had arrived back at Phemie's she had discussed her denial with her aunt, and this precipitated discussion of the murder. Then Nan had psychologically collapsed. This I think is the end she primed us for: is her literariness a way of coping with the horror of her material?

> I felt suddenly alien and cool, with the trembling gone. I was not talking rationally so much as seeing in pictures. I was not arguing from what the radio called 'the wave of crime' sweeping the country. The aftermath of war. The gas chambers. The mass butcheries. Jewish families are taking off their clothes, folding them, placing them in little heaps where they are told. They do this tidily. You can hear the whining sounds in their nostrils. Love sounds and love words and farewell. The naked family, one family and another and another, in the trenches they have dug. A young man is sitting on the edge of the trench with a tommy gun on his knees. He is smoking a cigarette. You hear it on the radio. You get used to it. But what I see in pictures – I can't go on. Ran, Ran, do you hear me crying to you? It's not for myself I'm crying. Shall I ever be able to tell you – (39–40)

Nan cannot escape her visualising emotion. The connections she makes between the Holocaust and the murder of the crofter prevent her from being 'escapist'. Both are recognised as a modern and monstrous dislodging of the comprehensible motives for killing. Rationalism and nihilism lurk behind them. 'Murderers were normal now. They just murdered. When you believe in nothing, why should you believe in not murdering ...?' (39).

Elaine Showalter has drawn attention to Woolf's use of the shell-shock victim, Septimus Smith, in *Mrs Dalloway* to highlight the parallel social constrictions affecting man and woman in the early part of our century.[7] Smith, she argues, is as much a victim of gender control as Mrs Dalloway and many of the other women in the book. Indeed, by introducing the issue of shell shock Woolf focuses on the very phenomenon in British culture which had compelled society to reassess that 'primarily female malady', 'hysteria'. In *The Shadow*, Gordie MacMaster, a shell-shock victim from the First World War, seems to be used in a similar way. It is he who introduces the 'stalking shadow' of the title (44). Nan feels pity and even responsibility for Gordie (45), and when she shudders at the idea of his being put in an institution we realise she partially identifies with him, too. A third dimension is the intellectual milieu in which Ranald is immersed. For Nan, Gordie's derangement, her own illness, and Ranald's intellectual ferocity (especially in his condescension to her own emotionalism or 'escapism') are inseparable issues. Because in her view Ranald is as sick as she is, her letters are for them both. This is true even though she is not going to send them. By making writing a way of understanding herself, and a way of making herself understood, she is also writing for Ranald. '[…] some day perhaps we'll be able to read them together and laugh,' she says (55) but 'meantime this narrative, though it has you in mind, is all mine.'

> I am making a story of myself to myself. This will help me. At least I think it will. [...] The queer thing about it all, Ranald, is that I must write it to you. If I hadn't you, I couldn't write. Writing would be impossible, unthinkable. [...] Alas – for I must be honest or all would be mockery – I feel that I am doing this for you. And I am not just thinking selfishly of my getting well for your sake and mine. (46–7)

The righteousness of 'doing this for you' is what McCulloch is referring to, I think, when she accuses Nan of glorifying 'the little woman's instinct beloved by writers of romance.' Nan wants to 'clean up' Adam, and Ranald, too (61). But remembering her London critics, Nan emphasises the reality of her. She has much more vitality, I think, than McCulloch's assessment suggests:

> It angered me that I could not even tell you of beautiful real things without getting messed up by such memories. I know they obsess me and I must get free of them. I could not even write these three words *beautiful real things* without a qualm, without hearing the echo of their jeering laughter,

> without a feeling of being detected in pulpy sentimentality.
> Oh, there I go again! What an extraordinary power and
> vitality the destructive mind has! How sickening the mere
> quiescence of *good* is to *evil*! (48)

Nan is sick. She knows she has not quite got right the balance
between reality and affirmative ideal. But she is more intellectual
and unsentimental than one might immediately allow. It is not
intellectualism she despairs of, it is the destructive mind. Her
analysis of J. M. Barrie, for instance, is right on target, if brief: he is
'one that's never grown up' (25). And her remark that 'it is a pity
all the psychoanalysts are men, all the famous ones' (24) would not
be out of place as an epigraph for any one of the fine feminist
critiques of Freud that have emerged in the last twenty years. The
metaphoric appropriation she makes of the venereal disease in
Ibsen's *Ghosts*, hardly light or usual reading for the standard
female of popular romances, shows her set quite apart from the
stereotype McCulloch would have us see (25).

It is important, too, to see Nan as one part of complex human
dialectic or argument and counter-argument, of half-people
whose personalities strike off each other. One part of that argu-
ment is encapsulated in the poet and painter, Adam. His
Lawrentian emphasis on Love-and-Death is epitomised by his
story about a stoat he saw in his childhood mesmerising a hare.
The hare, at the last minute, didn't quite stay for lunch, and Adam
had been deprived of 'the final enthralling spectacle' (65). Other
moments show Adam's rather painful concentration on matters
elemental and animistic: his glee at a blackbird's literal close shave
with a hawk, his love and knowledge of alpine flowers (a Law-
rence trait), and his seemingly unlascivious observation of Nan
bathing naked. Nan sees in Adam, however, the destructive im-
pulse she identifies in Ranald, though she is also attracted to him:
'He is like myself in so many ways' (79).

Ranald Surrey's method is that of the social planner, a role
based on a sharp use of Marxist analysis and an understanding of
freedom as, in Communist Party terms, 'the recognition of ne-
cessity' (19). He takes this into the realm of his personal relations
with the result that Phemie finds him unassailably confident and
matter-of-fact, 'a cool casual sort of fish' (82). Nevertheless, from
the first few pages of his actual presence in the novel we see that he
is not quite so on target as he might think. He is soon theorising

about creating a glen soviet, an idea complete with condescension to women and a terrible disregard for personal feeling and sound tradition (153).

In his discussion with Phemie about the rat epidemic (a metaphor Gunn reintroduces from Nan's letter), he stresses the infallibility of planning. Phemie, who is more a farmer than Ranald gives her credit for, is also more realistic:

'[...] when you have got to get the real work done, the actual grain and calves and what not produced, the land ploughed, and so on, with real human beings working at it – it's not easy. You're only a human being, and the other person is a human being, and if you're going to respect him as an individual with a right to some freedom of his own – it's difficult to plan him in your way.' (169–70)

This is the closest we get in this novel to Gunn's thoughts as expressed in his non-fiction work.

All that is left in the novel is for Nan to get better, and Adam, too. This both duly do. Nan's view that Ranald needs saving from his own intellectual arrogance becomes a personal mission:

'I am going back to London. I have made up my mind, Aunt Phemie. I am going to help Ranald all I can. I shall give him all that's in me. But I shall never betray – this world – all this, that's in me and you. That's maybe, all I have to give.' (240)

'This world', Phemie's land and Phemie's values, offers a challenge to the metropolis and its inhuman musings and, since Nan is part a product of the metropolis also, to its occasional twinges of sentimentality. Phemie is the only character clearly anchored in both optimism and a sense of reality. Though Adam and Ranald and Nan have all suffered (Ranald had been shot down while on an RAF mission), Phemie's transcendence of pain – the death of her husband and then the death of her child – seems to be the most enduring, the most hopeful. The book does not have a complacent closure. The relationship between Ranald and Nan is unresolved and their different points of view are still at thesis and antithesis stage. But in Phemie, a kind, self-assured and successful protofeminist, Gunn does present possibility. *The Shadow* ends on that feeling of hope.

Hope blossoms on *The Silver Bough* and the fruit is comedy.

Travelling by bus into the Highlands to excavate a previously unopened cairn, the archaeologist Simon Grant asks the man sitting next to him if the local landlord, Donald Martin, is likely to be at home. The man replies in the negative, and only when they arrive is Grant given to understand that the man was in fact Martin himself. Martin's dourness is set at an extreme from the hapless archaeologists well-meaning good humour, and the result is a novel which polkas around a Conradian horror.

The book goes from mistake to *faux pas*, from accident to act of idiocy. On his way to find lodgings, Grant catches up with Martin who suggests a nearby labourer might be available to help in the heavier work of excavation. When Grant goes to employ him he finds out the man is mentally handicapped and therefore (he thinks) a definite risk in archaeological work. Even so, his sympathy for the 'idiot boy', Foolish Andie, and especially his mother, Mrs Mackenzie, wins through. He even justifies Andie's employment to himself by musing on the affinity between his helper and the paleolithic civilisation under scrutiny. Andie is not the only person seen as a throwback to primitive times. Martin's skull, the first thing the book opens with, is recognised as Neolithic (9–10), but the joke is on Simon when he later acknowledges that he himself is a 'Mousterian ass' (48). Grant's behaviour is deliberately set against Andie's. At the end of one chapter, embarrassed at another of his own foot-in-mouth comments, he curses himself, 'What an idiot!' (72). At the beginning of the next he sees the dignity and calmness of 'the idiot and his mother sitting on the edge of cairn, its grey bulk behind them, waiting for him'. He wonders why 'if anyone could tie himself in knots he was the man' (73). The fact that his colleagues refer to him as 'Simple Simon' is further evidence of the play Gunn is making on the meaning and implications of being not quite the shilling and, indeed, of being a good deal less. One of the social achievements of the book, as with Robin Jenkins' *The Cone-Gatherers* (1955), is the compassion with which a victim of mental handicap is portrayed.

Grant finds a place to stay at the house of Mrs Cameron, who lives with her daughter, Anna, and Anna's illegitimate child, Sheena. At the house he hears Mrs Cameron telling her granddaughter the tale which gives the book its title. A king gives up his wife and child for a silver branch which produces the most wonderful music. After a while, however, the king beings to miss his family and sets out to find them. When he finally arrives at a palace, Manannan (the Gaelic magician) he gives him his family back and returns them all home. The silver bough is there, too. This is Sheena's favourite story; the family break-up it portrays offers a resolution which her own circumstances would seem to make impossible. The various parallels between ancient and new in *The Silver Bough*, not least that between the skeletons of the mother and child found in the cairn and Anna and Sheena, indicate a theory of constancy in the nature of fundamental human situations. Recurrence also emphasises the presence of authorial control. While this is not yet at the unbelievable pitch of *The Well at the World's End* or *The Other Landscape*, where realism is left clutching at a cliff-edge, the dissatisfaction with the norms of naturalism and realism can be found in work at least as early on as the heroic ventures of Finn, who is cast in a kind of living fable. Here, however, Gunn, and Grant, make a deliberate attempt to interpret various experiences as recurrences of fundamental 'fable'; recurrence is made to be significant.

Frazer's *The Golden Bough*, quoted in the text (231) and echoed in the title, had charted 'universal' myths, and Gunn's book deals with some more. Grant's point of view goes further than simply noticing paradigms of human behaviour. The quest for the crock of gold is a good example of this. After penetrating the cairn, Grant foolishly goes back to it at night to follow up a hunch. Behind a false wall, he finds an urn full of gold artefacts, collectively of enormous archaeological significance, but Andie comes upon him and snatches it away, leaving him unconscious. The urn is never recovered because Andie is killed some days later when the major standing stone topples down on him. Despite Grant's initial frustration, he comes to accept the loss as 'inevitable' because the fable of the crock of gold, through which Grant interprets his own experience, is a story about striving and disappointment. He has placed himself in a narrative structure he can identify with, and in this he finds a good degree of solace. Not only does myth anticipate future action, future action shapes itself to myth. It is as least satisfying to know that the crock of gold story exists for oneself, though the rainbow at Andie's funeral, which to Grant is the pot-of-gold rainbow, shows again Gunn's beautiful artifice ignoring any mean idea of 'likelihood'.

Grant does not leave the crock at that, even so. Keats's 'Ode on a Grecian Urn' is brought into his increasingly elaborate philosophising ('La Belle Dame Sans Merci' had already entered Grant's thoughts earlier in the book). Andie's death is a terrible thing, but the particular joy he had in the days preceding mitigates its effect. Mrs Mackenzie's terror of his being institutionalised because of her inevitable inability to cope, puts his death, only in hindsight of course, within the rightness of things. Keats's poem, because it presents both unfulfilment and unfading beauty, is used by Grant to encapsulate his mixed feelings about Andie's death and the loss of the archaeological urn.

> No, things did not happen to romantic order. In that sense, nothing had 'come right'. Andie had been killed and the crock of gold had been buried under the rainbow. Not actually under the rainbow, but near enough to give immortal sense to Keats and the figures on his Grecian Urn [...].
> The crock of gold seemed to have brought Keats to life in him after many years! And it would not help much now to be jealous of the rainbow! After all, a crock of gold under the rainbow would be only an urn in a museum. Even irony had its over-all balance. The poets needed a myth to feed on. It was their secreted honey. Keats took over from the archaeologist. (326)

'Only an urn in a museum' is an extraordinary way for a dedicated archaeologist to refer to an artefact. This shows how much he is compensating for his own disappointment, and how humane and self-critical he manages to be. The interweaving of Keats, urn, and crock, illustrates the sophistication Gunn's techniques have reached. It also shows how he saw myth as a force for understanding the human condition, and for compassion.

Gunn had long been a 'creative archaeologist'. *Sun Circle* writes a prehistory and an anthropology of northern Scotland that predates the approaches which have emerged in the last twenty years. Grant is a New Archaeologist, though he existed before the term had been forged. Collecting local folklore, he tries to assess the cairn not so much as an isolated artifact but more as an element within a human social structure. He is not averse to imagining what the extinct society was like, even though he is aware that this could lead to suspect romanticisation. Once again, the Celtic

Twilight surfaces as a bogus unreality in Gunn's fiction, but this time as a metaphor for the problems of Grant's adventurous style of archaeology.

> The trouble with this half-light was that it made the word 'scientific' magical, and as the mood of the twilight grew in its airy and subtle delight, a silent and delicious mockery translated 'scientific' into a mumbo-jumbo word, stripped in its portentous solemnity from it and left it naked as any totem-pole. Once he had written an essay called 'The Heresy of the Twilight', but feeling that its irony was insufficiently concealed and its wit concealed only too well, he had modestly refrained from offering it for publication. (61–2)

The gentle scepticism is also Gunn's. A cameo appearance of a schoolmaster who could easily be from *The Grey Coast* continues Gunn's self-scrutiny and clarification of stance. McCowan joins Grant briefly for a discussion on the origins of the cairn people. His inappropriate Celticism sees Celtic excellence in every rock with a scratch on it. Grant reminds him that the Gaels were 'mere newcomers, parvenus', and that the cairn people probably came from 'England'. McCowan's amateur scholarship, Grant remarks to himself, is loaded with 'silly racial arguments' (91). Not that Grant has been immune: in connection with the henge he had chuckled at 'some ever-youthful theory of sun-worship' (65). Gunn can smile at his own previous imaginative susceptibilities.

Even so, Grant is at his most winning when he is recreating prehistory. His conclusion that the local belief in the ghost of the circle had guaranteed the cairn's undisturbed sanctity seems substantiated by his tremendous find, but his assembled explanation of the mother and child is inspired. The filament between fiction and scientific investigation, the other half-light Grant had been thinking about, allows him to go further than his tightly circumscribed colleagues. This is one of the topics he discusses with Mrs Sidbury (Martin's sister) and Colonel Mackintosh (Grant's superior).

> On the command to fire ahead, Grant gave a quite vivid description of the ceremonies accompanying and following a burial in the chamber when it was 'the cathedral of its time.' He borrowed from recent anthropological field work among primitive peoples in Eastern archipelagoes, from Homer, from extant religious practices, but without parade

> of knowledge, for he had been thinking the matter over, or
> rather – though he did not put it like this to the Colonel – the
> matter, the reconstruction, had flowed into his mind. (207–
> 8)

It is interesting that forty years later another Scot, Neal
Ascherson, should draw attention to this process of academic
assimilation. Reviewing in 1985 an exhibition on prehistoric Brit-
ain he writes (without reference to Gunn, of course):

> For generations, prehistorians have played safe by sticking
> to 'fact', to recording and comparing pottery fragments,
> postholes, arrowheads. Fantasy and generalising were dis-
> reputable. Museums became the dull places they mostly
> remain. No wonder the later Sir Mortimer Wheeler barked:
> 'We have been preparing timetables: let us now have some
> trains!'
>
> Then, some 15 years ago, the 'New Archaeology' began to
> hit this country. It sent trains rattling off in all directions. It
> demanded that scholars and diggers should have ideas and
> prejudices. It said that it was nonsense to expect 'facts' to
> 'speak for themselves': the archaeologist was merely listen-
> ing to his own preconceived ideas without admitting it. [...]
> Archaeology had been blown up. And in the confusion
> archaeology darted about looting other disciplines: anthro-
> pology, cybernetics, sociology, aesthetics. A frightful jargon
> rose and mercifully fell [...] But the profession was liber-
> ated.[8]

Grant, without the jargon, brings out freshness and liberation. His
archaeological story for Sheena, for example, shows him vigor-
ously popularising his discipline and extending it theoretically,
without trashing it in the process (233). This is why he is treated as
'Simple Simon' by his more arid and narrow colleagues. In his
intellectual outlook he is a radical integrator. In his human rela-
tions he is an accidental hero who, when he overcomes the clumsy
initial reactions of his warm personality, behaves delicately and
compassionately.

Donald Martin counters this good-naturedness. His attitude is
not so much anti-social as dark. To Grant 'He's either an egoma-
niac or a walking death' (102). What lies behind the distance he
keeps from Anna and their child, to the extent that he fails to react
at all when Grant inadvertently mentions their parallel with the

skeletons, is only revealed towards the end of the novel. The reason for Mrs Sidbury's sensitivity towards her brother, incidentally, is rather clumsily spelt out by Gunn at the end of Chapter 13, despite the more relaxed revealing of Martin's fatherhood later on. The last two paragraphs, I would suggest, were Gunn's concession to Geoffrey Faber who felt that the common reader needed the connection to be made in a more obvious fashion.[9]

After Grant's strained talk with Martin at Clachar House he had felt the need to escape from 'out of the jungle' (102). This proves to be a prophetic metaphor. Later, when Grant is trapped inside a cave, he is rescued by Martin who, now rather more communicative, recounts his experience in the war-time forests of the Far East. The Second World War had made Martin see 'the horror' (the horror, the horror) at first hand (252). Japanese soldiers, after killing a white colonial, had raped and tortured the wife, and then killed her. After Martin had observed this, he had 'gone native', living on his wits to survive in the jungle, but shadowing the soldiers to enact his revenge. Like Kurtz in *Heart of Darkness* Martin had become almost a witch-doctor figure, and he had eventually killed all five of the soldiers, the last ritually. The killing instinct he had developed then, he theorises, also allowed him to understand the energies unleashed at a national level in the last war. There is a suicide-wish, culturally (Europe destroying itself), personally, and finally, even globally. '"Do you mean," and Grant had the odd sensation that something was suddenly shouting the final question in him, "that humanity has got the wish to destroy itself, that – that the death instinct has got charge?"' (254). Martin does not answer the question. There has already been an insinuation that his rowing on the sea has been a kind of death-wish and when the storm drives them to grief on a spit, it seems as if the death-wish has been fulfilled. Anna and Martin's chauffeur, however, come to their rescue and Grant looks on as Martin, despite himself, is resuscitated. It is then that Grant realises Anna's passion for her ex-lover, a passion so profound she cries out with 'the elemental cry of the woman to her mate' (263).

These are the emotional depths behind the silver bough tale of the title. The tale is taken from M. H. d'Arbois de Jubainville's *The Irish Mythological Cycle*, the most significant change being the change in nomenclature from the 'branch of silver' to which de Jubainville refers.[10] This brings the bough into line with the more famous golden one. Gunn enriches the obvious parallel between the story of the bough and Anna's real-life predicament in a number of ways. Grant is so taken with the tale, and Sheena's love of it, that he has a jeweller make a 'real', musical one. When it arrives, Simon plays 'Home Sweet Home' (270). The childlike simplicity and, in the circumstances, the bitter-sweetness of the tune, exemplify the poetry and concision of much of *The Silver Bough*. When Anna sees the bough, 'it might have been jewels for her wedding from the way she looked'. When Mrs Cameron hears it she is transported back to her childhood, and sings like a girl. Sheena associates its chiming with the magical properties of the fabled bough and when she hears it ring out imagines herself transported to the White Shore, a good way down the coast. In the closing paragraph Grant sees Sheena playing the bough in front of Martin down by the sea. The distance means nothing can be heard and this gives the effect of a mime, as if Sheena and Martin, and finally, Anna, have become part of a mythical tableau. Anna and Sheena join Martin in his boat and Grant supposes that they are embarking for the 'wonderful place' in the story (314), Sheena's White Shore.

The central ambiguity of the bough – an instrument of a dangerous escapism as well as of untold beauty – is not denied here. The 'strange and adventurous journey' (320), the quest for familial unity, is not going to be an easy one, given what we know of the strained relations between Anna and her deeply troubled ex-lover. The potential for a 'happy ending' is only a potential.

Despite Martin's turmoil and Andie's bloody death, *The Silver Bough* is ultimately a gentle, thoughtful book, and *The Lost Chart*, a spy thriller, comes as a surprise. There is, however, a thematic development. The 'watching' that Grant had pleasantly resigned himself to has become espionage. His intrusion into a dead culture's everyday life, an activity Martin had held to be 'spying', has become intrusion into the lives of ordinary people very much alive.

Dermot Cameron, a shipping executive, has a part-time job as a British secret agent. In the event of nuclear war, his task is to take a boat of people to the apparent safety of the secret western island of Claddy. Unfortunately, he loses his chart of the island when he tries to foil two bagsnatchers, and it falls into 'enemy' hands. The fight reintroduces him to Christina, a young woman he had not seen since his war-time visit to Cladday, some ten years ago. This suspicious coincidence proves, nevertheless, to be genuinely accidental. The story follows Dermot's attempts to recover the chart, a job he does partly with the assistant of his Intelligence chief, Grear, and partly on his own vigorous initiative.

Gunn makes full use of many of the conventions of the thriller. With a Cold War backdrop, the novel proceeds with sinister footsteps heard in steady pursuit, a suspicious colleague, punch-ups with enemy agents, a police raid, and corruption in the civil service. This genre has been very accommodating for Scottish writers, from Stevenson and Buchan through to Maclean; quite simply, though, *The Lost Chart* lacks their complexity. Instead Gunn builds on a very simple plot by emphasising aspects of spying which the spy novel usually skimps. The issues of privacy and trust, rather than the mechanics of spying, become the focus. The novel is deliberately tilted away from exotic settings by being based in an anonymous city recognisable as Glasgow. The distant, romanticised, business of being a secret agent is brought close to home. The trappings of spying become both metaphor and indicator of a modern and sick consciousness where intrusion is the new brutality. Although it is implied that the enemy is the Soviet Union, and the enemy ideology Communism, there is no explicit naming. This supports the notion, which the increasingly sceptical protagonist espouses, that the question of good versus evil cannot be seen in terms of one political state having a moral advantage over another. The very act of spying is the work of a decadent society.

The memory of Cladday dominates the novel. Dermot remembers his naval days there, when the delicate sensitivities of the islanders had been offended by his officially necessary surveillance. He and his colleagues had been torpedoed by a U-boat, and the islanders had come to their rescue, not without loss of life on the Cladday side. Dermot's recovery of the chart becomes, then, a very personal imperative – it is a gesture of recompense as well as a commitment to the kind of life lived on Cladday. For the same reason he tries to protect Christina from the suspicions of Intelligence. The idea of foreign or impersonal intrusion is alien to the islanders, and though Christina is by no means an *ingénue* the slightest contact with a policeman is a traumatic event. This is compounded by her association with underground socialists who are deeply distrustful of the police, not least because (unknown to her) they are subversives.

To Dermot, Cladday is also more than itself. When his artist friend Joe Duguid enquires about it, Dermot calls it 'the land of light; it's the place where you see light being made. Literally – you can watch God painting out there,' (56). A Gaelic prayer from the island celebrates the light, too.

> Glory to Thyself, O God of life,
> For Thy lamp of the Ocean,
> Thine own hand at the tiller,
> And Thy love behind the wave. (77)

Originally, the novel was to be called 'Behind the Wave', an indication of the importance to Gunn of this little poem. Its phrases recur through the text, particularly in Dermot's thoughts. Faber did not like the name, however, and Gunn changed it.

> The title [...] is a difficulty, because I mean it to be an answer
> not to the Gaelic part only. Let me be naive enough to
> confess when I'm at it that *Behind the Wave* was not thought
> of in the original conception as a thriller but rather as a
> serious (cannot think of the right adjective) book with the
> excitement of a thriller.[11]

Understandably, Faber wanted to emphasise the thriller aspects of the book even if Gunn was insisting that his use of the genre was only secondary. In common with previous work, Gunn was offering a particular kind of rural ideal to the world at large, and insisting on its wider applicability. To be behind the wave was to be set in a kind of spiritual home, and in the prayer light, 'Thy lamp', is an important part of that. Dermot remembers the Cladday people's empathy with their environment, and their sense of dignity, and he remembers the extraordinary beauty of the island. Their way of life, or rather their attitude to life, seems to have been lost everywhere else.

The place of light contrasts strongly with the dark and dingy Glasgow Gunn portrays. Joe's translation of different psycho-spiritual attitudes into light terms, the 'drama of the light' (178), is an explicit parallel to the use Gunn makes of light and darkness throughout. Most of the action in the city part of the novel is restricted to evenings and late nights. Talk makes it plain that crime is on the increase in town, but Dermot has an affection for the ordinary people there. He respects their urban tradition – 'Ships sailed out of their blood' (47) – and finds fault only with the type he dislikes in every society, the ideologue. The Glasgow Gunn describes is an extraordinary one. In some ways it can be seen as *Wild Geese Overhead* revisited. He makes sure that the reader knows the locale is Glasgow, but he makes sure that it is a distorted unreal Glasgow, too. Spoken language, normally important in Gunn's indication of location and culture, is here uniform and rootless. The few working-class characters have vocabularies indistinguishable from the 'standard' English spoken by everyone else in the book. The implications of Gunn's unGlasgow are manifold. The peasant and working classes are ill-represented in the book because in political terms they simply do not matter: a fact borne out by the pawn Christina becomes in the espionage game, and the frailty of the whole 'classless' society of Cladday. The old trade unionist at St Patrick's Close is taken in by the secret agents in the same way. Middle-class secret service officials plot against their class equivalents. Perhaps the city is portrayed without its language because Gunn is unwilling to fully recognise a specific culture and vibrancy which, by its very nature, would militate against his argument of just such a culture existing in superiority and isolation on Cladday. To show Glasgow in too good a light would detract from his symbolic intentions. Alternatively, he may have been avoiding a detailed portrayal, simply because he knew his limitations: as *Wild Geese Overhead* shows, he did not know city life well enough for anything more than symbolic expression. But the use of 'standard' English also tends to effect a sense of the universal. The debates which occur in the city's private talking shops, the more aggressive Dial Club, and the conservative and academic Parthenon, are the intellectual arguments which probably exist in every other city, too. The city has become The City, a deliberate shadow of Glasgow's reality. Once again, Gunn's novel occupies a symbolic landscape where realism is eschewed.

Through this stylized landscape of signposts rather than landmarks, Dermot moves warily. Though his fondness for Christina and for her island explains his attempts to protect her from Grear he also does the same for his Dial Club colleague, Basil Black. He knows that Black is more than an adversary in debate, and suspects him of being a fifth columnist, but he still tries to keep him out of his reports. He had told Basil that people in totalitarian countries have the secret police as their new Devil (121). At times Dermot sees counter-espionage in similar terms. A good example of this occurs when the folk-singer he is very fond of is singing especially for him at his flat. Ellen reaches back to a place of light with her voice, as Christina reaches back to it as a woman from Cladday. The telephone interrupts her like a 'machine gun ripping right through.' (157).

Grear is at the other end. MI6 is inescapable and the violence it does to the moment is indicative of the contempt it has to individuals. 'The sad thing is that *you* and *me* are not beginning to matter much any more,' Dermot tells Ellen. He had earlier realised that Christina's bagsnatchers were probably working for Grear, and at times he feels that Grear and Basil Black are just the two sides of the same coin – 'which side came down didn't matter a lot' (147).

When the telephone had interrupted Ellen

> it had destroyed the country where they [Dermot and Ellen] journeyed, that country which he was always a little afraid of, because its beauty, its containing harmony, was sad with the mute cry of the forever lost. (157)

This country is the country of love for Dermot and Ellen, as well as the country of the Gael, but Hart and Pick are right to hear in this 'the cadences of Fiona Macleod,' too.[12] *The Lost Chart* does have snatches of the Twilight lament, though its artistic distance from Macleod is marked by the ultra-modern context of nuclear apocalypse.

In my view, Gunn no longer assigns to the Twilight the literary or national implications he once did, and of course it does not have here the archaeological significance it had in the preceding novel. In essence, the country of the forever lost is an actual place. Unlike the world of the London hack Fiona Macleod, Gunn's Cladday and the Gaelic way of life it represents have been and are 'real'. The Cladday people have extremely hard lives and though Dermot romanticises life on the island, the Cladday folk do not. Cladday has its problems, too. The young clearly do not find they can live off its idyllic ambience, otherwise Christina would not have been a maidservant for years, and there might not be the emigration to the Antipodes which does exist.

There is also the difference between just being and admiring the act of just being. Dermot feels that Ellen's singing 'had a whole civilization behind it, an attitude to life and to death over a long time,' but of course Ellen just sings (306). This is not to say that Dermot is wrong, but that his conceptualising is merely inappropriate. Similarly, Christina is loath to repeat 'Behind the wave' because it is a private prayer (like the sea and moon ritual Dermot saw on Cladday, Gunn took this from *Carmina Gadelica*). To be self-conscious is, paradoxically, to demean self. Gunn sets up both the thing-in-itself and the analysis. He allows them to appear together so that he can depict on the one hand a way of life unfettered by thinking and idealising about itself, and on the other hand, a sympathetic observer who cannot help but contemplate and idealise. Because Dermot's comments argue passionately for the values of Cladday while the novel as a whole endorses those values as 'instinctual', Gunn is able to tell the uninitiated about them while also insisting on the problems of re-expression. This is a commendable state of being, he says in the first breath, and in the next, but of course the idea of commendability never occurs to those who achieve it. No wonder Zen, which Gunn explored more fully after *The Lost Chart*, was so appealing to him.[13] When we first meet Dermot , he is staring into a fishing-tackle shop, daydreaming. His shipping firm colleague interrupts what had been a reverie of childhood: catching his first sea-trout (an act Gunn readers immediately recognise as a moment symbolic of an almost metaphysical absorption and 'arriving at self'). That time in his life '"was simply another age"' (5) and irretrievable. '"However you go back, you must take yourself with you – and your age. Humanity never goes back."' (6). Dermot is not only referring here to the unsatisfactory practice of 'recreating the past', the nostalgia game, or even his own self-conscious feelings as one who is now older and wiser. He is referring to a change in mankind's sensibility in general: he must bring the shrivelling looks of the modern era back to the childhood of his memory, a process which inevitably destroys the sanctity of the first moment. This is 'the new Dark Age' (6).

Dermot rescues the chart of Cladday, captures an enemy agent, and tips off Intelligence as to the location of the enemy's lair. Even so, on the world scale which nuclear weapons now make it necessary to contemplate, these triumphs matter very little. The novel does not end as Dermot hands over the baddy and spills the beans on the rest of the political crooks. He is no Richard Hannay. Instead, he returns to his flat in terror of the global war Intelligence believe will probably break out, despite his success, in a matter of days. On Thursday in fact.

When Friday comes, Dermot wakes to the knowledge that war has been averted. But as Grear later explains, the reasons for the continuance of peace are out of the hands of ordinary folk, and in this case had been maintained only on the 'interpretation of a clause in an international agreement which they [the enemy] had hitherto tended to overlook,' (343). This sort of arbitrary lurching from heightened alarm to numbness and back again is no different, perhaps, from other periods in history, except that now the stakes are so much higher. In addition, a distant bureaucracy seems to have usurped the position of the old dictators. Dermot has returned to the rather grim beginning of the novel. Yet it is not just a return to the status quo. Grear reveals plans for Cladday to be fortified. Dermot is to collaborate with a power whose 'higher aims' are destined to maim Cladday even in peace-time, and then make it a target during any war. He is to go on a reconnaissance of the island in a matter of weeks. This problem is not resolved. Though angry and frustrated, by the end of the novel Dermot is still going to go along with Grear's plan. He accepts his divided loyalty as part of 'the ultimate duality in human destiny' (349). The last few pages see him diverting his concerns away from the immediate world scheme of things, which appears to be impervious to individual influence, and into his own personal affairs. Throughout the novel, his relationship with Ellen had been one of intimacy without commitment. He had felt the world crisis disallowed contemplation of any deeper relationship (44–5). At the end of the book, however, he proposes to her. Despite the harrowing atmosphere of the Cold War Dermot is making the best of a bad world (marriage returns as a Good Thing).

There is more to Dermot's decision than this. He also plans to use the reconnaissance mission as an opportunity to sail Joe and Christina (now definitely a couple) and Ellen to Cladday. In this way the four will be a 'salvage party' (352), a kind of spiritual rescue team. On the one hand, Gunn seems to have gloomily rejected the possibility of any individual seriously influencing the entrenched political structures consolidated by the war. On the other hand, Dermot is shown reacting against his feeling of helplessness on the level of personal quest. Though the real lost chart, trivial in itself, has been retrieved, another reality and another kind of chart is still missing. We have seen why Ellen and Christina are the 'right crew' to rediscover the world behind the wave: they tune into a world unfragmented and well-balanced. It could also be said that this world is dead or near death. Because of this, Joe has a special significance. His art is decidedly modern, abstract, and though he is called 'simple' by some, his directness, his honesty, have that quality Dermot so admires. He is a comic figure, too. He is wet behind the ears in matters of love, and Christina flusters him at first. Thinking and expressing himself most clearly in images, and images which are abstract, Joe is very much a part of that instinctual sensitive world which Cladday typifies, yet he is also Gunn's example of a modern. 'God's fool', the butterfly Finn encountered in *The Silver Darlings* (taken again from *Carmina Gadelica*), becomes a description of the feelings behind Joe's inarticulacy, the inarticulacy or at least indirectness which seems associated with most matters of the heart. 'Joe was exactly God's fool,' (126). The butterfly, which just *is*, 'translates' the precious elusive meanings which Joe is trying to express, yet Joe is doing so as well simply by being himself. The supposed fool, Nan in *The Shadow*, 'Simple' Simon in *The Silver Bough*, and now Joe, turn out to have a wisdom of substance and quality. Yet they are only part of a more complex vision. In the same way that Nan and Ranald and Phemie contribute to an intricate and dynamic political and personal presentation of dilemma and possibility, Joe, Christina, and Ellen, are each only exponents of a nebulous ideal. Dermot, skippering his ship of holy fools, is in search of what they have already found and carry with them.

Though *The Lost Chart* seems out of place between the less furious novels which surround it, that it ends on a wish to retrieve a spiritual conception of reality makes it closer to them than is first recognised. In *The Well at the World's End* (1951) Dermot's parting proposition of a personal quest is taken up by the central character, Peter Munro. Peter's developing search for epiphany re-introduces us to that rich particularity of characterisation and description which had been substantially and deliberately absent in *The Lost Chart*.

The plot outline is very simple, and its form and tone are largely established in the first four chapters. Peter, a professor in ancient history, and his wife, Fand, are on holiday in the Highlands. Their car has broken down, and Peter has been told by an old woman that he can find water in a nearby spring. When he reaches it, however, it is dry. The old woman still insists that there *is* water there, and when Peter actually puts his hand into the well he proves her right. The clarity of the water had misled him. How Peter explains his reaction, and how Fand responds, sets up part of the pattern for what is to follow.

> 'At first I laughed. That there should have been water in the well when we were so certain it was dry! Water so clear we thought it wasn't there! Then – all at once – the queer feeling came over me that we were at the beginning of an adventure – setting out to find the – the something in life that we think isn't there.'
>
> 'You have long been wanting to do that,' she said.
>
> 'Do what?'
>
> 'Go away and find the well at the world's end.' (10)

A relaxed humour pervades the book. Peter is a slightly ridiculous figure who is not above self-parody. His use of 'we' in the passage above is wrong-headed, and Fand is quick to show him that it will be *his* search, alone. *She* needs no such adventure. Soon after, as they dabble in a river pool Fand secures the salmon which has just escaped him. Later, he will find himself in other situations where his poor judgement teaches him a little humility. As she explains, Fand is the name of a goddess in Celtic legend who failed to observe the correct ritual before approaching the well at the world's end, the well of knowledge and poetry. Because of this the well had risen up and drowned her. Peter's behaviour is to show that he, too, fails to act correctly, especially in situations where more sensitivity is required. Men, much more than women, have to begin to think about the sensitivity of their approach to life. The simplicity of the plot is dictated by what becomes Peter's long circular hike. Mention of wandering in search of 'windmills' (27) establishes a Quixotic parallel, and in this modern picaresque the touch is generally light. At first you laugh, the book advises us, then you realise you are looking for, and at, something more. Delight, yes, but also a rather hard-headed understanding of one's self-deceptions and a better sense of what is personally valuable. Approaching *The Well at the World's End* requires the same balance between levity and sensitivity as approaching the legendary well and the real well, but it may reward as highly. Peter reminds us of Gunn's literary project when he asks: 'I wonder if this feeling of something magical is as rare as some of our misery-ridden plays and novels make out?' (20).

The narrative is continually reminding us of the well motif. On his lone trek, Peter encounters a series of 'wells' – a haunted river pool, a whisky still, a loch with romantic associations, the sea itself, and even the life-saving qualities of a ewe's milk. Almost all these episodes appeared in short story or essay form elsewhere, and Gunn's biographers have noted their large debt to real experience. This suggests that Gunn was deliberately laying out a series of special occurrences the essential truth of which he could validate. At each point, Peter either experiences or hears of another such moment where the fabulous is also a matter of fact. But he also sees the potential for harmony being torn asunder: in terms of the myth, where the well is approached improperly. This occurs perhaps most sharply when Peter quietly colludes in a practical joke in which Lowland workers are almost scared to death (literally) by two locals, Alastair and Lachlan. It is seen by Peter, though almost apologetically, as piercing a surface, as going 'through the boundary of superstition'. With a watery pun, Peter looks on it as 'all source material' (73). It is precisely this refusal to be actively sympathetic to human vulnerability, however, that militates against deeper understanding. When the pranksters succeed in frightening the wits out of their victims, one Lowlander goes near insane. He recovers from his apparent death-bed only by chance. In terms of the well myth, Peter had approached the pursuit of knowledge incorrectly. He had ignored what he had intuited: that the delicate but potentially ferocious power of folk knowledge is not one to be subjected to casual experimentation. The gothic motif we have already noted in *Second Sight*, and which occurs more subtly, for example, in the superstitions of the fishermen in *The Silver Darlings*, resurfaces here as a lesson in respect for human credulity, and respect for received custom.

If that joke isn't funny any more, it is a rarity in the book. The 'wells' Peter visits are reinforced by the author's frequent puns on the word 'well', among others: 'Well, he had started on his travels!' (31). 'If a man is going to do something it is well that he should do it thoroughly' (101), 'laughter welled up' (134), and 'he might as well go home now' (237). The word itself is ideal for Gunn because most of its meanings collude with the central symbol: pleasure, satisfaction, surprise. Tongue very much in cheek, this kind of humour reminds us that it would be as well for us not to be too po-faced in our approach to the book. It also emphasises, as the picaresque plot does, that once again here is a novel subversively antithetic to notions of realism.

As in form, so in general subject. Reflecting on his adventures, Peter is to come to understand that 'his quest for the well at the world's end had been light-hearted and poetic rather than stern and realistic' (237). Gunn takes Peter to privileged look-out posts which strain believability, from inside a secret cave where moonshine whisky is being made, to a remote and misty loch where, as if by chance, he witnesses the successful reunion of a previously unhappy husband and wife. Peter's experience is a poetic one, in the sense of deriving intimate meanings and charge from occurrences with are mostly relatively mundane in themselves. The *form* is poetic in the way that the book's metaphor extrudes and transforms itself. In addition to his interest in myth, Peter engages with different philosophical ideas. John Burns explains in a fine chapter in *A Celebration of the Light* that Peter is also, in Zen terms, on 'the way'.[14] This sense of spirituality through being is readily accommodated in a book which smiles and doffs its cap at Cervantes. However, the engagement with Chinese and other Eastern traditions is a light one. The book's assertion that the existence of spiritual sensation is proven empirically, and occurs in all manner of people independent of class or any religious view, has clear affinities with Zen. Though the Far East had very little concrete influence on the later novels, the 'moment of delight', an idea with Gunn since the 1920s, is deliciously at home with satori.

P. D. Ouspensky's *In Search of the Miraculous* (1950) was probably a suggestive text.[15] This is a first-hand account of the teachings in Moscow of the mystic Gurdjieff, recounted by his at first rather green 'student'. Gurdjieff is evasive about the origins of his philosophy, though the implication is that it is 'Eastern', though probably from not further east than India (in fact he was influenced by Sufism). In *The Well at the World's End* the desire for a personal *breaking through* into another level of understanding, a desire that can be identified in earlier novels, finds a companion in Ouspensky. At the beginning of his book,

Ouspensky describes how he set himself a task not dissimilar to Peter's:

> I had come to the conclusion a long time ago that there was no escape from the labyrinth of contradictions in which we live except by an entirely new road, unlike anything hitherto known or used by us. But where this new or forgotten road began I was unable to say. I already knew then as an undoubted fact that beyond the thin film of false reality there existed another reality from which, for some reason, something separated us. The 'miraculous' was a penetration into this unknown reality.[16]

The metaphor is analogous to Peter's putting hand into air and discovering water. The idea that the 'miraculous' might be 'forgotten' or 'new' is also in line with Gunn's looking back to go forward. Gunn appreciated Gurdjieff's phrase, 'remember yourself'. Ouspensky's initial belief that enlightenment can probably be learned formally, that one can 'get miraculous', has affinities with some of Gunn's endearing intellectual fools, of which Peter is here the latest. In the same terms of 'approach' and 'source' that Gunn uses, Gurdjieff warns Ouspensky that hard work lies ahead:

> 'He who wants knowledge must himself make the initial efforts to find the source of knowledge and to approach it, taking advantage of the help and indications which are given to all, but which people, as a rule, do not want to recognize. Knowledge cannot come to people without effort on their own part. They understand this very well in connection with ordinary knowledge, but in the case of *great knowledge*, when they admit the possibility of its existence, they find it possible to expect something different.'[17]

Peter's search for the miraculous in other people's lives is not always as arduous as this, but his own journey towards self-discovery is ultimately almost fatal. Despite the necessarily individualistic nature of such moments, in Gunn they are not always anti-social affairs. Most of Peter's experiences are centred on people's relationships with each other: the moment that brings estranged husband and wife together again, the unworded understanding between the officer and private who have been through war together, the joy in dancing. Apart from Peter's personal quest, he has a desire to see how the kind of spirituality in which he is interested affects other types of people, too. He wants to find if this aspect of the individual is actually 'shared' by everyone (20), and finds that it is experienced by all sorts of people.

The novel also takes cognizance of another fairly recent text. Robert Graves published his book on myth, folklore, magic, and poetry, *The White Goddess*, in 1948. Its mixture of scholarship, speculation, and anthropology had considerable appeal for Gunn. Graves cites some old favourites: Carmichael's *Carmina Gadelica*, Keats, Blake, Aldous Huxley, Dunne's *Experiment with Time*, and Frazer's *The Golden Bough*. His culminating argument, that poetic inspiration of an authentic kind can only occur when the male poet rediscovers the appeal to a feminine principle of truth, the Muse, has certain affinities with Gunn's appeal to 'female values'. Like Gunn, Graves widens this to a thesis on all social activity, not art alone.

Gunn's use of *The White Goddess* is concentrated in one episode within the book. When Peter meets up with an English friend, the ridiculously named Cocklebuster, the latter is out hunting with his dog, Sally. At first they venture into a Forestry Commission plantation. The 'sterile' nature of the forest confuses Sally which proves ineffectual at tracking and prey. Peter suggests jokingly that the trees have been 'psychoanalysed' (163). Sally then leads the two men to a mixed deciduous wood.

> Presently Peter began to hear something. And then, as if suddenly waking up (he had let go) in paradise, he became aware of bird song. His opened eyes roamed among leafy branches, oak and ash and elm and even a beech, a beech with drooping foliaged branches gracious and widespread, like the skirts of the woodland mother, the ancient matriarch, the first and only goddess. (172)

This reverie is closely related to Graves's interest in the connection between an ancient tree cult, matriarchal in structure and aspiration, and writing itself. The names of all the trees in Peter's wood, which Peter senses has 'been left behind' (172), are all constituent parts of what Graves argued was an alphabet based on trees. Peter and Cocklebuster develop a conversation about trees that is closely based on Graves's speculations.[19] There are, nevertheless, some rather more subtle allusions. The difference between a Forestry Commission plantation and a deciduous wood is not only a purely aesthetic one – hence the gibe about psychoanalysis – it is one of modernity versus tradition. More specifically, Peter

remembers the guilt of his first stolen apple from an orchard and
Cocklebuster recalls the guilt of shooting a sitting pheasant out of
season, and guiltily taking the bird into the concealment of woods.
The Englishman had felt as if he was Adam or Eve hiding in the
trees and awaiting nemesis. Soon after these confessions which tie
in the personal with the archetypal, the conversation moves fur-
ther into Graves's territory.

'Over immense aeons of time the only god was a goddess – '
'The Savage Goddess,' said Cocklebuster.
'That's right,' said Peter, whose eyes were on the beech
tree, 'though doubtless she would have had her gracious
moments, her poetic – uh –'
'Personal conjecture of so-called civilised man.'
'But is conjecture impermissible?' (176)

Peter's argument that the goddess 'would have had her gracious
moments', even 'poetic' ones, refers back to the positive and
inspiring quality of the feminine as Gunn sees it. But Gunn takes
Graves's initiative in making this a peculiarly *writer's* font of in-
spiration. Peter's glance at the beech tree, the tree that he had
earlier seen as 'the first and only goddess' (172), has creative
significance. As Graves explains (on the same page from which
Cocklebuster's alphabet speech had been derived), in the roots of
European languages '"Beech" is a common synonym for "litera-
ture"'. This connection between trees and writing is repeated,
again 'innocently', when Peter recalls his 'poaching adventure in
boyhood and how to him it had seemed that the leafless branches
wrote upon the air' (178). When Cocklebuster makes his remark
about the tree alphabet, therefore, he is following on from much
more delicate echoes. Even if the reader is not familiar with
Graves's book, these establish an intimate connection between
myth, language, and real feeling.

This type of allusion continues with Russell's *History of
Western Philosophy*. Gunn's use of Russell is almost as direct as his
use of Graves. Russell: 'The Bacchic ritual produced what was
called "enthusiasm", which means, etymologically, having the god
enter into the worshipper, who believed that he became one with
the god.'[20] Gunn: '"Enthusiasm" was the old word of the Bacchic
ritual, and the word meant having the god inside, so that the
worshipper became one with the god' (229). Though specific
significance arises from Gunn's placing of his re-arranged allu-

sions (here, 'enthusiasm' is captured, like elsewhere, 'primal sub-
stance', for Gunn's special version of hedonism), general obser-
vations can be made as well. Firstly, Peter, as a professor in ancient
history, is supposed to think in terms of the early myths and
philosophers. Secondly, this layering of what is accepted as light
scholarly commentary upon everyday happenings both legiti-
mises and seeks to explain, or at least re-express, the spiritual
'truths' Peter is discovering. Gunn ultimately is not anti-intellec-
tual in his outlook. To paraphrase Peter, in Gunn conjecture is
always permissible.

The effect of this episodic structure is to make the book in
schematic terms a string of pearls. In *The Well at the World's End*,
the necklace is fastened when Peter nears the point from which he
started. Peter knows that he is now in the region where he had
earlier encountered 'the wild man'. A ghillie who had been made
unemployed some years ago, Peter MacKay had taking to living
rough rather than leave Caithness or live on the dole there. The
professor had had a moment of intense terror when he met him at
the edge of a deep gully. The two Peters are physically alike and
the silent meeting had been 'beyond even the nightmare' (37).
MacKay had left before a word could be spoken. So strong is the
feeling of an almost supernatural occurrence having taken place,
that Peter questions his own faculties. Was the man his own
'doppel-ganger [...] from another plane'? (38). It is only later that
Peter hears his namesake's personal history, but already the idea
of a kind of alternative Peter had been laid. Back within the wild
man's usual territory, Peter hopes to meet his mysterious double.

> In a few moments he could see the meeting taking place. He
> knew how to behave. He had, as it were, the trick of it.
>
> And a very simple trick it was. All he had to do was to
> forget himself. Immediately the ego with its demands was
> forgotten, everything was alive naturally in its own place,
> everything was given its own place, nothing intruded any
> more than the wind upon the heath. Yet the wind came upon
> the heath.
>
> He smiled, for the trick was a cunning and delightful one.
> As he had proved, once you pushed through the boundaries
> of personal importance things opened out; a wider range of
> freedom, an ampler air; the sky was the limit. As bargains
> went it was jam for no money. (263)

Peter seems a little too pleased with himself, a little too compla-
cent of success. Though he has described losing 'personal impor-
tance', it appears that he is doing so to exploit the wild man. In
other words, Peter's 'trick' fails in forgetting self, because its
intention is self-gratification. He soon realises this.

> For in this trading account it is equally blessed to give and to
> receive. Giving and receiving are aspects of the same thing; as
> time and space are aspects of the one time-space continuum,
> according to the latest mode of scientific deliverance.
>
> By blessing the community you bless yourself.
>
> Conversely, by destroying the community you destroy
> yourself.
>
> Results may take a little time to come in, but they come in,
> one way or the other. This trading account never fails to
> balance. (264)

Though this is another example of Gunn wishing to integrate the
findings of modern science with a spiritual sensibility, this moral
balance of payments which seems to have left its narrow self-
interest behind clearly derives from New Testament teaching:
'…remember the words of the Lord Jesus, how he said it is more
blessed to give than to receive.' (Acts, 20: 35). In the Gospels,
however, Christ stresses more of an equilibrium:

> […] go rather to the lost sheep of the house of Israel.
>
> And as ye go, preach, saying, The kingdom of heaven is at
> hand.
>
> Heal the sick, cleanse the lepers, raise the dead, cast out
> devils: freely ye have received, freely give. (Matthew 10: 6-8).

Gunn's Christian echo also anticipates what proves Peter's literal
downfall. Soon after his discursive essay on the act of blesssing, he
comes across a lamp stranded on a precipice a good distance down
the cliff on which he is standing. His first impulse is just to leave it
and so avoid what looks a near impossible clamber down the
perpendicular, but his habit of seeing symbolically intervenes. The
lamb is *the lamb:* 'that slight emphasis on *the lamb,* the tincture of
blasphemy in the irony, was just a bit too much' (268). In a self-
critical sense, he knows his own mind. He decides that the lamb,
just possibly, can be saved, and he descends down the cliff. The
lamb becomes over-excited and seems about to jump off the edge.
Peter lunges to save it and both fall out and down…

Waking up, he gradually realises that the sticky mess beneath him is the little sheep, and though he is partially paralysed, he sees that the lamb, cushioning his fall, had died that he might be saved. This is both black comedy and a reminder that even Peter's moral schema of things admits both the blood and the rose of human existence. With Peter now only able to crawl, the comic levity of the book seems to have vanished, and the possibility of death seems very real. What had earlier been a philosophical celebration of the easy-going frame of mind – 'The only real appointment man had was with death. That would come soon enough' (263) – now seems to have been prophecy. Peter makes his painful way to a cave in the cliff-face, and realises that the cave is one used by the wild man: there is a blanket and a rough bed. He sleeps there and during the night wakes to an awareness that another man is in the cave. The man makes no response to his greeting, however, and Peter wonders if it is a ghost. Recovering a little strength and the use of his legs, he decides that his first impulse, to wait for the wild man to come and save him, could be fatal. He leaves the cave, and is saved from starvation by the penultimate 'well': the milk from the udders of the lamb's mother, which Peter manages to subdue.

Making his painful way towards Fand's rendezvous point, Peter encounters the last twist of all. At the point where he had first met the wild man he sees a man in tweeds, but instead of approaching, the man retreats with a frightened gait. This seems to be the end of all hope. Why had the man made such a hasty escape? Peter realises that his resemblance to the wild man is stronger now that he is dishevelled and unshaven, but why should a local hillman be afraid of a harmless recluse? With fabulous providence, a crumpled newspaper on the moorland tells the story: the wild man has just died. That he had been in some sense Peter's doppelganger is brought out by the similarities between the wild man's death and his own. Both Peters had fallen from a cliff, and both had crawled to the cave. Peter Mackay, however, had not survived. He had been discovered, presumably only just before the professor's accident, by a shepherd looking for the two sheep. The hillman had clearly seen the man's ghost in the professor.

This closeness to death, both in Peter's physical state and in his haunting connection with his namesake, gives the novel both a late dramatic tension to be solved – will Peter survive? – and an intimation of the otherness which until now has been more to do with a celebration of life than a contemplation of death. 'An intuition of the state of death came very close to Peter now. From the wild man a shadow touched him.' (288). Gunn seems to be reminding the reader of the hard-headed implications of that earlier ethical and spiritual 'trading account'. Peter and Peter are now on either side of the scales, but the complexity of 'spiritual economics' by no means obviates the professor's death. Like the time-space continuum of which Gunn is so fond, life and death may be part of the same thing. If so, Providence works itself out with a higher logic beyond understanding, though possibly within the scope of glancing intuition. Anticipating the metaphysical speculation of *The Other Landscape*, therefore, Gunn places the delights of his book, occasionally seen as sentimentalisations, against an acceptance of life's very real severities.

He does not kill off his gentle hero, however. Fand, who has been concerned over his now over-long absence has been out looking for him. Stripped of the false wish for 'the lure of transcendence' (294), Peter finds the 'ultimate vision' (292) to be Fand herself, and then Fand finds him. She is the 'springing fountain, and was crystal as the well from which a man could drink and be strengthened' (292). In other words, Peter's quest for self has been a quest whose prize has been the refutation of such purposeful questing, however light-hearted. To enrich our relations with each other – this is the most important quest. Man's egotism is humbled before a woman when the last chapter delivers Peter, literally on his knees, into the sanctuary of the last well: Fand, herself. With a modest, but fabulous, cup of milk, 'She had control' (295). As self-possessed as ever, Fand receives and saves her foolish husband who, in these final moments before reunion, has become a little less foolish.

10

A New Commandment

Bloodhunt and *The Other Landscape*

Bloodhunt (1952), is generally acknowledged to be among the most dramatically honed of Gunn's novels. A precis of the plot reveals that, once again, we are on the margins of an established popular genre. This time it is the suspense thriller. A young man, Allan, has murdered the seducer of his ex-girlfriend, Liz Murison, who is pregnant by the victim, Robert. Nicol Menzies, Robert's brother, is also the local policeman and the novel opens with his bursting in on an elderly crofter suspected of harbouring the murderer (if unintentionally). Sandy, a retired sailor, had been friends with Allan a few years ago when several of the local boys had helped with farmwork, using the croft as a base for poaching as well. Instinctively, Sandy tries to delay Nicol in his thorough search, and he succeeds in protecting Allan who is indeed taking refuge on his property.

There are three main movements in *Bloodhunt*, each taking up about a third of the book. The first establishes the book's tense atmosphere: Nicol's methodical investigation and the suspicion that the croft and its immediate surroundings are being constantly watched, Allan's precarious survival in the open, and the secret help he receives from Sandy. The second movement begins when Allan's young brother comes to Sandy's croft with stolen money from a recent church bazaar. The boy hopes to find his brother there, and so help him to make a safe getaway. This actually begins a largely comic section. Sandy contrives to secretly replace the money when he visits the minister, Mr Davidson. He is caught at the last minute, however, and so confesses in such a way that Mr Davidson is moved to protect the boy. We learn later that word has it that the lost money had been found in the minister's lavatory, a joke that propagates others. Soon after, Sandy has his shoulder dislocated by his frisky cow, and this introduces the main comic predicament. Confined to bed and descended on by the rather too neighbourly Widow Macleay (who is rumoured to have matrimonial intentions), Sandy is beleaguered by kindness and a lively tongue. Allan is due to visit the house that night, but, even when Sandy has managed to say goodbye to Widow Macleay, the visiting doctor compels him to take sleeping pills.

In the end, Allan doesn't arrive. Sandy is all set to expect him the following night when Liz turns up. This begins the final movement which belongs to the mother-to-be. Sandy reluctantly accepts her into his household and manages to help Allan without the two meeting. He even tempers Mr Davidson's holier-than-thou condemnation of Liz. Her straightforwardness and her vulnerability impress him. Allan seems to have escaped for good, and for a moment all is as well as it could be. The odd little 'family' is workable:

> There was something soft in Liz that touched the heart. That was the truth of the matter. And if he had helped Allan on his way there was no reason why he shouldn't help Liz on hers. Indeed it would give him considerable satisfaction. And the woman who would know just what to do for her in her trouble, where to put her or send her or what not, would be the widow. (210)

But all is not well. Allan appears before Liz in the barn and the shock precipitates her labour. Though Sandy copes with this, it is clear that Allan is very close to being captured. Nicol, now almost psychopathic, catches up with him on the moors and kills him. Sandy is only in time to conceal the body. The novel ends with his deciding to say nothing: he goes back to Liz who he finds singing to her baby. His priority now is to look after them.

Hart and Pick have called his plot 'the most classical of all his novels'.[1] *Bloodhunt* has affinities with Greek drama, in its theme, tripartite structure and tight plot. The issue of justice, divine and man-made, and Aeschylus' conclusion of mercy in the bloodhunt of *The Oresteia*, even its symbolic female singing at its close, have their parallel here. But it is to Euripides that Gunn seems more attracted, his interest kindled perhaps by Russell's *History of Western Philosophy* where Euripides is quoted extensively. Alive to the ways of intra-family conflict, Sandy realises that Nicol's search for vengeance has an out-of-the-ordinary motivation behind it. This is confirmed later when he learns that Robert had

been his mother's favourite and, moreover, that Nicol's going into
the police force had been against her will. These circumstances
have made Nicol's hunt a dark opportunity to prove himself.
Sandy recalls *Medea* when he senses that Nicol's mother has been
exerting especial pressure on him to find Robert's murderer.

> Into his wonder about Nicol's mother came the perform-
> ance of an old Greek play in Buenos Aires. Two or three of
> the crew had gone, and though the play had looked high-
> brow and the whole affair a bit posh, still the company was
> English and they would see a bit of stuff from home. The girl
> who had played the part of Media had let herself go. Terrific.
> Sandy himself had felt uncomfortable, and when his mates,
> afterwards, turned on him and jeered at him for having
> inveigled them into going to the show, he had defended
> himself by saying that at least they had seen what a woman
> could do in the way of murder and slaughter when the lid
> was off. The talk after that! The confessions! (38)

The reference to *Medea* avoids Sandy's seeming inappropriately
'highbrow'. Clearly it is only the behavioural aspect in which
Sandy is interested. In the play, Medea murders her rival and her
own children in revenge for the unfaithfulness of her former lover,
Jason. Such a fable seems even more appropriate for Liz than it
does for Nicol. This suggestion surfaces when Sandy thinks at first
that killing her child, Robert's child, might not be beyond her
(175). Gunn has introduced *Medea* as one of the fundamental fa-
bles – 'what a woman could do in the way of murder and slaughter
when the lid was off' (38) – but, since Liz does not kill her baby,
Bloodhunt is a counter-fable. In fact, a number of destructive
myths are presented in the book and finally rejected.

The hunt for the murderer is another of these universal stories
which needs answering. 'Somewhere he [Sandy] had seen that
many famous scientists and poets read detective stories. Now he
knew why. They were after the murderer. They were on the old
blood hunt. The satisfaction of the final kill' (99). For Gunn, the
murder story taps deep – even the learned (MacDiarmid and Eliot
for example) respond to the structure, the myth, of the 'old blood
hunt'. To Sandy, the hunt had moved beyond the individual to the
institution, so that the crisis in which he is immersed is recognised
as one that has parallels in society at large (99).

Can Sandy's contemplative sensibility cope with crisis? 'What an ancient sage has achieved in the way of aphorism did not hold the insistence, the urgency, of a human life wandering in the dark, hiding and hunted. Hunted by other humans, after him like dogs,' (28). Sandy's instincts take over, and he shelters Allan from the sinister policeman. He is, even so, self-protective. Hard-headedly, he does not want to get involved, he feels his graceful winding down to the end of his life has been profoundly interrupted, and as far as possible he avoids incriminating himself in his dealings with Allan. In this way Gunn has produced a character who is utterly unsentimentalised.

The croft, once 'an oasis of grey light in darkness', is now 'a trap with the jaws flattened out and covered over' (28). 'If Alan came to the front door he [Sandy] was to invite him into the trap' (30). In Sandy's terms the straightforwardness of hunting animals is travestied by the human hunt. Allan's temporary shelter on a crannog, possibly originally built for protection against wolves, highlights the distance between the two types of hunting relationship. Wolves, now long gone, would be 'simple enough' an adversary today (52), but the crannog may not protect Allan from the determined manhunt. For Sandy the animal hunt 'was clean and swift' (96), but this human pursuit is messy and complicated. He would prefer Allan to die of hypothermia than to go to the gallows. The court proceedings would only bring so many others into the net, and would measure out Allan's last days intolerably. Even the eventual outcome – Nicol's anonymously murdering Allan – is to be preferred. The snare with the rabbit in it which Sandy discovers just before he finds Allan's corpse implies the same thing, and as Sandy quickly kills the rabbit, the idea of mercy killing is reiterated.

As Nicol is trapped in his relationship with his mother, so, too, is Liz in her relationship with almost everyone. Almost everywhere, what should be living relationships are disrupted, distorted, or smothered. The first murder has its basis in a lover's misunderstanding and an affair on the rebound. When Sandy remembers the summary execution of his one love, Maria, during the First World War, he is showing that the sort of brutality one normally only associates with war and terrorism exists, at another level, in the personal everyday sphere, too. Medea's story and Liz's story meet in the one story of the broken family, and infanticide seems to hover close. *Bloodhunt* seeks a way out of the net.

Gene Pick suggested to Gunn that the Sandy had been 'infiltrated' by Christian teaching. In his reply Gunn played down the Christian element and cautiously suggested that a more general 'goodness' was at work. Yet he was unhappy even with this.

> [...] this 'infiltration' of goodness belongs to us all and is not of north or south, so there you are. But now the next thing: assuming it could be evoked (for I am placing no value on my effort) would we like it or would we react against it, find it too soft, too kindly; finding it too much of a good thing? I am beginning to wonder. I am beginning to wonder if our talk of wanting this goodness isn't a bit of a fake, a literary gent's nostalgic moment.[2]

Sandy's ongoing debate with the minister establishes the Christian context Gunn had denied. Davidson and Sandy, who is a well-read atheist, exchange biblical quotations and allusions in a banter that has an underlying seriousness. The minister sees the recent murder as part of 'the materialism of the age', and from this he seeks comfort in the existence of the Kirk. '"Spiritual power to be effective needs a vessel, it needs an institution, it needs the Church'" (24). Sandy is numbed by the crime and is not so sententious. But he, too, is disquietened by the problem of appropriate redress. His knowledge that justice is being evaded, 'the violence unpaid for', (69), is not helped by his own complicity. He is actually helping Allan to 'avoid tribal law' (69), his own vision of justice which seems anthropological in a knowledgeable amateurish way, befitting, perhaps, a retired sailor. This issue of moral repayment, the wish that 'In the long run the sum is added up, the balance squared' (172), is a development of the 'trading account [which] never fails to balance' (264) in *The Well at the World's End*. Indeed, the peculiar type of existentialism posited and only finally put into practice on a small scale in the previous book (trying to rescue the lamb) is here incarnate.

In Davidson's company again, Sandy strips Christianity down to tradition and story. It is these, not the Church or any other orthodoxy that are important. '"In profound matters, as I have heard you say, it is often possible to talk only in parables [...]'" (80). Perhaps here, in the novel, the parable mode is the only one available to Gunn for his own purposes. Sandy's reliance on an essential story is paralleled by the author's construction of a new one.

Murder and Liz's pregnancy are prime examples, in Sandy's terms, of the polar myths of Cain and Christ. These, absorbing Sandy's view of tribal elders as well as the story of Medea, re-emerge like the ancient Greeks in Muir's poetry to offer Sandy in the modern world their difficult options.

> As it had been in the beginning so was it here in his croft now. And outside and beyond – the remorseless Nicol was hunting Allan, no longer as a policeman, no more as a keeper of the laws of the tribe, but as one man on the track of another with that hidden in his blood which the tell-tale dream or 'sight' saw as a dead body. The manger and the hay and life's new cry; beyond it, that hunt. Of all the stories man had made only two were immortal: the story of Cain and the story of Christ. (233)

Liz's association with Christian example begins with the minister's visit to the croft. At first he is outraged that Sandy should have encouraged her to stay away from the family who in fact drove her out (her father is 'a worthy man and a deacon in the church' (190)), and he calls her the cause of all the 'Sex and sin and murder' (190). Typical of the 'godless young', her alleged iniquities launch him on an attack against youth in general and, comically, on 'picture houses' in particular. To the likes of her he would 'give them the fear of God' (191). To this Sandy answers: "'Either that or the love of Christ.'" This is where Cain and Christ meet. Because the minister is not a caricature, Sandy's upbraiding is persuasive, as his pleas for Allan's younger brother had been. It is now that the minister remembers, from John 13:34, Christ's plea for compassion:

> 'I bring you this new commandment,' said the minister, and paused, as though somehow words that Sandy had dropped so lightly stole now upon him unawares and troubled him. There was a short silent travail of the spirit, then humbly, yet not too humbly, the minister repeated the most revolutionary saying the world had yet heard: 'I bring you this new commandment: love one another.' (193)

To love one another is revolutionary because it is almost too much to expect from mankind. Almost. Sandy in his small way makes the transition by not initiating a further blood hunt for Nicol and, most importantly, by providing the outcast, Liz, with a permanent home. Her child is delivered by a man who had brought 'many a lamb [...] into the world' (220), and the little boy is placed in a manger. The Christian parallels proclaim a new hope.

What Gunn creates in *Bloodhunt*, then, is a synthesis of opposing stories. Brought into the spiritual equation are the extremes of age, so that as the elderly Sandy contemplates his own death, a death made the more uncomfortably close by the demise of his old neighbour, Murdo, Liz and her infant declare that life still has a grip, and is worth the holding. Allan tenderly and painfully buried, Sandy makes his commitment to life by privately guaranteeing Liz his small fortune, and by pledging, as it were, a kind of surrogate paternity for Liz; an active grand-paternity for the boy. To encourage a broken home (rejecting Liz's 'worthy' father) in this case is to support a new family. This goes against Sandy's previously strong inclination to be left alone, and for this reason as well, like his refusal to turn Nicol in, it is not an easy decision. As he walks back to the croft he hears Liz's lullaby, a song which resonates all the way back to his own childhood. Here then, despite the fragmentation and violence of what has gone before, is a restorative continuity. The new commandment seems worth striving for.

On the face of it, *The Other Landscape* (published 1954) is utterly different from all the preceding novels and in particular *Bloodhunt*. The most immediate distinction is the use throughout of first-person narrative, a technique Gunn had used only once before, in *The Shadow*, and then only for the first part of the book. The challenges raised by Nan's telling of her own story are magnified here by Walter Urquhart who, though not suffering a breakdown, can be a deceptive guide. The novel is Gunn's most self-consciously 'literary' work. The first-person, as one might expect, immediately sets up a special barrier between the reader and 'what actually happened', and the initiating factor in the book is actually an intriguing short story. The occasionally hostile reception of Gunn's own work, and the jabs in the book at metropolitan critics, have supplied an irresistible parallel for some commentators, and Hart has called it 'the parodic self-allegory of an author having his final joke at London's expense.'[3]

In some sense, then, *The Other Landscape* belongs to those novels concerned with textuality and point of view (*The Private*

Memoirs and Confessions of a Justified Sinner, Wuthering Heights, The Turn of the Screw), and with artists, art and their exploitation (*The Aspern Papers, Humboldt's Gift*). These connections mark a very clear division between *The Other Landscape* and its immediate predecessor, and that the novel features so many characters little associated with northern Scotland contributes further to the relative singularity of the book. Nevertheless, there is an underlying structure shared by the last two novels, and I will argue that in spite of their technical differences, they are closer in concern than might be thought.

Urquhart, normally an anthropologist, has come up from London to a coastal hamlet in the Highlands. He is investigating the author of a short story, 'The Cliffs', which had been submitted to a journal edited by one of his friends. The editor had recognised it as a work of genius. Urquhart had agreed, and because no address had been supplied had undertaken to find the apparent author, Douglas Menzies, and to check if indeed it was Menzies' work. Urquhart soon learns that Menzies is the author, but that he is first and foremost a composer. When they meet, Menzies feels the irony of being recognised for what had been only an artistic diversion. The narrator is shocked when he learns that Menzies' wife, Annabel, had died following circumstances very similar to those described in the story: that he should have been so callous as to use personal tragedy and for a pecuniary purpose. His shock deepens, though, when Menzies tells him that the story has been written before Annabel's death. This epitomises the concept of 'recurrence' in the book (perhaps a development of Gunn's sustained interest in second sight).

Menzies has been a recluse ever since Annabel's death, but Urquhart manages to gather information about him from neighbours and later from contacts in London. Once a rising composer, he had moved back to Scotland with Annabel after she had had a miscarriage. Annabel had managed to support Menzies as he worked on a new symphony but had died in childbirth while he had been trying to help the crew of a ship going down off the point. The child had died too. Now suspected of drinking himself into an early grave, especially by one hotel lodger, Major Thornybank, Menzies has not been seen by the locals for weeks. Urquhart's visits are therefore rather special. Gradually, the narrator realises that Menzies is trying to come to terms with his wife's death by using an intense form of metaphysical speculation whose discoveries seem ultimately to be beyond expression. With each visit Menzies seems less ironic and hostile towards Urquhart, though not less enigmatic. When another storm blows up Menzies saves the lives of two men at sea, and it appears that the tag of suicidal recluse has been ill-judged.

As a gesture of thanks, the locals suggest that Urquhart take some whisky to him. Though accidentally dropping the bottle, Urquhart does go along and it is then that their last conversation takes place. In the early hours of morning, the composer notices there is no alcohol left in the house. He sets off down the nearby cliff-face at the bottom of which is a concealed barrel of rum, providential flotsam which Menzies has been partaking of for some time. He slips and falls to his death. When Urquhart gets down to him he finds the expression on the corpse's face characteristic of 'having heard the struck note and knowing what the note meant' (314).

The foregoing has been a serious distortion of *The Other Landscape*, yet it is the scenario which has formed the focus of critical commentary to date. It ignores the whole of the last chapter, which reveals Urquhart's marriage to a hotel servant and their subsequent child, and it ignores most of the intimations leading up to what is rather more than a coda. There is a fine analogy here with the difference between the popular remembrance of *Wuthering Heights* and what Brontë actually writes. The story of Heathcliff and Cathy is the one that generally comes to mind, and, like the love story of Annabel and Menzies, this does seem to be the passionate focus. But following Cathy's death a good deal of *Wuthering Heights* is devoted to the second Catherine, and especially her relationship with Hareton, the two rising above the twisted, petulant, intense, infantile behaviour of their elders. Similarly, Urquhart and Catherine are the second chance, succeeding where Annabel and Menzies had tragically failed. Unfortunately, modest successes seem to be intrinsically less interesting than catastrophes, but this should not mean we ignore such phenomena as we read.

The motif that brings all the main characters together is music, When Urquhart's editor-friend describes 'The Cliffs' as 'in the nature of an overture' (12), Urquhart agrees: 'In fact I got haunted by a sort of mad music. Cliffs and storms and the almighty

Wrecker.' This introduces the first and most obvious aspect of the
novel's association with music: Menzies. It also begins what is to
be a series of shocks and repetitions, almost as if they, too, were
part of the musical theme resonating throughout the whole novel.
In chronological order (which is not the order of their appearance)
these include: Menzies' soundtrack for a film in which there is a
wreck at sea; Menzies' *Cliff Symphony*; the short story derived
from the symphony and posted just before Annabel's death (on
the night a ship went down just off the shore); and Menzies' own
death after rescuing two men from their wrecked boat, and after
playing the symphony Urquhart regards as his masterpiece.

Menzies' modern music draws on the folk themes he had heard
Annabel singing. In this way, as in earlier novels, forward-looking
art is presented with a solid basis in tradition and locale. Annabel's
music has a further relevance to Menzies' symphony because to
Urquhart her songs derived their very rhythm from the elements,
especially the sea and the wind, so that the symphony in some way
has an extraordinarily close affinity with its subject matter. This
relation between music and environment reaches its haunting
climax when Urquhart approaches Menzies' house for the last
time and can almost hear music on the wind. His idiomatic nar-
rative contributes to what at first seems an illusion.

> [...] The cliffs had all their stops out. The boom, the thunder
> and the depth. A primordial performance with the wind
> tossing the overtones into space [...]
>
>   As I gathered myself and my wits I became the prey of a
> delusion that hit my back like a cold sheet. The cliffs in the
> freedom of their night had gone a stage beyond their wild
> uproar and were now producing a fantastic but coherent
> symphony of sound. I heard it, lost the theme and heard it
> again. I stalked the unblinded window – and saw Douglas
> Menzies at the piano. (295–6)

If Urquhart is 'prey' he is also one who 'stalks': his identity and
role seem as transformational and unstable as the dissolving line in
the book between art and nature. To 'pull all the stops out' is a
phrase which derives from organ playing (in such a way as to give
maximum resonance). Mention of 'performance' and 'overtones'
consolidates this musical metaphor, as a metaphor only, until it
emerges, instead, as the reality of 'Menzies at the piano.' As
Menzies' tragic personal life and work testify this type of interplay

is of the novel's essence.

Another importance example of this occurs when Urquhart and Menzies are in a boat:

> [...] The sea moved under us and we were suspended. The three words he let fall irradiated that seascape with so profound a humour that they matched it. 'The slow movement.' If I say the moment was translated in some divine way I can only appear to exaggerate. I did not look round at him. I could not even be quite certain that he meant the slow movement of his own symphony. [...] (226–7)

This 'matching' of phrase with sea, and (by implication) music with sea, has a charge of significance in itself, but it is also a yardstick for Menzies' apparent understanding of 'the other land-scape', the metaphysical dimension towards which his thoughts seem now to be directed. When Urquhart talks to him about this it is clear that Menzies can only attempt explanation in symbols, symbols which bear the same relation to 'the other landscape' as his ultimately inadequate music, despite its emotional richness, bears towards the sea-scape (itself unpredictable, ineffable; in its moods, infinite). Because Menzies' other landscape can only be approached by symbols, themselves always on the verge of rede-fining and decomposing themselves, this supernatural world re-mains a mystery to Urquhart and therefore to us all. Menzies' death at the foot of the cliffs, at the changing interface between land and sea, ends any hope of understanding the extra-world which Menzies only in death has, apparently, entered fully. In-creasingly Urquhart realises the unsettled nature of his own insights. 'Extraordinary how this sudden shift in "certainties" had been happening to me ever since I had come to Dalaskir. Always dead sure I knew what was what ... then in a moment it wasn't that at all. An invisible hand shakes the kaleidoscope and the scene is startlingly new' (257).

Because of a misreading of the enigmatic nature of Menzies and his ideas, *The Other Landscape* is sometimes regarded as a pre-tentiously philosophical book, positing an unconvincing philo-sophical system. McCulloch's objections to the disconcerting na-ture of the first-person narrative and the reported 'incoherence' of Menzies' talk[4] miss the point entirely. What *The Other Landscape* presents, in an unphilosophical way, is both the possible close-ness, and the ultimate disjunction, between language and meaning.

In anticipation of certain literary critics who allege that we exist solely as language-tuna in a sea of discourse, this novel presents situations where language simply cannot keep track of meaning: 'we do experience in certain reaches of the spirit what we cannot communicate' (296). All this makes for an an extremely slippery text, one which, like Menzies, should be approached with friendly caution.

In counterpoint to Menzies, there is the bullish prickly atheist Major Thornybank, a retired diplomat staying at the local hotel, whom Urquhart also engages in conversation. Music contributes to signifying what type of person he is, too. Their discussion of Fitzgerald's translation of the *Rubaiyat* works round to the phrase 'the beating of a distant drum' (20). When the Major asks if Urquhart has ever literally heard such a thing, the narrator does not reply. The implication is that for all Urquhart's expertise as an anthropologist, the Major still knows a thing or two from real experience. Urquhart is nonplussed. At an artistic level this introduces the drum as the instrument with which the Major is to be associated. 'Hell's drums!' he exclaims when he burns his fingers on a match (21). Though later he accuses Menzies of 'going to hell his own way' (94) and, indeed, Menzies' house and dog finish their days in an inferno complete with the smell of brimstone (310, 315), the Major has the whiff of the Bad Place about him, too.

In conversation, the Major admits he is an atheist. Urquhart says that certainly this 'makes things tidier', and supposes that though such a trait has 'a Roman dignity' it also had psychologically hellish consequences – '"So we come back to hell all roads"' (198). The Major takes up the challenge:

> If the Major flouted the Roman dignity that was in him, it found itself now and then in the orotund phrase. 'A Daniel come to judgement,' and his mocking interest crawled like the worm.
>
> 'In profound moments it is difficult to get away from the literary. We go in hearing the beating of that drum.'
>
> 'Boom! boom!' said the Major in unexpected but expressive criticism. I was glad to be able to smile again.
>
> 'That's all,' said the Major. 'Boom! boom!'
>
> Laughter shook me in an empty place. 'Ta-ra-ra-boom-di-ay,' I agreed.

'Hell's back roads,' said the Major.

'And heaven's back teeth.' (198–9)

This verbal playfulness – the translation of Persian poetry, musical hall repartee and song, Scripture, and fragments of aphorism – is another example of the Gunn's cunning use of turns of phrase, dwelt upon and transformed later on in the text. The hell parallel is taken up when Urquhart's initial wish that the Major's room 'might go up in flames' (27) comes true. The Major accidentally sets himself and his room alight, a 'belching fiery hell' (207); it is a comic scene, and he survives with little more a light sauté and the explosion of a fire-hose in his direction. That this inferno is placed in comparison with the one which consumes Menzies' house points, I think, to the inadequacy of both self-isolating modes of being, even though Menzies appears to have been on the brink of rising above his seclusion.

The Major's 'Roman dignity' and his drum-beat recur, transfigured, when Urquhart rows a boat out to sea and looks back to the shore.

> [...] Far as my eye could travel not a soul moved. Not even the dotted sheep and three if not four cows. Peace. Tearing across this scene of primeval good will and summer sleep came a motor car from the gap in the mountains like a large black beetle stung fiercely behind. Toward what end?
>
> How people rushed on for nothing, to miss the tide at the end of it most likely, not the mention the ferry boat that plied to the Land of Heart's Desire.
>
> My perilous reflections were answered by the sea at the south end of the island with a faint: Boom! boom! I lay on my oars listening. It would not come again, and then it came from inside the high dark rock structure: Boom! boom! A jut of cliff above me was like a Roman jaw. (221)

The Major's Roman dignity and his bang of the drum have 'become' the sinister cliffs, the ironic 'answer' to modern civilisation hurtling toward the edge. Once again, Urquhart finds the landscape 'reiterating' what has affected him in his various human encounters. This is yet another factor in the destabilisation of the text. Clichés become heavy with meaning to the extent that the book seems at times on the edge of announcing itself as the intricately sculpted work of art that it is; yet it holds back as 'plain speaking', too. In a way the sheer cross-referential density of *The*

Other Landscape, (the Land of Heart's Desire, for example, also refers back to further significant events), the book's consciousness of itself, makes it Gunn's most complex work. As John Burns has shown, the philosophical aspect is worthy of attention, even if it is not to be found in Menzies' speech as such,[5] but its complexity is not in its philosophy, it is in its art.

Urquhart's relationship with Catherine, Lachlan's daughter, is of more importance, I think, than has generally been recognised. While not studying at Glasgow University Catherine works as a chambermaid at the hotel, and it is in this capacity that Urquhart encounters her:

> I paused as I heard a girl's voice humming in that mindless or unconscious way that is, in a moment, so intimate. And it was one of the old sea melodies or seal songs, it seemed to me, that had affected me that morning. Actually it wasn't, as I later found out, but for the moment I was swept into that region. Though 'swept' is quite the wrong verb: I simply was there, still as a tree in a landscape. This kind of 'translation', if I may use the word, gives me at least more insight into the meaning of 'magic', in my professional sense, than any amount of effort at intellectual apprehension. It was a very old Gaelic air; it went back so far that it was timeless or had transfixed time; it had words and these words told a story of human tragedy; yet that tragedy had been so winnowed by the generations that it could be sung, hummed, as a lullaby to a child. I know of no essentialising process more profound than this. (54)

Urquhart's analysis of the tune is rhapsodic, but, like his first vision of Catherine, it is also far more than romanticisation. Importantly, he sees that Catherine's music is transcending its own subject matter, which is tragic. This faculty is of the essence of *The Other Landscape*, since it anticipates the last chapter's reaching beyond Menzies' lamentable life and death. To come out of tragedy into a lullaby, the very thing that Liz Murison and Sandy do in the final page of *Bloodhunt*, is metaphorically what Catherine and Urquhart do when they come back to Dalaskir with their little boy. This is the important similarity between the last two novels: that after taking his readers into human devastation Gunn presents, with pain and respect, hope.

After a conversation in which the Major discusses Catherine's background, Urquhart realises what is happening. There was 'not much use in disguising any longer the fact that this vague state of wonder had been induced when Catherine had been mentioned' (130). He sees, too, that with her singing, her education, Catherine has a likeness to Annabel: 'they met in that mutual place behind the events of the world where life is a joy.' In short, Catherine 'was starting off on the same path as Annabel … (131). When this seems clear, however, Urquhart shrinks from the comparison, and rationalises the similarity as typical of hundreds of Highland women. The idea of 'recurrence', even the odd shipwreck recurrences which surround Douglas Menzies, are refuted as eminently possible events. This, though, proves unsatisfactory, too. He realises that his attempts at explanation were actually a way of extricating Catherine from any association with Annabel (132). Bad dreams and fear follow in Urquhart's disturbed night, but when he wakes he listens 'with a sort of greed' for Catherine (135). That day he tries unsuccessfully to pay Menzies' rent for him, and in the evening he manages to talk to Catherine about what has now become a matter of some urgency. In his conversation he reaches new heights of awkwardness, especially as she seems to use the gift of remaining silent to urge him on into further embarrassment. His consciousness of this makes Menzies peripheral: it is his relationship to Catherine that has become important, and Menzies has fast become a mere way of introduction. It is during this talk that he learns the name of the song he had earlier heard her humming. It is 'Land of Heart's Desire' (150), a title which startles him (and us) because it is the phrase Menzies had used when describing the short story, 'The Cliffs'. The two lovers in the story had been 'coming back to the land of their hearts' desires' (151). As we have seen, Urquhart also uses the phrase in his ironic passage about the car beetling towards the edge of the 'Major-like' cliff. When he coaxes Catherine into singing the song he is euphoric, and it is here that the love element introduces itself as that which may go beyond Menzies' tragedy: 'Menzies affected me no more than the man in the moon' (152).

Catherine closes Menzies' last living chapter. Urquhart, at the foot of the cliff with Menzies' corpse, thinks of Annabel in 'The Cliffs', looking down on the fictional body on the rocks. After the landlord appears at the top of the cliff, Urquhart sees Catherine's face looking down – another of those tingling 'recurrences', and another uncanny parallel between the two women. Finally back on firmer ground, Urquhart walks toward Catherine to explain, and the penultimate chapter is finished. The last chapter, which brings the reader 'up to date' with the narrator, describes his return to Dalaskir some three years later. The atmosphere is of both hope and serenity. Things are improving in the Highlands in general with the oncoming of hydro-electric power, the boat that has been wrecked in the terrible storm has been replaced with a new one, and, most importantly, where Annabel's pregnancies had each been a story of death, here is Mrs Catherine Urquhart with a little boy. The landscape is radiant.

The last chapter returns the reader from Menzies' ineffable speculations to a celebration of ordinary happinesses. The matter of fact has become fabulous, the human condition has become the stuff of marvel. This is very close to the perspective Sandy attains at the close of *Bloodhunt* when he transfers his commitment away from the implications of Allan's death and towards the new life for Liz and her child. Menzies' expressed ideas, vaguer in Urquhart's memory even than they were originally, cease to have the importance that they had when compared with the challenge to survive and make a life for oneself.

By remembering and respecting Annabel and Menzies, and also by being themselves, Catherine and Urquhart show that it is love, that which had been so diverting to Urquhart throughout most of the book, it is love, in *Bloodhunt* the subject of Christ's new commandment, it is love that must rise from and transform humankind's suffering. Ultimately, Gunn's vision is as matter-of-fact and fabulous as that.

Conclusion

Gunn's first novels arise in part from the three-fold intersection of a nationalist aspiration, a critique and revision of Celtic Twilight values, and a personal anger with northern Scottish enervation. In artistic terms, *Morning Tide* marks a triumph over these problems. An understanding of the distortions of the whole carpet-bag of Unionist, elitist, centralist history-making underlies his history novels of the early 1930s, and in *Butcher's Broom* there is a major anticipation of the now established social-history perspective of Scottish historiography.

A wide spectrum of modernist writers, including Joyce, Proust, Eliot and MacDiarmid, were important to Gunn. Eliot and MacDiarmid in particular paid special attention to Gunn, and that attention was reciprocated in his work. But he was also very much a product of late Victorian sensibilities, and his fondness for the poetry of this era surfaces throughout the *oeuvre*. Rising above the intellectualising of some of the later 1930s novels, *The Silver Darlings* incorporates personal historical research with folklore and myth in a rich, highly readable narrative. It is not only a highpoint in Gunn's work, it is also representative of his integrating technique and vision, and expresses his realistic optimism.

Gunn's reaction to the Second World War was complicated by his friendship with Germans and by his almost overshadowing horror of Stalinism. H. G. Wells's dream of a world state had been long feared and often criticised by Gunn, and now that the dark dream seemed nearing reality his skills as a novelist were put to their greatest political test. In *The Green Isle of the Great Deep* he produced a dystopian novel of the stature of *1984*, of which it is a forbear. The novels from the later 1940s onwards, though arguably his most various in subject matter, are generally increasingly concerned with human vulnerability in the face of authoritarian control and authoritarian intellect. Technically, these novels are marked out by a literary occupation of different genres of popular fiction. They reach their apotheosis in the tense but deeply moral thriller of 1952. *Bloodhunt*. His last novel, *The Other Landscape*, is a technical masterpiece in its layered use of first-person narrative, and is a paean to spiritual love.

Given his achievements, why is Gunn insufficiently appreciated in his own country, and generally unheard of elsewhere? There is every reason now for Gunn's work, his importance to literature and to Scotland, to be celebrated for its intelligence, compassion, and life-affirming qualities. In a letter to Francis Hart, Gunn wrote one of his very last sentences: 'Dear me, that I should have to be silent.' Today it is as vital as ever for Gunn to be heard, and to be understood.

References

Where possible, I have quoted from the editions of Gunn's work that are currently in print. These, along with details of the originals, are listed in the Bibliography; only page numbers are given in the text. The original is cited when a work is out of print.

Full references to magazine articles are given below. Author and title references to books are expanded in the Bibliography.

The abbreviations used are:

HL   *Neil M. Gunn: a Highland Life*, F. R. Hart & J. B. Pick
SL   *Selected Letters*, ed. J. B. Pick
SM   The Scots Magazine

1: CRAWLING FROM OUT THE HINTERLAND

1 *The Scottish Chapbook* 1: 12 (July 1923), 329.
2 Letter to Gunn, 26.7.23, *The Letters of Hugh MacDiarmid*, 196.
3 Letter to Gunn, 14.10.25, op. cit., 201-202.
4 'Visioning', *Scottish Nation* 1: 12 (July 1923).
5 See 2 above.
6 'The White Hour' was published in *Dublin Magazine* (March 1924), 'The Hat Box' and 'A Tight Corner' in the *Glasgow Herald* (13 and 20 October 1923).
7 Letter to Gunn, 21.1.[25], op. cit., 199-200.
8 'Half-light', *Cornhill Magazine* (November 1925); 'Hidden Doors' originally 'Musical Doors' in *Cornhill Magazine* (March 1927), both collected in *Hidden Doors* (1929).
9 *Hidden Doors*, 53.
10 Ibid., 61
11 Ibid., 63.
12 'From Ioana. To George Meredith', preface to 'The Sin-eater', *The Works of 'Fiona MacLeod'*, vol. 2, p. 5.
13 Ibid.
14 McCulloch, *The Novels of Neil M. Gunn*, 16.
15 'Symbolical', *Hidden Doors*, 82-91
16 Ibid., 85.
17 *SM* 14: 5 (February 1931), 396.
18 'Caithness and Sutherland', in George Scott Moncreiff (ed),

Scottish Country; reprinted in Alistair McCleery (ed), *Landscape and Light*, 27.
19 R. C. Reid, 3.9.26, NLS Dep. 209, Box 21.
20 See Mairi Robinson (ed), *The Concise Scots Dictionary.*
21 Letter to Gunn, 1.11.23, *The Letters of Hugh MacDiarmid*, 197.
22 *HL*, Chapter 4.
23 Gifford, 'Myth, parody and dissociation: Scottish fiction 1814-1914' in Douglas Gifford (ed), *The History of Scottish Literature*, vol. 3, p. 235.
24 Letter to Gunn, 22.3.26, op. cit., 204-06.
25 'Caithness and Sutherland', *Landscape and Light*, 28.
26 Gunn was much affected by Melville's *Moby-Dick*, which forms the nucleus of his short story 'The Black Woollen Gloves' (*SM* 8: 4 (January 1928), 261-8). There the female protagonist reads the 'chapter on whiteness' [Chapter 42] and observes that 'Melville's "incantation of whiteness" seemed the light side of an incantation of darkness.' White occurs elsewhere in Gunn's fiction of this period, usually symbolising the life-power in those compelled to defence at the edge of their being. Turner, the tragic figure in 'Hidden Doors', is possessed by a 'remorseless white light', and Ewan in *The Lost Glen* has 'the final core of integrity that was himself, the white core before which the flesh shivers in exaltation and fear' (43). Gunn described the novel as having a 'white heat' (SL, 15).
27 *To Circumjack Cencrastus, The Complete Poems*, 218.
28 *The Works of 'Fiona MacLeod'*, vol. 2, p. 14.
29 Ibid., 7.
30 Muir, *Scott and Scotland*, 113.
31 MacLeod, *The Winged Destiny*, 165-6.
32 Ibid., 162-3.
33 'The Hidden Heart', *SM*, 9: 5 (August 1928), 335 (under the pseudonym 'Dane M' Neil).
34 Letter to Gunn, 6.2.24, op cit., 198-9.
35 Cairns Craig (ed), *The History of Scottish Literature*, vol. 4, 5.
36 Alexander Carmichael (comp. 0, *Carmina Gadelica*, vol. 1, p. xv.
37 *The Novels of Neil M. Gunn*, 20.
38 'Half-light', *Hidden Doors*, 63.
39 Gifford, *Neil M. Gunn and Lewis Grassic Gibbon*, 27.
40 Carswell, *Open the Door!*, 32-3.

2: TWILIGHT AND NEW MORNING

1 *The Poaching at Grianan, SM* 11: 6 (September 1929) – 13: 2 (May 1930); *The Lost Glen, SM* 9: 1 (April 1928) – 10: 2 (November 1928). See also McCleery, 'The Early Novels of Neil M. Gunn', *The Bibliotheck* 10: 6 (1981), 127-38.

202 *The Fabulous Matter of Fact*

2 *SM* 11: 6 (September 1929), 419.
3 *A Bibliography of the works of Neil M. Gunn*, 21.
4 *SM* 1: 6 (September 1929), 419.
5 Ibid., 424.
6 Ibid., 426.
7 Ibid., 418.
8 Ibid., 425.
9 Ibid., 426.
10 *SM* 12: 1 (October 1929), 26.
11 Ibid., 33.
12 Ibid., 26.
13 Ibid., 419-20.
14 *SM* 12: 2 (November 1929), 130.
15 Ibid.
16 *SM* 13: 1 (April 1930), 65.
17 *SM* 12: 3 (December 1929), 208.
18 Ibid., 209, 210.
19 *SM* 12: 6 (March 1930), 458.
20 *SM 13: 1* (April 1930), 63.
21 *SL* 7.
22 *SM*, April-November 1928.
23 McCleery, 'The Early Novels of Neil M. Gunn', op. cit.
24. Ibid.
25 Munro, *The Lost Pibroch and Other Shieling Stories*.
26 *SM* 9: 4 (July 1928), 294.
27 Wittig, *The Scottish Tradition in Literature*, 270-73.
28 Fred T. Macleod, *The MacCrimmons of Skye* (Edinburgh: Henderson & Hamilton, 1933), 139-54.
29 *SL* (30.11.27), 6.
30 Letter to Gunn [1927], *The Letters of Hugh MacDiarmid*, 212.
31 George Malcolm Thomson, letter to Gunn, 5.12.30, in NLS Dep. 209, Box 20.
32 Henry Patterson, *The Politics of Illusion: Republicanism and Socialism in Modern Ireland* (London: Hutchinson/Radius, 1989), 8.
33 Ibid., 10.
34 Munro, *The Lost Pibroch and Other Shieling Stories*, 20-21.
35 *SM* 9: 1 (April 1928), 23.
36 *SM* 9: 4 (July 1928), 288.
37 McCulloch, *the Novels of Neil M. Gunn*, 28.
38 Ibid.
39 Carswell, *Open the Door!*, 109.
40 The book was originally intended to be published in December, thus the 1930 date in the first edition. See Stokoe, *A Bibliography of the works of Neil M. Gunn*, 25.
41 McCleery, *The Porpoise Press*, 1922-39, 65.
42 Muir, *An Autobiography*, 37.
43 'Hans Carossa' in Butter (ed), *The Truth of Imagination*. 178.

44 Letter to Gunn, 16.2.31, in NLS Dep. 209, Box 17.
45 Letter to Gunn, 30.1.31, in NLS Dep. 209, Box 21.
46 *Glasgow Herald*, 19 June 1926, 4; collected in *Hidden Doors*.
47 See Simpson, Chapter 2 'The Joy of Grief', *The Protean Scot*, 41-69.
48 *HL*, 21.
49 McCulloch, *The Novels of Neil M. Gunn*, 43.
50 Letter to Gunn, 8.6.30, NLS Dep. 209, Box 12.

3: MAKING HISTORY

1 'Newer Scottish Fiction (2)', *Scottish Educational Journal* (2.7.26), collected in *Contemporary Scottish Studies* (1976), 110-11.
2 NLS Dep. 209, Box 1, Notebook 6.
3 Letter to F. R. Hart, 19.3.70, NLS Dep. 209, Box 18.
4 Letter to Gunn, 6.8.35, NLS Dep. 209, Box 17.
5 See James B. Caird, 'Gaelic elements in the works of Neil Gunn', *Studies in Scottish Literature* XV (1980), 88-94.
6 Letter to Gunn, 13.3.30, NLS Dep. 209, Box 20, Folder 8.
7 'The Hidden Heart', *SM* 9: 5 (August 1928), 331-5 (as 'Dane M'Neil'); collected in *Gairfish* (1990), 13-20.
8 'The Caledonian Antisyzgy and the Gaelic Idea', *Selected Essays of Hugh MacDiarmid*, 70.
9 Gunn interviewed in the series 'What Scottish writers must do', *Daily Record and Mail*, 11.6.29.
10 Letter to gunn, 21.11.34, NLS Dep. 209, Box 17.
11 'Lewis Grassic Gibbon', *Left Review* 2: 5 (February 1936), 220-25.
12 'Scotland a Nation', *Left Review* 2: 14 (November 1936), 735-8.
13 'The Hidden Heart', op. cit.
14 Cf. C. G. Jung, *On the Nature of the Psyche*, trans. R. F. C. Hull (Princeton University Press, 1980). This first appeared in English as 'On psychical energy' in *Contributions to Analytical Psychology* (London: Kegan page 1928).
15 Grieve, 'The New Movement in Scottish Historiography: George Pratt Insh' (18.12.25), collected in *Scottish Educational Journal* (1976), 68-70.
16 'The New Community of Iona', *SM* 30: 1 (December 1938), 169-74; collected in *Landscape and light*, 224-7.
17 John Dowden, *The Celtic Church in Scotland* (Society for Promoting Christian Knowledge, 1894), 120.
18 See Alfred P. Smyth, *Warlords and Holy Men* (London: Edward Arnold, 1984), 258.
19 John Mackay, *The Church in the Highlands* (London: Hodder & Stoughton, 1914), 28.

20 Rescanieres, 'Scottish Saga' in Scott and Gifford (eds), *Neil M. Gunn*, 89.
21 Letter to Grieve, 28.5.33, *SL*, 30.
22 McCulloch, *The Novels of Neil M. Gunn*, 46.
23 McCleery, *Landscape and Light*, 4; Burns, *A Celebration of the Light*, 30.
24 Letter to Grieve, 28.5.33, *SL*, 30.
25 Letter from Revd Archibald Scott, 25.10.34, NLS Dep. 209, Box 21.
26 *The Listener*, 14.11.34.
27 *Whisky and Scotland* (1977 edn), 65-9.
28 Pick noted in a letter to me (28.2.90) that Gunn privately thought 'Joyce became increasingly self-indulgent and ended down a cul-de-sac'.
29 Tolstoy, *War and Peace*, trans ??? (London: Dent, 1911), vol. 3, 1-4, 65-9.
30 *Selected Essays of Hugh MacDiarmid*, 67.
31 Daniel Corkery, *The Hidden Ireland: a study of Gaelic Munster in the eighteenth century* (Dublin: M. H. Gill & Son, 1925), x-xi.
32 *A Journey to the Western Islands of Scotland* (Penguin edn), 116.
33 *HL*, 104-05.
34 Letter to Agnes Mure Mackenzie, 7.4.42, *SL*, 166.
35 Review of *Scott and Scotland*, *SM* 26: 1 (October 1936), 72-8; collected in *Landscape and Light*, 123.

4: DIFFERENT SOURCES

1 *HL*, 137.
2 'Rannoch, by Glencoe', *the Complete Poems and Plays of T. S. Eliot* (London: Faber & Faber, 1969), 41. I am grateful to Robert Crawford for informing me that the poem was originally published in the *New English Weekly*, October 1935.
3 Letter to Grieve, 14.11.33, *SL*, 35.
4 See Gunn's letter to George Blake, 28.1.39, NLS Dep. 209, Box 17.
5 Robert Crawford, 'A Drunk Man looks at the Waste Land', *Scottish Literary Journal* 4: 2 (November 1987), 62-77.
6 Letter to Morley, October 1935, NLS Acc. 5412; *HL*, 138-9.
7 Review, *The Listener* (9.6.37), 1164.
8 J. B. Pick, personal letter, 28.2.90.
9 Giford, 'The Source of Joy: *Highland River*', in Scott and Gifford (eds), *Neil M. Gunn*, 119.
10 Saul Below, 'The Distracted Public', lecture delivered in the Sheldonian Theatre, Oxford, 10.5.90.
11 'The Green Linnet', *William Wordsworth*, ed. Stephen Gill (Oxford University Press, 1984), 249.

12 Proust, *Remembrance of Things Past*, trans. C. K. Scott Moncrieff and Terence Kilmartin (Penguin, 1989), vol. 1, 94.

13 See Gifford's fine chapter on *Highland River* in *Neil M. Gunn and Lewis Grasic Gibbon*

14 Ivan Turgenev, *Rudin*, trans. Richard Freeborn (Penguin, 1975), 77.

15 C. J. Jung, *On the Nature of the Psyche* op. cit., 37.

16 See n. 7 above.

17 *On the Nature of the Psyche*, 54.

18 Patrick Crotty, 'From Genesis to Revelation', *Scottish Literary Journal* 15: 2 (November 1988), 5-23.

19 Letter to Gunn, 15.7.32, *The Letters of Hugh MacDiarmid*, 246.

20 McCulloch, *The Novels of Neil M. Gunn*, 81.

21 Burns, *A Celebration of the Light*, 61.

5: CITY WORK AND COUNTRY PLAY

1 *SM* 28: 3 (December 1937), 186-94.

2 Letter to Gunn, 14.5.40, NLS Dep. 209, Box 19.

3 McCulloch, *The Novels of Neil M. Gunn*, 142.

4 'President of Eire: the true value of tradition', *SM* 29: 3 (June 1938), 177-80.

5 *HL*, 170-71.

6 *Journey to the Western Islands*, 112.

7 Ibid.

8 Ibid.

9 *The Listener* (9.6.37), 1164.

10 *HL*, 167.

6: PROGRESS AND PROGRESSION

1 *HL*, 173.

2 Murray and Tait, '*The Silver Darlings*', *Ten Modern Scottish Novels*, 35.

3 Ibid.

4 'Tradition and Magic in the Work of Lewis Grassic Gibbon', *SM* 30: 1 (October 1930), 28-35.

5 *HL*, 96.

6 'New Golden Age for Scots Letters', *Daily Record and Mail* (28.5.30), 5.

7 'The Wonder Story of the Moray Firth', *Anarchy 86* 8: 4 (April 1968), 122-5.

8 Carmichael (comp.), *Carmina Gadelica*, 224.

9 Gifford, 'The *Silver Darlings* and the Song of Life', 131.

10 *HL*, 31-2.

11 Gifford, 'The *Silver Darlings* and the Song of Life', 129.

7: THE WAR AT HOME

1 'Memories of the Months: a balance sheet', *SM* 34: 4 (January 1941), 258-62 (as 'Dane M'Neil').
2 Letter to George Blake, 13.10.43, *SL*, 77.
3 McCulloch, *The Novels of Neil M. Gunn*, 116.
4 *HL*, 194-6.
5 Ibid., and 'Nationalism in Writing III', *SM* 31: 4 (July 1939), 275-82.
6 Arthur Koestler, *Arrival and Departure* (1940; Penguin, 1964), 147.
7 H. G. Wells, *The World of William Clissold* (London: Ernest Benn, 1926), 613.
8 Clifton Fadiman (ed), *I Believe*, reviewed by Gunn in *SM* 34: 1 (October 1940), 51-5.
9 *SM* 15: 3 (June 1931), 185-8.
10 Ibid.
11 Letter to John MacCormick, 4.12.39, *SL*, 59-61.
12 *HL*, 163.
13 Christopher Harvie, 'Labour and Scottish Government, the age of Tom Johnston', *Bulletin of Scottish Politics* 2 (1981), 1-20.
14 *SM* 31: 1 (April 1939), 30-35; *SMT Magazine* 25: 5 (May 1940), 21-3.
15 McCleery, *Landscape and Light*, 13.
16 Notebook, NLS Dep. 209, Box 1, Folder 2.
17 *HL*, 163.
18 'Scotland a Nation', *Left Review* 2: 14 (November 1936), 735-8.
19 *HL*, 183.
20 Edwin Muir, *The Listener* (15.7.43), 78.
21 Joseph Freeman, *An American Testament: a Narrative of Rebels and Romantics* (London: Gollancz, 1938). Margaret MacEwen had lent Gunn the book – see *SL*, 55.
22 *HL*, 40.
23 Smout, *A Century of the Scottish People* 256.
24 Freeman, *An American Testament*, 52.
25 Fyodor Dostoevsky, *The Brothers Karamazov*, trans David Magarshack (Penguin, 1982), 298. Andrew Noble has drawn attention to the Dostoevskian dilemma Gunn confronts in his essay 'Fable of Freedom' in Gifford and Scott (eds), *Neil M. Gunn*, 194-5.
26 Notebook, NLS Dep. 209, Box 1, Folder 2.
27 *HL*. 191-2.
28 Stokoe, *Bibliography*, 49-58.
29 Letter to Douglas Young, 17.7.39, *SL*, 59.
30 *HL*, 126-7.
31 'Memories of the Months...: Land and Sea, Twin Halves of the

Mystery', *SM* 34: 2 (November 1940), 118-22.
32 Noble, 'Fable of freedom', op. cit.
33 'Memories of the Months: a balance sheet', op. cit.
34 Dostoevsky, *The Brothers Karamazov*, 302.
35 Koestler, *Arrival and Departure*, 147.
36 Letter to F. R. Hart, 25.7.61, *SL*, 159.
37 Edwin Muir, *The Listener* (27.7.44), 106.
38 F. R. Hart, *The Scottish Novel*, 362.
39 Letter to Ian Grimble, 5.10.64, *SL*, 203.
40 *HL*, 180-81.
41 Gunn, 'Awakening of a nation', *Daily Record* (13.10.44), 2.
42 Wittig, *The Scottish Tradition in Literature*, 338.
43 Gunn, 'The Novel at Home', *SM* 45: 1 (April 1946), 1-5.
44 J. M. Reid, *Modern Scottish Literature*, 24.

8: THE GOOD SHEPHERD

1 Francis R. Hart, 'Neil Gunn's Drama of Light', in Cairns Craig (ed), *The History of Scottish Literature*, vol. 4, 97.
2 Letter to Nan Shepherd, 7.8.43, *SL*, 75.
3 J. B. Pick, 'A Neglected Major Novel: Neil Gunn's *The Key of the Chest*', *Scottish Literary Journal* 17: 1 (May 1990), 35-45.
4 McCulloch, *The Novels of Neil M. Gunn* 129.
5 'The Man who Came Back', *SM* 8: 6 (March 1928), 419-29; *Back Home* (1932); *Tilleadh Dhachaidh*, produced by Hugh MacPhee for the Scottish Home Service, broadcast 13.3.47.
6 Gifford, 'Myth, Parody and Dissociation: Scottish Fiction 1814-1914' in Gifford (ed), *The History of Scottish Literature*, vol. 3, 223.
7 Francis R. Hart, 'Neil Gunn's Drama of Light', 97.
8 Letter to Ian McKillop, 29.8.46, *SL*, 88.
9 Letter to Naomi Mitchison, 4.2.46, *SL*, 86.
10 'Scotland Moves', *Sm* 39: 6 (September 1943), 447-50; '…And after the war', *Daily Record* (22.8.44), 2; 'Questions for Scots', *Daily Record* (24.11.44), 2; 'Awakening of a Nation', *Daily Record* (27.12.44), 2; 'Scotland isn't a "region"', *Daily Record* (15.1.45), 2; 'Belief in ourselves' *Sm* 43: 6 (September 1945), 424-7.
11 'Belief in ourselves', op. cit.
12 J. A. Symon, *Scottish Farming Past and Present* (Edinburgh: Oliver & Boyd, 1959), 256-7.
13 Ibid., 363.
14 Department of Agriculture for Scotland, *Report of the Committee on Hill Sheep Farming in Scotland*, (Edinburgh: HMSO, 1944) Cmd 6494.

9: GOD'S FOOLS

1 Daisy Gunn posted the manuscript in late November, and Faber had already responded in detail by the 29th: letter to Gene Pick, 24.10.46, *SL*, 90; letter to Geoffrey Faber, 29.10.46, *SL*, 92.

2 'Convalescence', *SM* 42: 1 (October 1944), 1-13. There are slight variations between the two texts, most notably the inclusion in the novel of an explicit admission of the heroine's mental illness.

3 'Snow in March', *SM* 29: 3 (June 1938, 191-9..

4 McCulloch, *The Novels of Neil M. Gunn*, 146, 147.

5 Virginia Woolf, *A Room of One's Own* (1929; London: Grafton, 1989), 7.

6 Letter to F. R. Hart, 27.8.62, *SL*, 169-70.

7 Elaine Showalter, 'Male Hysteria', *The Female Malady, Women Madness and English Culture 1830-1980* (London: Virago, 1987), 167-94.

8 Neil Ascherson, 'Stonehenge and its power struggles', *Games with Shadows* (London: Hutchinson/Radius, 1988), 70.

9 Letter to Geoffrey Faber, January 1948, *SL*, 96.

10 M. H. D'Arbois de Jubainville, *The Irish Mythological Cycle*, trans R. I. Best (Dublin: O'Donoghue, 1903).

11 Letter to Geoffrey Faber, 10.11.48, *SL*, 100-01.

12 *HL*, 215.

13 Burns's *A Celebration of the Light* explores this sensibility in an illuminating way.

14 Ibid., 105-24.

15 *HL*, 243.

16 P. D. Ouspensky, *In Search of the Miraculous: Fragments of an Unknown Teaching* (London: Routledge & Kegan Paul, 1950), 3.

17 Ibid., 39.

18 Ibid., 87.

19 Robert Graves *The White Goddess: a Historical Grammar of Poetic Myth* (London: Faber, 1948), 33, cf. *The Well at the World's End*, 178.

20 Bertrand Russell, *History of Western Philosophy* (London: Allen & Unwin, 1946; 1962), 36.

10: A NEW COMMANDMENT

1 *HL*, 237.

2 See Gunn's letter to Gene Pick, 24.6.52, *SL*, 112.

3 Francis R. Hart, 'Neil Gunn's Drama of Light', op. cit., 101.

4 McCulloch, *The Novels of Neil M. Gunn* 165-8.

5 Burns, *A Celebration of the Light*, 147-67.

Select Bibliography

C. J. L. Stoke *A Bibliography of the Works of Neil M Gunn* is the standard bibliography. The work of many years, it is a vital resource, and at first glance indicates Gunn's range and sheer output. The only articles I have found which are not included there are: 'Scotsman's English', *Pictish Review*. 1: 8 (June 1928) [under the pseudonym 'Nial Guinne']; 'Scotland a Nation,' *Left Review*, 2: 14 (November 1936); 'How the German sees the Scot', *SMT Magazine*, 25: 5 (May 1940) [Collected in McCleery's *Landscape and Light*]: 'Tradition and Violence', *The New Alliance and Scots Review*, 7: 7 (October 1946); and 'Appoint a Psychiatrist' in *The New Alliance and Scots Review*, 8: 10 (February 1948).

The following lists all the non-drama books, as well as selected other works and manuscripts used in this study. Gunn's periodical articles are cited in detail as they appear in the text and are not repeated here.

1 BOOKS BY NEIL M. GUNN

Books are listed in chronological order as they were written not as they were published, as far as this can be ascertained. Where I have used a more recent reprint or edition to help readers' accessibility to Gunn, the recent text is quoted in brackets after the original. Though *The Poaching at Grianan* was never published as a book it is included here as a 'proto-novel'.

The Grey Coast, London: Cape, 1926 (London: Souvenir, 1976). A revised Porpoise edition (Edinburgh) was issued in 1931 with losses and gains in expression, but Souvenir happily reprints the original.
The Poaching at Grianan, serialised *SM*, September 1929-April 1930 [written 1927].
The Lost Glen, serialised *SM*, April-November 1928; rev. - Edinburgh:

Porpoise, 1932 (Glasgow: Richard Drew, 1985). [written late 1927?]
Hidden Doors, Edinburgh: Porpoise, 1929. [Short stories]
Morning Tide, Edinburgh: Porpoise, 1931. (London: Souvenir 1975).
Sun Circle Edinburgh: Porpoise, 1933 (London: Souvenir, 1983).
Butcher's Broom, Edinburgh: Porpoise, 1934 (London: Souvenir 1983).
Whiskey and Scotland, London: Routledge, 1935 (London: Souvenir, 1977). [Essay]
Highland River, Edinburgh: Porpoise, 1937 (London: Arrow, 1960).
Off in a Boat, London: Faber, 1938 (Glasgow: Richard Drew, 1988) [Travel]
Wild Geese Overhead, London: Faber, 1939.
Second Sight, London: Faber, 1940 (Glasgow: Richard Drew, 1986).
The Silver Darlings, London: Faber, 1941 (1969).
The Serpent, London: Faber, 1943 (London: Souvenir, 1978). [written 1941?]
Young Art and Old Hector, London: Faber, 1942 (London: Souvenir, 1976).
Storm and Precipice, London: Faber, 1942. [Anthology of extracts]
The Green Isle of the Great Deep, London: Faber, 1944 (London: Souvenir, 1975).
The Key of the Chest, London: Faber, 1945 (London: Souvenir, 1986).
The Drinking Well, London: Faber, 1946 (London: Souvenir, 1978). [Actually published early 1947]
The Shadow, London: Faber, 1948 (Glasgow: Richard Drew, 1989).
The Silver Bough, London: Faber, 1949 (Glasgow: Richard Drew, 1985).
The Lost Chart, London: Faber, 1949 (Glasgow: Richard Drew, 1987).
Highland Pack, London: Faber, 1949 (Glasgow: Richard Drew, 1989). [Essays]
The White Hour, London: Faber, 1950 (Glasgow: Richard Drew, 1990). [Short stories]
The Well at the World's End, London: Faber, 1951 (London: Souvenir, 1985).
Bloodhunt, London: Faber, 1952 (London: Souvenir, 1984).
The Other Landscape, London: Faber, 1954 (Glasgow: Richard Drew, 1988).
The Atom of Delight, London: Faber, 1956 (Edinburgh: Polygon, 1986). [Philosophy]

2. OTHER WORKS AND MANUSCRIPTS BY GUNN

Back Home: a Play in One Act, Glasgow: Walter Wilson, 1932
National Library of Scotland, Deposit 209 (N. M. Gunn Papers): notebooks, journals, typescripts, correspondence to and by Gunn, poetry, government papers, newspaper cuttings, etc.
Landscape and Light, ed. Alistair McCleery, Aberdeen: Aberdeen University Press, 1987. [Essays]
Selected Letters ed. J. B Pick, Edinburgh: Polygon, 1987.

3. SECONDARY SOURCES AND BACKGROUND MATERIAL

The following lists individual articles not collected elsewhere, collections of essays and books.

Aitken, W. R., 'Neil Gunn's revision of his first novel.' *Bibliotheck*, 6 (1971-2), 114-7

Anson, Peter F., *Fishing Boats and Fisher Folk on the East Coast of Scotland*, London: Dent. 1930

Atlas of British Social and Economic History since c.1700, ed. Rex Pope, London: Routledge, 1989

Barke, James, 'Lewis Grassic Gibbon', *Left Review*, 2: 5 (February 1936)

Blake, George, *The Heart of Scotland*, 3rd edn, London: Batsford, 1951 (first edn 1934)

Bold, Alan, *MacDiarmid: Christopher Murray Grieve: a Critical Biography*, London: John Murray, 1988

Bold, Alan, *Modern Scottish Literature,* London: Longman, 1983

Burns, John, *A Celebration of the Light: Zen in the Novels of Neil Gunn*, Edinburgh: Canongate, 1988

Caird, James B, 'Gaelic Elements in the Works of Neil Gunn'. in *Studies in Scottish Literature*, 15 (1980)

Carmina Gadelica, compiled by Alexander Carmichael, Edinburgh: N. Macleod, 1900 (2 vols)

Carswell, Catherine, *Open the Door!*, London: Virago, 1986 [originally published 1920]

A Celtic Miscellany, ed. Kenneth Hurlstone Jackson, London: Penguin, 1971

The Concise Scots Dictionary, ed Mairi Robinson, Aberdeen: Aberdeen University Press, 1985

Crawford, Barbara E, *Scandinavian Scotland*, Leicester: Leicester University Press, 1987

Dodgshon, Robert A, *Land and Society in Early Scotland*, Oxford: Clarendon Press, 1981

Dunne, J. W, *An Experiment with Time*, 3rd edn, London: Faber, 1934 (first edn 1927)

Eliot, T. S, *The Use of Poetry and the Use of Criticism*, London: Faber, 1987 [originally published 1933]

Essays on Neil M. Gunn, ed. David Morrison, Thurso: Humphries, 1971

European Unity in Context: the Interwar Period, ed. Peter M. R. Stirk, London: Pinter, 1989

Frazer, J. G, *The Golden Bough: a Study in Magic and Religion*, abridged edn, London, Macmillan, 1941, c.1922

Gibbon, Lewis Grassic, *Sunset Song*, London: Hutchinson, 1932
Gibbon, Lewis Grassic, *Cloud Howe*, London: Hutchinson, 1933
Gibbon, Lewis Grassic, *Grey Granite*, London: Hutchinson, 1934
Gifford, Douglas, *Neil M. Gunn & Lewis Grassic Gibbon*, Edinburgh: Oliver & Boyd, 1983
Graeme, Alan, 'The Modern Novelist and the Scottish Highlands: Neil M. Gunn's Accomplishments', *SM* 16: 6 (March 1932)

Hart, Francis Russell, *The Scottish Novel: A Critical Survey*, London: John Murray, 1978
Hart, F. R. and Pick, J. B, *Neil M. Gunn: a Highland Life*, London: John Murray, 1981 (Edinburgh: Polygon, 1985)
Harvie, Christopher, 'Labour and Scottish Governments: the Age of Tom Johnston'. *Bulletin of Scottish Politics*, 2 (1981), 1-20
Harvie, Christopher, *No Gods and Precious Few Heroes: Scotland 1914-1980*, London: Edward Arnold, 1981
Harvie, Christopher, *Scotland and Nationalism: Scottish Society and Politics, 1707-1977*, London: Allen & Unwin, 1977
The History of Scottish Literature, vol 3, 'Nineteenth Century', ed. Douglas Gifford, Aberdeen: Aberdeen University Press, 1988
The History of Scottish Literature, vol 4 'Twentieth Century', ed. Cairns Craig, Aberdeen: Aberdeen University Press, 1987
I Believe, W. H. Auden ... [et al], London: Allen & Unwin, 1940 Johnson, Samuel, *Journey to the Western Islands of Scotland*, London: Penguin, 1984 [originally published 1775

Jukes, H. R, *Loved River*, London: Faber, 1935

Koestler, Arthur, *Darkness at Noon*, London: Penguin, 1964 (originally published 1940)

Lindsay, Maurice, *Francis George Scott and the Scottish Renaissance*, Edinburgh: Paul Harris, 1980

McCleery, Alistair, 'The Genesis of *The Green Isle of the Great Deep'. Studies in Scottish Literature*, vol 22 (1987), 157-72
McCleery, Alistair, 'The Lost Novel of Neil Gunn.' In *The Scottish Literary Journal*, Supplement no 17, Winter 1982
McCleery, Alistair, *The Porpoise Press, 1922-39*, Edinburgh: Merchiston, 1988
Mac Colla, Fionn, *The Albannach*, London: Souvenir, 1984 [originally published 1932]
Mac Colla, Fionn, *And the Cock Crew*, London: Souvenir, 1977 [originally published 1945]
McCulloch, Margery, *The Novels of Neil M. Gunn: a Critical Study*, Edinburgh: Scottish Academic Press, 1987
MacDiarmid, Hugh, *The Complete Poems: 1920-1976*, eds Michael

Grieve and W. R. Aitken, London: Penguin, 1985.

MacDiarmid, Hugh *Contemporary Scottish Studies,* Edinburgh: *Scottish Educational Journal,* [1976] [reprinted from *Scottish Educational Journal,* 1925-7]

McDiarmid, Hugh, *The Letters of Hugh MacDiarmid,* ed. Alan Bold, London: Hamish Hamilton, 1984

MacDiarmid, Hugh, *Selected Essays of Hugh MacDiarmid,* ed. Duncan Glen, London: Cape, [1969]

Mackenzie, Agnes Mure, *The Arts and Future of Scotland,* Edinburgh: Oliver and Boyd for Saltire Society, 1942

Mackenzie, Alexander, *History of the Highland Clearances,* Perth: Melven Press, 1979 [first published 1883]

MacLeod, Fiona, *Poems and Dramas,* London: Heinemann, 1910

MacLeod, Fiona, *The Sin-Eater, The Washer of the Ford, and Other Legendary Moralities,* London: Heinemann, 1910

MacLeod, Fiona, *The Winged Destiny: Studies in the Spiritual History of the Gael,* London: Chapman and Hall, 1904

Mitchison, Naomi, *Among You Taking Notes,* ed. Dorothy Sheridan, London: Gollancz, 1985

Morley, Frank, *Literary Britain: a Reader's Guide to Writers and Landmarks,* London: Hutchinson, 1980

Muir, Edwin, *An Autobiography,* London: Hogarth Press, 1987 [originally published 1954]

Muir, Edwin, *Collected Poems,* London: Faber, 1984 [originally published 1963]

Muir, Edwin, [Review of *Butcher's Broom*] in *The Listener, 14.11.34*

Muir, Edwin, [Review of *Highland River*] in *The Listener,* 9.6.37

Muir, Edwin, *Scott and Scotland: the Predicament of the Scottish Writer,* Edinburgh: Polygon, 1982 [originally published, 1936]

Muir, Edwin, *Selected Letters,* ed. P. H. Butter, London: Hogarth Press, 1974

Muir, Edwin, *The Truth of Imagination: the Uncollected Reviews and Essays,* ed. P. H. Butter, Aberdeen, Aberdeen University Press, 1988

Muir, Edwin, *Uncollected Scottish Criticism,* ed. Andrew Noble, London: Vision, 1982

Munro, Neil, *The Lost Pibroch and Other Shieling Stories,* Edinburgh: Blackwood, 1896

Murray, Isobel and Tait, Bob, *Ten Modern Scottish Novels,* Aberdeen, Aberdeen University Press, 1984

Neil M. Gunn: the Man and the Writer, eds. Alexander Scott & Douglas Gifford, Edinburgh: Blackwood, 1973

Pottinger, George, *The Secretaries of State for Scotland, 1926-76,* Edinburgh: Scottish Academic Press, 1979

Power, William, *My Scotland,* Edinburgh: Porpoise Press, 1934

Reid, J. M, *Modern Scottish Literature,* Edinburgh, Oliver & Boyd for the Saltire Society, 1945

Sar-Obar nam Bard Gaelach, or, The Beauties of Gaelic Poetry and the Lives of the Highland Bards, [collected by] John Mackenzie, Glasgow: MacGregor, Polson & Co, 1841

Scotland in Quest of her Youth: a Scrutiny, ed. David Cleghorn Thompson, Edinburgh: Oliver and Boyd, 1932

Scottish Country, ed. George Scott Moncrieff, London: Wishart, 1935

The Scots Week-End and Caledonian Vade-mecum for Host, Guest and Wayfarer, eds. Donald and Catherine Carswell, London: Routledge, 1936

Simpson, Kenneth, *The Protean Scot; the Crisis of Identity in Eighteenth Century Scottish Literature*, Aberdeen, Aberdeen University Press, 1988

Smout, T. C, *A Century of the Scottish People, 1830-1950*, London: Fontana, 1987

Stokoe, C. J. L, *A Bibliography of the Works of Neil M. Gunn*, Aberdeen: Aberdeen University Press, 1987

Thomson, George Malcolm, *The Re-Discovery of Scotland*, London: Kegan Paul, 1928

Victorian and Edwardian Highlands from Old Photographs, [compiled by] Francis Thompson, Edinburgh: Tantallon, 1989

Watson, G. J. 'The Novels of Neil Gunn', *Literature of the North*, eds. David Hewitt and Michael Spiller, Aberdeen: Aberdeen University Press, 1983

Watson, Roderick, *The Literature of Scotland*, Basingstoke: Macmillan, 1984

Wells, H. G, *An Experiment in Autobiography*, London: Gollancz, 1934

Wittig, Kurt, *The Scottish Tradition in Literature,* Edinburgh: Oliver and Boyd, 1958

Index

222 *Index*

Hebrides, 11-12, 74, 83, 85, 86

Helmsdale, Sutherland, 95

Hodder and Stoughton
(publishers), 22, 26, 29

Hogg, James, *The Private
Memoirs and Confessions of
a Justified Sinner*, 188-9

Huxley, Aldous, 176
Brave New World, 127

Ibsen, Henrik, 153
Ghosts, 156

Internationalism, 107

Inverness, 5

Iona community, 50

James Henry
The Aspern Papers, 189
The Turn of the Screw, 189

Jenkins, Robin, *The
Cone-Gatherers*, 158

Johnson, Samuel, 57
*Journey to the Western Islands
of Scotland*, 85-6

Johnston, Tom, 128, 147, 148

Jonathan Cape (publishers), 2

Joyce, James, 55-6, 80, 198

Jukes, H. R., *Loved River*, 62

Jung, Carl, 'On psychical energy',
68-9

Kafka, Franz, 75

'Kailyard' concept, 3, 22

Keats, John, 176
'La Belle Dame Sans Merci', 160
'Ode on a Grecian Urn', 160

Koestler, Arthur, 105
Arrival and Departure, 105,
126-7
Darkness at Noon, 105

Landseer, Sir Edwin, *Monarch of
the Glen*, 21

Lawrence, D. H., 15, 46, 153

Left Review, 44-5

Lybster, Caithness, 5, 90

McCleery, Alistair, 22, 24, 109

The Porpoise Press, 1922-39, viii

MacColla, Fionn (T. D.
MacDonald), *The
Albannach*, 55

MacCormick, John, 107, 109

MacCoul, Finn, 94, 97, 118, 130

McCulloch, Margery, *The Novels
of Neil M. Gunn*, vii
on 'Clare' in *The Lost Glen*, 30
on *The Drinking Well*, 143,
144
on *The Grey Coast*, 12
on 'Half-light', 3-4
on *Morning Tide*, 39
on 'Nan' in *The Shadow*,
151-2, 155-6
on NMG's philosophical
works, 72
on *The Other Landscape*, 192
on *Young Art and Old Hector*,
104

MacDiarmid, Hugh *see* Grieve,
Christopher

MacDonald, Thomas Douglas *see*
MacColla, Fionn

MacEwan, Sir Alexander, 109

Mackenzie, Agnes Mure, 58

Maclean, Alistair, 165

Macleod, Fiona *see* Sharp, William

Macpherson, James ('Ossian'), 38

Mavor, O. H., 89

Mitchell, James Leslie ('Lewis
Grassic Gibbon'), 44-5, 92,
Gay Hunter, 86
Sunset Song, 98-9

Mitchison, Naomi, 105, 145

modernism, 26, 55-6, 80, 86, 198

Morley, Frank, 31, 62-3

Muir, Edwin, 62, 74, 111, 127, 187
on *Highland River*, 64, 68, 88
An Autobiography, 31, 69
Scott and Scotland, 9-10, 59

Munro, Neil, 3, 25-6
The New Road, 26
'The Secret of the Heather
Ale', 25, 26-7

Murray, Isobel and Tait, Bob, 91